Jewish Life and Culture in Germany after 1945

Jewish Life and Culture in Germany after 1945

Sacred Spaces, Objects and Musical Traditions

Edited by
Katrin Keßler, Sarah M. Ross, Barbara Staudinger and Lea Weik

DE GRUYTER
OLDENBOURG

This publication is based on the research project "Objects and Spaces as a Mirror of Religious Practice of Jewish Communities: Traditions and Transformations of Judaism in Germany after the Shoah", funded by the Federal Ministry of Education and Research (BMBF) under the grant number 01UO1828A-D. The responsibility for the content of this publication lies with the authors.

SPONSORED BY THE

Federal Ministry of Education and Research

ISBN 978-3-11-075071-3
e-ISBN (PDF) 978-3-11-075081-2
e-ISBN (EPUB) 978-3-11-075085-0
DOI https://doi.org/10.1515/9783110750812

Library of Congress Control Number: 2022933745

Bibliographic information published by the Deutsche Nationalbibliothek
The Deutsche Nationalbibliothek lists this publication in the Deutsche Nationalbibliografie; detailed bibliographic data are available on the internet at http://dnb.dnb.de.

This book is published with open access at www.degruyter.com.

Cover illustration: Dortmund Synagogue (Photograph: Ulrich Knufinke, Bet Tfila – Research Unit for Jewish Architecture, Braunschweig, 2007).
Typesetting: Integra Software Services Pvt. Ltd.
Printing and binding: CPI books GmbH, Leck

MIX
Papier | Fördert gute Waldnutzung
FSC® C083411

www.degruyter.com

Contents

Katrin Keßler, Sarah M. Ross, Barbara Staudinger, Lea Weik

Introductory Remark

From the general perspective of historiography, quite a bit has already been written about the early social and institutional history of Jewish communities in post-war Germany. But what can we learn about Jewish communal life in Germany since 1945 when looking through the glasses of ritual objects, synagogue architecture, liturgical practices and their music? These and other research questions guided the interdisciplinary project on "Objects and Spaces as a Mirror of the Religious Practice of Jewish Communities: Traditions and Transformations of Judaism in Germany after the Shoah." The project was conducted between September 2018 and August 2021 by two university institutes and two Jewish museums, and was funded by the Federal Ministry of Education and Research. The research teams involved visited several Jewish communities and archives, and conducted narrative interviews with contemporary witnesses, community members and clergy to reveal the history and narratives behind Jewish spaces and their architecture, behind ritual and cultural objects as well as liturgical practices and their musical expressions, in order to gain insight into their meanings for post-war Jewish communities in Germany.

The research teams dived into the world of a reconstructed and revived Judaism in Germany after the great break through the Shoah: A world that revealed itself through the layout of prayer halls and synagogues (their partitioning, wall paintings, stained-glass windows, etc.), through prayer books, synagogue organs, Torah arks and their curtains, through bimot, pews and prayer desks, but also through Torah scrolls and their decoration (crowns, rimonim, mantles). The history of these tangible forms of Jewish heritage is made vivid by contemporary witnesses, by historical audio and film documents (such as radio recordings of synagogue inaugurations), newspapers and other publications, picture collections (photo albums), historical interviews and autobiographical testimonies. Beyond the material manifestations of the post-war history of Jewish life in Germany, an ethnographic study on synagogue music in today's Jewish communities, on intangible Jewish heritage, completed the research undertaken in the project mentioned above. Through fieldwork among selected Jewish communities, a contemporary *emic* (internal) perspective of Jews in Germany themselves is added to the stories that have unpacked through the analysis of objects and spaces mentioned above. First results of the three-year project, as well as further complementary contributions discussed at an online workshop held in July 2021, are presented in this volume.

Those Jews who survived the Shoah, who left the DP camps and decided to stay in Germany, as well as those who re-migrated from exile were the ones who founded the first synagogue communities from 1945 onwards. These communities initially consisted of Jews originating from Germany and other, mostly Eastern European countries. Later on, that is since the fall of the Iron Curtain in 1989, the cultural

https://doi.org/10.1515/9783110750812-001

composition of the communities was expanded by the influx of Jews from countries of the former Soviet Union. Throughout the second half of the twentieth century, the post-war communities experienced many social, economic, demographic and cultural challenges, resulting for example in emigration waves of those who did not see a perspective for a permanent stay "in the land of the perpetrators," and those, who regarded the newly established communities as a "liquidation community" only.

In order to maintain the small congregations despite their cultural and religious diversity, the nineteenth-century idea of a "unified congregation" gained new meaning, although one has to ask to what extent the desired unification originated from the congregations or was imposed from the outside by means of a "new Germany" political agenda. Within the context of synagogue worship, compromises had to be found between differing religious and cultural traditions: that is between Central and Eastern European forms of Orthodoxy and former German practices of Reform Judaism. The effects of these developments can be traced to the present day. Having become a "tradition" themselves, liturgical forms of the post-war period have experienced and still are experiencing renewed change since the influx of Jewish immigrants from the states of the former Soviet Union after 1990, which is also expressed in a diversification of the religious practices of present communities. These changes and their different aspects are presented in the chapter "Liturgy and Music."

It was only towards the end of the 1940s and increasingly after 1950, when most of the emigrants had left Germany, that permanent community structures developed. New community centers and synagogues were built, while many prayer halls, especially those of the Displaced Persons, disappeared. Now they saw themselves as a *Wiederaufbaugemeinde* ("rebuilding community") – although the feeling of having to live on "packed suitcases" remained. The structures – temporary prayer rooms or built synagogues – became research objects themselves, exemplifying the development of Jewish post-war history and the changing meaning of objects of the early post-war period. These questions are examined in the first chapter "Synagoges and Spaces." The heterogeneity of post-war Jewish life in Germany becomes visible in a range of religious, educational and cultural spaces and institutions, as well as in "new" Jewish self-understandings. Both find their expression in a wide range of buildings and facilities provided by the Allies and set up in DP camps, partly in barracks, in assigned houses but also in synagogues that had not been completely destroyed in 1938. This regained Jewish life also reveals itself in historical, sometimes reused ritual and other objects that have been used in these provisionary and later on in permanent communal spaces. Such paths of ritual objects are examined in the chapter on "Ritual Objects."

The project also considers the ideas, objects, rooms and liturgical practices that have been brought into the communities by the new community members, including numerous converts. Thus, older (pre-war) forms and remains of Jewish life in Germany were supplemented and sometimes even replaced by new cultural and religious values, practices and their material expressions. Most often, associated

Jewish knowledge has simply been forgotten. Objects and spaces from the early post-war period that continued to be used in today's congregations became "symbolic objects." By means of these symbols, contemporary Jewish communities seek to preserve the memory of their early post-war history. At the same time, the gradual forgetting of their significance due to the change of generations must be stated, too.

The objects and documents have been handed down in various contexts: in Jewish communities in Germany itself and abroad, in Jewish and general museums (e.g., in the Jewish museums in Berlin, Frankfurt am Main, Munich etc., but also in numerous smaller museums), in archives (e.g., Zentralarchiv für die Geschichte der Juden in Deutschland, Heidelberg, Centrum Judaicum Berlin), in private collections or estates, and last but not least: in memories, cultural and liturgical practices, and thus in the actual lives of Jews in Germany today. A few early places of worship have been preserved in situ but are no longer used as such (e.g., in Augsburg-Kriegshaber as a branch of the Jewish Museum Augsburg Schwaben, but also in Ampfing, Gelsenkirchen, or Trutzhain), others still serve Jewish communities today (in Berlin, Celle, Frankfurt am Main, Magdeburg, Munich or Weiden).

On the basis of the objects, spaces, written, ethnographic and acoustic sources to be identified and contextualized, the team approached the question of religious life of Jewish communities from different perspectives. The aim of the interdisciplinary research project was to examine and interpret Jewish places of worship in Germany after 1945 (Bet Tfila – Research Unit on Jewish Architecture in Europe, Technische Universität Braunschweig), the ritual objects used by their Jewish communities (Braunschweigisches Landesmuseum and Jüdisches Museum Augsburg Schwaben) as well as their liturgical-musical practices (European Center for Jewish Music, Hanover University of Music, Drama, and Media). From the perspective of the two participating museums, the task was to record and research their own holdings and those still to be documented and to incorporate them into museum practice in an appropriate manner. The results of the research are to be presented in a planned exhibition in Braunschweig and Augsburg.

The contributions published in this volume were presented and discussed in detail at the international online conference "Jewish Communities in Germany in Transition: Objects, Spaces and Traditions as a Mirror of Religious Transformation Processes after the Shoah" held in July 2021. The editors would thus like to express thanks to all contributors. And of course, the team would like to thank all Jewish communities and their representatives who opened their doors and archives for this research project.

In addition, the research project and this publication would not have been possible without the financial support of the Federal Ministry of Education and Research (BMBF), to whom we would like to express our deepest gratitude.

Part 1: **Synagogues and Spaces**

Katrin Keßler and Ulrich Knufinke

Introduction to Part 1: Synagogues and Spaces in Post-War Germany

To conduct a Jewish service, no dedicated room or building is needed and many services took place in the open field, in liberated concentration camps, etc.[1] Despite this, efforts to establish a prayer room – even if only for a limited period of time – can be noted everywhere, where Jewish survivors gathered immediately after the end of their liberation. The aim was to re-establish Jewish worship in a "safe space" as quickly as possible and thus – at least for the time of prayer – to re-establish a little normality, or the memory of it.

The first Jewish religious services after the Shoah were held in many places, even before the surrender on May 8 in areas liberated by the Allies – such as on April 29, 1945, in the air raid shelter of the Roonstraße Synagogue in Cologne[2] or a week earlier at one of the most symbolic places in the German Reich – the speaker's pulpit of the Nuremberg Nazi Party Rally Grounds (*Reichsparteitagsgelände*), where US Chaplain David M. Eichhorn, five American Jewish soldiers and five Jews liberated from a prison camp celebrated an almost symbolic service on Hitler's last birthday, April 20, 1945. The speaker's platform served as a base for the Torah scroll that was brought in a mobile Torah ark transported on a jeep.[3] Mostly organized by field rabbis with their ritual equipment, liberated Jews gathered in many places for first prayers – in the camps, in cities – and simple prayer rooms were quickly prepared in a simple way.

The architectural history of Jewish communal institutions since 1945 can be subdivided into various historical phases: The early phase of provisional and transitory beginnings until the founding of the two German states in 1949 was followed by decades of consolidation in the Federal Republic and the German Democratic Republic (until around the mid-1960s), after which a period of stagnation (until 1990) can be

---

1 Such services are mentioned for example by rabbis of the US-army, see Albert Isaac Slomovicz, *The Fighting Rabbis. Jewish Military Chaplains and the American History* (New York, 1999), or Greg Palmer, and Martin S. Zaid, *The GI's Rabbi. World War II Letters of David Max Eichhorn* (Lawrence/Kansas, 2004).

2 See Wolfram Hagspiel, *Köln und seine jüdischen Architekten* (Köln, 2010), 295. After a prayer room was established in the former Jewish asylum in Cologne-Neuehrenfeld, only special commemorative ceremonies were held in the Roonstraße Synagogue until it was finally rededicated after renovation on September 20, 1959.

3 See Palmer/Zaid, *The GI's Rabbi*, see note 1, p. 6; and for a similarly symbolic Pessach service in "Goebbel's castle," Schloss Rheydt see: Katrin Keßler, "Vom Kleiderschrank zum Toraschrein – Synagogeneinrichtungen nach 1945," in *Wandernde Objekte*, ed. Katrin Keßler, Andreas Brämer, and Ulrich Knufinke (Braunschweig, 2021), 79–91.

https://doi.org/10.1515/9783110750812-002

Fig. 1: Bad Nauheim Synagogue, Jewish servicemen attend a religious service in the synagogue in Bad Nauheim, 1946 (United States Holocaust Memorial Museum, courtesy of Gisela Eckstein Zamora, call no. 65637).

claimed. After the political changes in the Warsaw Pact, the Jewish communities in Germany often increased by several times due to Jewish immigrants from Eastern Europe, so that one can speak of a continuing phase of new beginnings, also in architecture.

In the beginning, it seemed highly unlikely to most contemporaries that there could ever be permanent Jewish life in Germany again after the Holocaust. More than 100,000 Jewish survivors liberated from the concentration and labour camps, deported from all over Europe, formed provisional communities as so-called Displaced Persons (DPs) in camps and other accommodation in the western occupation zones, usually separated from German society. Services were held in various premises – sometimes in preserved and quickly restored synagogue rooms (Ahrweiler, Amberg, Bad Nauheim (Fig. 1), Celle, Berlin, Munich and Straubing), but mostly in private flats, very often Jewish community centers and other Jewish institutions of the pre-war period, for example Jewish hospitals (Berlin, Essen, Frankfurt am Main) or homes (nurses' home in Nuremberg, Mannheim, old people's home). Synagogues were set up even in Jewish cemeteries – albeit with certain precautions to comply with religious law, the *halacha* (e.g., in

1950 in the converted cemetery hall in Dresden [1866], in Halle/Saale in the cemetery hall [1894] from 1948 on, officially inaugurated in 1953). But non-Jewish buildings too, like municipal buildings (e.g., rooms in schools, administrative buildings) or other institutions (cinemas, festival halls) were given to Jews for prayer. Although most of these early prayer halls were used for a short period – many only until 1946 – some remained in use for a longer time and served the communities until the 1950s and in a few cases even until the 1960s. However, these were usually located in exclusively Jewish institutions like the former Jewish hospital Frankfurt am Main (Gagernstraße, used from 1945 to the early 1970s),[4] and the Jewish nurse's home in Nuremberg (Wielandstraße, 1945–1966).[5] The only exception was a classroom in a public school-building in Osnabrück, used for Jewish prayer from 1945 until the 1960s. But, the reason for this use was obvious: the school was erected on the site of the destroyed synagogue.

Although the traces of this phase of Jewish life have disappeared almost everywhere today, the congregations founded at that time often formed the basis for further development, and mementos of this time of new beginnings can still be found in the synagogues and congregation halls in some congregations today. Currently, however, these are threatened by the generational change that has taken place or is imminent in many communities. If the stories of these objects are not passed on and if they are not equally appreciated by the next generation, they will fall into oblivion and decay, or even be lost. Most of the prayer halls established in the early post-war years have not been preserved with their furnishings, some of their buildings have been destroyed in the meantime, while others have been renovated several times since then and have been heavily remodeled.

Synagogues and prayer halls in DP camps

Although reintegration into German society might initially seem less difficult for Jews of German origin than for displaced persons from other states, the will to emigrate was also widespread among them. Nevertheless, this group of Jewish survivors led to the formation of new Jewish communities in many places, which, however, were subject to future emigration for a long time. In the large cities – due to the different religious ideas – it was not uncommon for "parallel" structures to emerge for DP congregations and congregations of the – here sweepingly called – returnees.[6]

4 Alon Tauber, *Zwischen Kontinuität und Neuanfang: die Entstehung der jüdischen Nachkriegsgemeinde in Frankfurt am Main 1945–1949* (Frankfurt am Main, 2008), 32.

5 Nicole Rinza, "Synagogenneubauten nach 1945 in Deutschland – von den Anfängen bis zur Gegenwart," [unpublished manuscript 2007], 113.

6 In Braunschweig, for example, the two communities were completely separated; the German Jews prayed on the upper floor of the Jewish community center, while the DP community was provided with a room in the headquarters of the British forces. See *"Wenn man ein Haus baut, will man*

The religious orientation of these communities, more or less shaped by survivors from Eastern Europe, was mostly traditional or Orthodox, which is reflected in the corresponding furnishing of the synagogue rooms, and – of course – the furnishing reflect the available possibilities.

All DP camps were closed by 1950, except for Föhrenwald, which remained in operation until 1956. After the dissolution, the conflicts described above continued within the now numerically much smaller communities, but compromises were found again and again. The fact that the different religious and cultural orientations of individual groups within the congregations did not remain without effects on the design of the synagogues can be seen above all in the buildings and furnishings of the 1950s and 1960s. But even in the early synagogue rooms and furnishings, the various currents and objectives can be discerned despite the predominantly provisional character of these facilities and the sometimes poor state of the sources.

The state of knowledge about the religious facilities in the Jewish DP camps varies greatly. Due to the difficulty of finding sources, no attempt has yet been made to provide a comprehensive account of the history of architecture or art. Files, photos or reports and, in rare cases, traces of buildings only provide a haphazardly assembled picture of the facilities of those years. For some there are indications of their existence for a very limited time, but details of their shape cannot be given according to current knowledge. It is likely that there were a number of other prayer rooms and other religiously designated facilities that are unexplored, overlooked and forgotten in the literature. Thus, the account of religious community facilities of the DP communities must be limited to a few examples.[7] Nevertheless, the known buildings and premises exhibit remarkable designs (see Ulrich Knufinke's contribution in this volume).

Early prayer rooms outside the DP camps

Returnees and survivors of German communities, who sometimes tried to make a new start in their old home towns or regions, lived together, especially in the larger cities, but also with former DPs who expected to make a medium- or longer-term living in Germany. The "packed suitcases" still remained in the cupboard, but new ties and more permanent institutions emerged with the stay, so that integration into German, non-Jewish society became necessary and possible. Especially in larger

---

bleiben" Die Geschichte der Jüdischen Gemeinde Braunschweig nach 1945, ed. Stadt Braunschweig (Braunschweig, 2005), 20.

7 However, individual facilities have been examined; see Sabine Glatter, et al, *Die Bauwerke und Einrichtungen der jüdischen Gemeinde in Celle. Synagoge, Mikwe, Friedhof* (Bielefeld/Celle, 1997), 54 on (synagogue) and 75–79 (*mikveh* and *sukkah*); and see more examples in Ulrich Knufinke's article.

cities, it was even possible for communities to merge: In Frankfurt am Main, two congregations merged in 1949 – the small congregation of survivors and returnees with the DP congregation of the camp in the Zeilsheim district (1945–1949), which numbered about 3,500 people, and thus provided the starting point for new congregational life in the city.[8] In Munich, where the Jewish Community of Munich and Upper Bavaria (IKG) was newly founded on July 15, 1945, the proportion of DPs among the community members was also rather large.[9] For both communities, the DPs are still an important part of the community's history today.

The gradual transition from a community oriented towards emigration to a community that saw a longer-term perspective in Germany can also be traced in the development of several other Jewish communities and their building activities, which were often complicated by the fact that building sites had to be reclaimed and that the penniless communities were forced to rely on restitutions and financial aid. After, in the Soviet zone and the early German Democratic Republic (GDR), a few provisional congregations had formed in renovated old synagogues (Leipzig 1945) and other rooms (Magdeburg, Rostock), the first new synagogue building was inaugurated at the same time as the first West German synagogues.

Erfurt synagogue

The only new synagogue in the GDR was built in 1951 to 1952 in Erfurt.[10] In 1945, fifteen returnees founded the first congregation and, due to the settlement of former Jews from Breslau, the number of Jewish inhabitants grew to around 350, so that a larger synagogue room became necessary. After another plot of land was rejected, it was decided to erect a new building on the site of the synagogue destroyed in 1938 on Kartäuserring (now Juri-Gagarin-Ring). On April 29, 1949, a first plan for a new synagogue was submitted to the building authorities; the Erfurt architect Willy Nöckel had already produced a corresponding design dated May 8, 1948.[11] The

8 See Helga Krohn, *"Es war richtig, wieder anzufangen" Juden in Frankfurt am Main seit 1945* (Frankfurt am Main, 2011); Tobias Freimüller, *Frankfurt und die Juden: Neuanfänge und Fremdheitserfahrungen 1945–1990* (Göttingen, 2020); and for DP camps see the publications of Jim G. Tobias, for example *Zeilsheim. Eine jüdische Stadt in Frankfurt* (Nürnberg, 2011).

9 On Munich, see *Beth ha-Knesseth, Ort der Zusammenkunft. Zur Geschichte der Münchner Synagogen, ihrer Rabbiner und Kantoren* (München, 1999); and on remigration, see Andrea Sinn, "Rückkehr aus dem Exil. Über die Aufnahme jüdischer Remigranten in München," in *"Auch in Deutschland waren wir nicht wirklich zu Hause" Jüdische Remigration nach 1945*, ed. Irmela von der Lühe, Axel Schildt, and Stefanie Schüler-Springorum (Göttingen, 2008), 101–120; and Richard Bauer and Michael Brenner, ed., *Jüdisches München. Vom Mittelalter bis zur Gegenwart* (München, 2006).

10 On the building history, see Eberhard Menzel, "Die neue Synagoge – eine Stätte der Hoffnung," in *Stadt und Geschichte*, ed. Arbeitskreis Stadt und Geschichte (Erfurt, 2002).

11 Menzel "Die neue Synagoge," see note 9, 16.

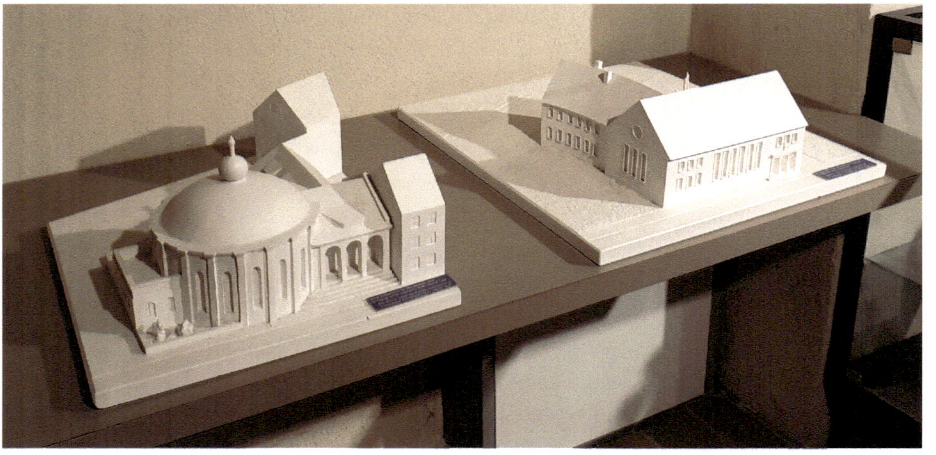

Fig. 2: Erfurt, plaster models of the synagogue designs of Willy Nöckel, ca. 1950 (Photograph: Maria Stürzebecher, Erfurt, 2020).

planning and realization of the Erfurt synagogue therefore took place at the same time as the first new synagogue buildings in West Germany.

The design was neither rejected nor approved, so Nöckel submitted two variants in early 1950.[12] By a special stroke of luck, the model of one of these variants has been preserved in the Museum Kleine Synagoge (Fig. 2).[13]

But even this architecturally interesting project of a circular building did not receive the go ahead. Instead, Nöckel had to completely revise his design: Facing the street, the synagogue room and the entrance area were to be enclosed in a uniform wing with a saddleback roof, while a slightly curved, angled wing was to house a weekday prayer room and the congregation rooms. The exterior of the synagogue, which was inaugurated on October 31, 1952, was kept deliberately simple, even inconspicuous:[14] Instead of being set back from other buildings, as initially planned, the building is directly adjacent to a row of houses in the west. The entrance is located in

12 Menzel "Die neue Synagoge," see note 9, 17. See also Eike Küstner, "Zurückhaltend und sachlich. Vor 60 Jahren eröffnete der einzige Synagogenbau der DDR," *Jüdische Allgemeine* (August 6, 2012), https://www.juedische-allgemeine.de/gemeinden/zurueckhaltend-und-sachlich/. Accessed February 2, 2022.

13 The plaster models were shown to the author in the early 2000s by Mrs. Rosita Peterseim, Erfurt. Since then, they were disposed of but fortunately found in a container and saved from destruction by Dr. Maria Stürzebecher, the city of Erfurt's UNESCO World Heritage representative. After restoration, they are now on display in the Small Synagogue Erfurt.

14 Construction work began on July 5, 1951, the foundation stone was laid on August 9. Menzel, "Die neue Synagoge," see note 9, 17.

the north façade facing the more important street, and a Hebrew inscription (*Patkhu li sha'arei tzedek*) is placed above the portal. Narrow vertical window strips divide the façade. The gable front of the east side shows a Star of David in a high oculus and three window strips (Fig. 3).

Three entrances lead to the foyer of the synagogue in the western part of the building, where there is a washbasin for the ritual washing of hands, and a memorial plaque for the victims of the Holocaust on the west side. A staircase takes visitors from the women's gallery to the upper foyer. The rectangular, flat-roofed synagogue hall is built according to the pattern of Liberal synagogues of the nineteenth and early twentieth centuries: The Torah ark, the bimah, the prayer lectern and the sermon lectern are grouped together on a raised platform in a niche in front of the east wall and thus face the congregation. Above the Torah ark is the U-shaped choir and organ loft which encloses the niche (Fig. 4).[15] For all its simplicity, recognizable value is placed on the distinction of the liturgically important area: While the walls of the hall are roughly plastered, that of the niche is smooth, and the balustrades, pulpit and steps are worked in natural stone. The Torah ark is highlighted by a red marble surround; two large brass menorah candlesticks stand on either side.

Fig. 3: Erfurt Synagogue, view from north-east (Photograph: Ulrich Knufinke, Bet Tfila – Research Unit for Jewish Architecture, Braunschweig, 2008).

15 The chancel and organ were raised on a gallery behind and next to the Torah ark. Such an arrangement has been used since Edwin Oppler's synagogue in Breslau/Wroclaw (1872) or Constantin Uhde's synagogue in Braunschweig (1875). This spatial allocation was further followed in the first third of the twentieth century, for example in the synagogues in Hamburg-Oberstraße and in Plauen.

Fig. 4: Erfurt Synagogue, interior towards east (Photograph: Katrin Keßler, Bet Tfila – Research Unit for Jewish Architecture, Braunschweig, 2019).

The less conspicuous exterior of the Erfurt Synagogue is quite similar to the one planned at the same time in Saarbrücken (1947–1951, Heinrich Sievers). Strictly speaking, this cannot be counted as the first synagogue in the Federal Republic, as the Saarland did not join the Federal Republic until 1956! Its smooth façade of light-coloured limestone is interrupted only by high-set windows and a large round window with a Star of David, the entrance almost casually had a flat Hebrew inscription above it. The generous gestures of demonstratively opening up the building to the public space that were customary in the architecture of the 1950s are also completely absent in this building.

In the GDR, membership stagnated and declined from the 1950s onwards, so that no further new buildings were erected. In the Federal Republic, on the other hand, after Saarbrücken and Stuttgart (1951–1952), a wave of new Jewish community centers was built in the mid-1950s. The newly founded communities had gradually become consolidated as permanent institutions and the payment of so-called reparations by the state offered financial opportunities for new building projects.

The "wave of new construction" in the 1950s and 1960s in the Federal Republic of Germany

The founding of the State of Israel in 1948 and the founding of the Federal Republic and the GDR in 1949 changed the situation of the Jewish population in Germany to a great extent. On the one hand, emigration to a Jewish state, the life goal of many survivors, was now possible; on the other hand, those who remained in the country had to position themselves in the new German state system. The young State of Israel, its symbols and buildings, soon became an important point of reference in Germany's synagogue architecture as well (see Katrin Keßler in this volume).

Those who decided – for the time being in the medium term – to stay in Germany and build new Jewish communities often experienced considerable rejection from the Jewish public all over the world: the World Jewish Congress had ruled out a Jewish future in Germany in 1948 and the Jewish Agency threatened two years later that Jews who did not leave the "cursed soil" within six weeks would no longer be considered Jews and would be excluded from all aid. Thus, the new communities were increasingly denied material and political support from international Jewish organizations. Only after a long process of dialogue was there acceptance of the German Jewish community in the world. Nevertheless, for many Jews in Germany there remained a dichotomy, stemming from a "feeling of guilt" towards those who had emigrated to Israel.[16]

The need to combine different ritual groups in a single congregation, for reasons of personnel and finances alone, is reflected in some features of the synagogue facilities of the 1950s and 1960s, which were intended to make services according to Liberal and Orthodox rites at least equally possible. Thus, although ritual baths (*mikvaot*) were installed in many new community centers, their use does not seem to have been common among all members by any means.

Jewish community life became increasingly concentrated in a few places, many communities in smaller towns ceased their activities, and the remaining Jewish inhabitants joined larger communities.[17] Nevertheless, it was difficult to build up a religious life: Only a small proportion of the community members regularly attended services, so that it was often difficult to form a *minyan*. The reasons for this were manifold and should not be generalized too broadly, but it can be stated that many Jews of German origin, a large proportion of whom had survived the persecutions under National Socialism as spouses in so-called "mixed marriages," remained non-

16 Michael Brenner, *Geschichte der Juden in Deutschland. Von 1945 bis zur Gegenwart* (München, 2012), 142 on. See also Anthony Kauders, *Unmögliche Heimat: eine deutsch-jüdische Geschichte der Bundesrepublik* (München, 2007), 95 on.

17 It was only possible in a few cases to find references to the religious institutions of these small congregations, which had been dissolved or had become inactive by the mid-1950s, and whose existence in the towns concerned is partly unknown today.

religious. However, as public representatives of the congregations – chairpersons, board members – they shaped their social appearance. Religious life within the congregations, on the other hand, was largely shaped by survivors from Eastern Europe, who were able to assert their commonly called "Orthodox" traditions.[18]

As the wave of emigration progressed, the international Jewish aid organizations reduced their work and the communities were increasingly left to their own devices. At the same time, it remained difficult to be recognized as successors of the destroyed Jewish institutions and to be compensated accordingly. Many post-war communities had to fight for land and properties, as the official successor organization of the pre-war communities in the American zone was the Jewish Restitution Successor Organization (JRSO) based in New York, which, however, was more interested in winding up the buildings than in building up new communities and their needs.[19] This referred not only to buildings, but to an even greater extent to ritual objects.

In 1951/52, however, agreements were reached with the various federal states, which now regulated the restitution procedures themselves. With the Federal Restitution Act of 1957, the Federal Republic committed itself to compensation for looting by state authorities or Nazi party organizations. This meant that the newly founded municipalities were also entitled to buildings, land and compensation for destruction during the Nazi era.[20] Thus, financial resources from state budgets were available – albeit sometimes only with great difficulty – to erect new buildings for the municipalities or to remodel existing ones.

In the first half of the 1950s, smaller projects oriented towards current pragmatic needs still predominated, alongside which the restoration of the Westend Synagogue in Frankfurt am Main (Fig. 5) must be considered an outstanding juncture on the path to a new Jewish architecture in terms of design. In September 1959, the *Jüdische Illustrierte* showed "Das Gesicht der Synagoge" [The Face of the Synagogue] with an array of pictures of restored and newly built synagogues: Bad Mergentheim, Berlin-Joachimsthaler Straße and Pestalozzistraße, Bielefeld, Bonn, Detmold, Dortmund, Düsseldorf, Frankfurt am Main, Cologne-Roonstraße, Saarbrücken and Trier (Fig. 6).[21]

---

18 Michael Brenner, "Als in der Synagoge die Orgel erklang. Reinheit des Glaubens oder Einheit der Gemeinden? Zur Geschichte des Streits zwischen orthodoxen und liberalen Juden," *Die Welt* (May 14, 2004), https://www.welt.de/print-welt/article313643/Als-in-der-Synagoge-die-Orgel-erklang.html. Accessed October 31, 2021.

19 On Würzburg, Ronald Flade, *Die Würzburger Juden. Ihre Geschichte vom Mittelalter bis zur Gegenwart* (Würzburg, 1987), 401, says: "If the reconstituted community had come into possession of the former community's real estate, built up over the course of several centuries, it would not have any financial problems today." Quoted in Alexandra Klei, *Jüdisches Bauen in Nachkriegsdeutschland. Der Architekt Hermann Zvi Guttmann* (Berlin, 2017), 196.

20 See Jürgen Lillteicher, *Raub, Recht und Restitution: die Rückerstattung jüdischen Eigentums in der frühen Bundesrepublik* (Göttingen, 2007), especially 357–369.

21 *Jüdische Illustrierte* 9 (September/October 1959): 4–5.

Fig. 5: Frankfurt am Main, Westend Synagogue (1910), inaugurated after reconstruction in 1950 (Photograph: Ulrich Knufinke, 2008).

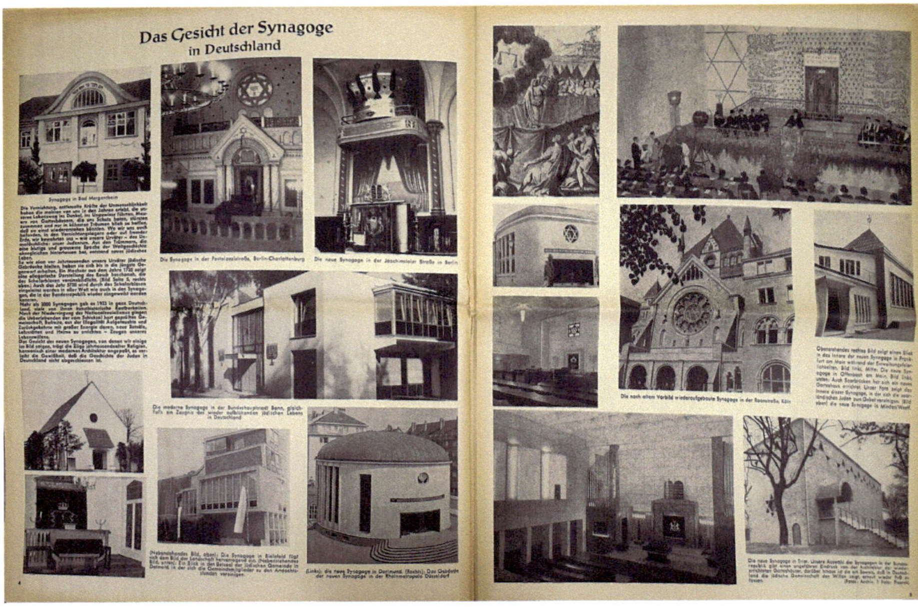

Fig. 6: "Das Gesicht der Synagoge," *Jüdische Illustrierte* 9 (September/October 1959), 4–5.

Not only the *Jüdische Illustrierte*, but also the numerous commemorative publications and extensive coverage in the press (and increasingly in the media of radio and television) provide a good insight into both the intentions of the architects and general conclusions about intentions and reception history. The political use of the construction of Jewish institutions can be clearly seen in the published speeches and greetings of the Federal Chancellor, prime ministers or mayors. In terms of the number of projects realized, the phase between the mid-fifties and the mid-sixties was the most productive period for Jewish buildings in Germany since 1945. The repertoire of functional-spatial, constructive and formal solutions for the Jewish building tasks that continued to develop here and internationally is correspondingly rich.

Synagogues of the phase of stagnation in the Federal Republic (1965–1990)

After a large number of synagogues and community centers was built in the twelve years between 1951 and 1963, there were only a few buildings in the more than twenty-five years that followed until 1990. In May 1966, the *Jüdische Illustrierte* entitled a picture report with the headline "In jeder Großstadt eine neue Synagoge" [In every big

Fig. 7: "In jeder Großstadt eine Synagoge," *Jüdische Illustrierte* 1 (May 1966), 6–7.

city a new synagogue] and showed a renewed review of the synagogues restored or newly built in the past years in Berlin-Fasanenstraße, Berlin-Kreuzberg, Bonn, Düsseldorf, Essen, Frankfurt am Main, Hamburg, Kassel, Cologne, Stuttgart, Worms (Fig. 7).[22] The decline in building activity in the subsequent years may be seen as a sign of stagnation: The membership of the existing congregations declined, so that no new buildings were necessary, and new communities in places where there was no congregation were no longer formed.

International synagogue architecture remained influential on the projects realized in the Federal Republic. Parallel to the late works of the two Jewish architects Hermann Zvi Guttmann[23] (Osnabrück 1969, Würzburg 1970, Frankfurt am Main 1977)

---

22 *Jüdische Illustrierte* 1 (May 1966): 6–7. The text reads: "Since the end of the war, 42 synagogues have been rebuilt in the Federal Republic, six in West Berlin. In some communities, one was content with the establishment of prayer halls (36 in the Federal Republic, five in West Berlin). The new synagogues in Germany were influenced by modern architecture. As far as the destruction was not total, the remains were harmoniously integrated into the new building. The interior style of the new synagogues also differs from the earlier ones. Today they often serve as a place of cultural exchange between Jews and non-Jews. One example is the new synagogue in Fasanenstraße in West Berlin. It was built on the same site as the earlier one, of which some stone ornaments and a few columns survived the destruction. These remnants decorate the entrance to the new cultural center. The new building not only provides space for religious devotions, but also for cultural events."

23 On Guttmann, see especially Klei, *Jüdisches Bauen in Nachkriegsdeutschland*, see note 19.

Fig. 8: Karlsruhe Synagogue, Torah ark (Photograph: Ulrich Knufinke, Bet Tfila – Research Unit for Jewish Architecture, Braunschweig, 2008).

and Helmut Goldschmidt[24] (Mönchengladbach 1967), buildings were constructed in Wiesbaden, Karlsruhe, Freiburg or Nuremberg that can be formally assigned to "late modernism" and the transition to so-called "postmodernism (Figs. 8 and 9)."

With the buildings and projects of Salomon Korn and his theoretical foundation of contemporary Jewish architecture on the basis of postmodern ideas,[25] a significant change began in the mid-1980s, not only in the generation of architects and clients, but also in the general interest in Jewish culture and history, of which the Mannheim Synagogue (1985–1987) by Karl Schmucker and the Darmstadt Synagogue (1988) by Alfred Jacoby also bear witness.

24 See Ulrich Knufinke, "Helmut Goldschmidt," *mr moderne regional 2015/1*, https://www.moderne-regional.de/fachbeitrag-helmut-goldschmidt/. Accessed October 12, 2021.

25 See Salomon Korn, *Geteilte Erinnerung. Beiträge zur ‚deutsch-jüdischen' Gegenwart* (Berlin, 1999).

Fig. 9: Karlsruhe Synagogue, view from south (Photograph: Ulrich Knufinke, Bet Tfila – Research Unit for Jewish Architecture, Braunschweig, 2008).

The political turnaround in the states of the Eastern Bloc around 1990 led to a fundamental change for the Jewish communities in the Federal Republic. With the end of the Soviet Union, thousands of Jews were able to immigrate to Germany as so-called "contingent refugees," so that the membership of the communities often multiplied. This not only confronted the communities with the problem of social integration of the immigrants, but also with the question of adequate premises.

Thus, since the beginning of the nineties, there has been a renewed wave of new synagogue buildings, which continues to the present day. The "built awakening" (*Gebauter Aufbruch*)[26] began only a few years after a changed awareness of German-Jewish history (and its material testimonies such as historic synagogues, cemeteries,

26 This is the title of an exhibition of 2010, in which nineteen synagogue designs of the previous fifteen years were presented: Stiftung Baukultur Rheinland-Pfalz, ed. *Gebauter Aufbruch. Neue Synagogen in Deutschland* (Regensburg, 2010).

etc.) had become manifest in the German public. In 1988, on the occasion of the commemoration of the fiftieth anniversary of the November pogrom, these questions began to be addressed again in the GDR as well as in the Federal Republic. If the Jewish immigration movement formed the "motor," as it were, for the construction of new community facilities, the historical-political interest of "commemorative culture" now played an essential role as a pattern of intention and interpretation in new buildings. Above all, it must be asked to whom the symbolic "messages" of the new synagogues and community centers – the artificial cracks, empty spaces, etc. – are addressed and how, in turn, a social expectation intervenes in the design possibilities when Jewish buildings increasingly enter the image of cities and are supposed to embody a new Jewish-German "normality."

The first decade of this new phase of Jewish architecture in Germany was marked by several major projects. After decades of stagnation and a hesitant new start in building activity at the end of the 1980s, the synagogues and community centers in Heidelberg (1994), Aachen (1995), Duisburg (1999) and Dresden (2001) as well as Mainz (competition 1999, inauguration 2010) set new standards both in terms of building volume and above all in terms of design, which was reflected in a hitherto unknown level of public interest. At the same time, a number of smaller new buildings and numerous conversions were constructed to supplement existing facilities or to prepare rooms that had previously been used for other purposes for the Jewish communities. While the large new buildings mentioned above took place in places where there had been at least small Jewish communities until 1990 (Duisburg being a certain exception as the new location of a merger of several communities), the remodeling of existing premises is a characteristic of the facilities of those numerous communities in cities where there had been no Jewish communities for many decades (such as in Gießen, Göttingen, Oldenburg, Potsdam or Hameln). Numerous other examples of provisional prayer halls could be mentioned. Those in Hameln and Hanover have since either moved to another provisional building, to a newly built community center (Hameln) or to a completely remodeled older building (Hanover) and are therefore no longer preserved. Similar to the new buildings of the 1950s and 1960s, it can be observed in part that individual elements of the "founding provisional buildings," for example Torah arks or artistically designed windows, are often adopted in the synagogues that are then permanently built.

Conversion of buildings: Synagogue Etz Chaim in Hanover

One of these prayer rooms, which had already ceased to exist, is the prayer room of the Liberal congregation set up in an office building at Freundallee 27 in Hanover (Fig. 11). It bears witness to a further development within the Jewish communities in Germany that only became possible with the general increase in membership – a differentiation

Fig. 10: Hanover, Synagogue Haeckelstraße (1963), (Photograph: Ulrich Knufinke, Bet Tfila – Research Unit for Jewish Architecture, Braunschweig, 2008).

into separate religious orientations of Judaism that have developed worldwide as a result of the Reform movement that started in Germany at the beginning of the nineteenth century. In Hanover, a Liberal Jewish community was founded in 1995, which wanted to provide an alternative to the traditional, ritually Orthodox synagogue in Haeckelstraße (1963, Fig. 10). Accordingly, the synagogue room is not divided into a men's and a women's area, the bimah and the Torah ark are close together. Instead of an organ, there is a piano for the musical accompaniment of the service.

This prayer hall was abandoned after the congregation inaugurated its new synagogue (Fig. 12) on January 25, 2009. Rabbi Dr. Gábor Lengyel had asked rabbis in Israel and the USA whether the building, the former Lutheran Gustav Adolf Church (1968,

Fig. 11: Hanover, Liberal prayer room in Freundallee (Photograph: Ulrich Knufinke, Bet Tfila – Research Unit for Jewish Architecture, Braunschweig, 2008).

Fig. 12: Hanover, Liberal synagogue Etz Chaim, 2009 (Photograph: Ulrich Knufinke, Bet Tfila – Research Unit for Jewish Architecture, Braunschweig, 2009).

Fig. 13: Hanover, Gustav Adolf Church (1968) that was later converted into a synagogue (Photograph: Ulrich Knufinke, Bet Tfila – Research Unit for Jewish Architecture, Braunschweig, 2006).

Fig. 13), could be used as a synagogue at all. The first synagogue to be built by converting a church was the Oldenburg Synagogue (1995), a neo-Gothic Baptist chapel from 1867.

The conversion to the new synagogue and community center "Etz Chaim," which was awarded the Lower Saxony State Prize for Architecture in 2010, was led by the architects Roger Ahrens and Gesche Grabenhorst. The synagogue is situated in the upper floor of the building, its interior is dominated by the Torah ark with a large red curtain framed by a textured gold aluminum sheet – mirroring the entrance façade. The bimah, parochet and candelabra were designed by the architects. The ark is situated in a stage-like niche of the eastern wall, elevated by three steps only. A playpen in the western part of the hall shows that the hall with variable seating may be used for several purposes.

Reoccupation of the traditional site: Braunschweig (2007)

The Jewish community in Braunschweig (Lower Saxony) took a different approach to redesigning the community center. The synagogue, consecrated in 1875 by the architect and professor of the Braunschweig Polytechnic Constantin Uhde (1836–1905),

Fig. 14: Braunschweig Synagogue (Photograph: Ulrich Knufinke, Bet Tfila – Research Unit for Jewish Architecture, Braunschweig, 2017).

was destroyed in 1938 and a high bunker was built in its place.[27] Only the adjoining community building survived the National Socialist era, and its façades are listed as historical monuments. Here, in the 1950s, a new congregation initially set up a small and very modest prayer hall on the upper floor. In 1985, a larger prayer hall was established on the ground floor.[28] With the influx of people from the former Soviet Union countries, this hall soon became too small, and there was also an urgent need for more space for the congregation's activities. In 2005, the decision was made to build a new synagogue in the inner courtyard between Uhde's community building, which is a listed monument, the bunker that still exists today on the foundation walls of the synagogue and the historical neighboring buildings. Therefore, the new synagogue could

27 On the Moorish-Romanesque synagogues of Uhde, see Ralf Busch, "Constantin Uhde als Synagogenarchitekt," *Artibus et historiae* 17 (1988): 39–48; Ulrich Knufinke, "Braunschweig und Wolfenbüttel," in *Synagogenarchitektur in Deutschland*, ed. Harmen H. Thies, and Aliza Cohen-Mushlin (Petersberg, 2008), 217–220; and on Uhde's oeuvre, see Christina Krafczyk, *Constantin Uhde. Bauen in Braunschweig* (Braunschweig, 2016).

28 Bettina Schmidt-Czaia, *"Wenn man ein Haus baut, will man bleiben,"* see note 6.

Fig. 15: Braunschweig Synagogue during the erection in a courtyard (Photograph: Ulrich Knufinke, Bet Tfila – Research Unit for Jewish Architecture, Braunschweig, 2006).

not be seen from the street. In a campaign, 1,938 Braunschweig residents purchased symbolic synagogue bricks at 100 euros each to financially support the construction.

The Oldenburg architect Klaus A. Zugermeier, who had already redesigned the community center of the Jewish community in Oldenburg in 2000 and added a mikveh, designed the building as a steel construction that skillfully incorporates the historic wall features.[29] On a diamond-shaped ground plan, the synagogue hall aligns itself to the east with the acute-angled corner of the courtyard, which forms between the concrete wall of the bunker left visible in the interior to the south and a historic quarry stone wall to the northeast. To the remaining part of the courtyard, the synagogue is glazed; to the other side, it adjoins the older community hall. The central main entrance, reached through the gateway of the community hall, is designed as a mighty rectangular portal, its natural stone cladding contrasting with the otherwise "light" steel and glass architecture, giving the structure the character of a perhaps only

29 Sincere thanks are due to the Jewish community of Braunschweig and its chairperson, Renate Wagner-Redding, for opening her archives and answering many questions, as well as to Dr. Klaus A. Zugermeier for providing information during the building process.

temporary installation. The rather high hall, in which round supports placed freely in front of the historic walls carry the roof structure, can be divided by folding walls so that two smaller halls are available. The Torah ark is situated in the apex of the triangle, the bimah is set free-standing at some distance in front of the ark. Its position is accentuated by a skylight shaft with an inset Star of David. The room can accommodate up to 200 worshippers, and there is no architectural separation of the sexes.

Compared to the synagogue in Munich, which was completed and inaugurated at the same time, the Braunschweig building is naturally modest and unspectacular. Due to the restriction to the historic community site in the middle of the old town of Braunschweig and there in one of the few building blocks with building fabric from the time before 1945, a building that could be recognized as a Jewish place of worship in the cityscape was not possible. More important here is the location at the historical site of the destroyed synagogue and the visualization of this wound in the form of the bunker wall.

Preservation of the early synagogue: Gelsenkirchen

Only in a few cases was it possible to preserve the appearance of the synagogue space used until then after a new building. Perhaps this circumstance also shows the upheaval that the communities that grew in the post-war period experienced in the nineties. The view of the "heritage" has inevitably become different; on the other hand, the often unloved architecture of the 1960s has a hard time asserting itself in other building tasks as well.

There are exceptions, especially when the preceeding synagogue has a special significance for the board or community members – as in Gelsenkirchen, where the chairperson of the Jewish community, Judith Neuwald-Tasbach (*1959), is the daughter of the former chairperson Kurt Neuwald (1906–2001), who returned to his hometown in spring 1945. As a child, she had witnessed the services in the previous synagogue.

The small synagogue with a schoolroom, offices and library, inaugurated on June 29, 1958, was located in an older brick building at 9 Von-der-Recke-Strasse. A prayer house was built in the courtyard of the house and consecrated on June 29, 1958 (Fig. 16). With the growth of the congregation since 1990, it became clear that these rooms would no longer be sufficient. A plot of land on a street corner near the pedestrian zone, i.e. in the middle of the city, was available for a new building; it is the site of the synagogue from 1885, which was destroyed in 1938 and was a striking example of the Moorish style.[30] With its community center, the Jewish community was thus able both to tie in

30 On the destroyed synagogue, designed by architect Peter Zingel, see Elfi Pracht-Jörns, *Jüdisches Kulturerbe in Nordrhein-Westfalen. Regierungsbezirk Münster* (Cologne, 2002), 245–276, especially 247–249.

Fig. 16: Gelsenkirchen, the first synagogue (1958) preserved as a museum (Photograph: Katrin Keßler, Bet Tfila – Research Unit for Jewish Architecture, Braunschweig, 2021).

Fig. 17: Gelsenkirchen, the new synagogue towards the Torah ark (Photograph: Katrin Keßler, Bet Tfila – Research Unit for Jewish Architecture, Braunschweig, 2021).

spatially with its own history and to return to the cityscape, in which it had hardly been recognisable since the time of National Socialism. Among the new buildings erected by Jewish communities in the region after 1990, the Gelsenkirchen Synagogue is the only one that could be built on the site of a predecessor destroyed in 1938. Nevertheless, the architects of the Gelsenkirchen office of Reinhard Christfreund and Benedikta Mihsler did not borrow anything from the architecture of the historic synagogue.

By 2007, a building had been erected that reveals its complex use as the religious and social center of the Jewish community in its structure. An open forecourt on the north side, separated from the street by a high wall into which vertical viewing slits are cut in close succession, makes it possible for passers-by to perceive what is happening inside the building. Access to the building is through the multi-storey administration wing on the west side of the site, from where one enters a foyer. An open staircase leads to the upper foyer and the synagogue room above the congregation hall. From the outside, the prayer hall is barely discernible, apart from a bay window for the Torah ark. The rectangular synagogue room is divided into three naves by round pillars (Fig. 17). The middle one is slightly elevated above the bimah and the Torah ark, so that the basilical structure already taken up in the 1920s for synagogues in abstract form is also recognisable here. The women's area on the west side is only separated from the men's pews by a few steps.

A tendency towards a new "functionalism," an accentuated simplicity, can be read in the Gelsenkirchen synagogue room, which gives it a dignified, though barely "sacralized" character. However, it is remarkable that elements of the predecessor prayer hall from 1958 are integrated in a significant place. A stained-glass window with symbolic representations is embedded as a light box in a wall of the upper foyer, which thus receives a strong colorful accent (Fig. 18). In the prayer room itself, the menorah chandeliers are from the previous synagogue and the Torah ark curtain was reworked and adapted to the new dimensions.[31]

The fact that the room of the predecessor synagogue could be renovated at the same time and is now accessible to groups of visitors is a special stroke of luck, which is mainly due to the awareness of post-war history on the part of the chairpersons.

Relocation and reconstruction of synagogues: Göttingen

Interesting enough, there have been two cases of translocations of preserved country synagogues to cities, for example, the Wohra Synagogue (ca. 1876) was moved

31 Interview with head of the community, Judith Neuwald-Tasbach, on February 26, 2000. The authors would like to express sincere thanks to her for the generous help during the research.

Fig. 18: Gelsenkirchen, the stained-glass window of the earlier synagogue transferred to the new building (Photograph: Katrin Keßler, 2021).

to Gießen in 1995 and the Bodenfelde Synagogue (1825) to Göttingen eleven years later. Only a few Jews lived in Göttingen after the war; they held services in a private flat and founded a congregation. Although the community was inactive for a long time, it was not officially dissolved and therefore could be revived in 1994. In order to move the small half-timbered building from Bodenfelde to Göttingen, a sponsoring association was founded in 1996, which collected donations. In the same year, a documentation and architectural research study of the building was carried out by the Technische Universität Braunschweig.[32] The building, which had been used as a barn until then and in which remains of the interior painting were still preserved, was finally acquired by the sponsoring association at the request of the Jewish community and dismantled in 2006. "Even the old window frames were packed individually in order to reinstall them – as far as it was possible – true to the original. However, many parts had to be repaired and supplemented, as they had suffered greatly as a result of decades of neglect."[33]

Even before the Göttingen translocation, the Jewish architect Alfred Jacoby criticized this way of dealing with synagogue buildings:

> The same rejection as the idea of reconstructing the old synagogue façade as a proposal in the competition in Aachen must therefore also provoke the idea of relocating an old existing village synagogue to Gießen as the centerpiece of a new center. As architects, we have every

32 Andrea Jensen, and Sabine Glatter, "Die ehemalige Synagoge in Bodenfelde. Ein Beitrag zum Dokumentationsprojekt '*Synagogen in Niedersachsen*' der Technischen Universität Braunschweig, Institut für Bau- und Stadtbaugeschichte," (Braunschweig, 1996), unpublished, archives of Bet Tfila – Research Unit Braunschweig.

33 Detlef Herbst, "Umzug in ein neues Leben. Die Geschichte der Synagoge der Jüdischen Gemeinde Göttingen," https://jg-goettingen.de/synagoge/index.php. Accessed October 14, 2021.

Fig. 19: Göttingen, the timber-frame synagogue transferred to Göttingen (Photograph: Katrin Keßler, Bet Tfila – Research Unit for Jewish Architecture, Braunschweig, 2020).

> reason today to give expression to the history of the Jews in Germany. But to do so by mummifying history would mean not actually taking note of it. If architecture was once described as "frozen music," it is certainly not a "frozen time" from which one can break out arbitrary set pieces.[34]

Relatively unnoticed by the scientific press, the small neo-Gothic brick synagogue in Herford was rebuilt in its outer appearance of 1892 next to the preserved community hall. Interesting enough, the rebuilding is not stressed in the publication by the Jewish community, which says only: "Since the beginning of the 1990s, the congregation [...] thought about a synagogue building on the site of the old place of worship. This has now been completed."[35] The building was inaugurated on March 14, 2010. The fact, that – for the first time in Germany (if we do not count Worms) – a synagogue was rebuilt in its original outer appearance (but with a modern interior) did not gain public attention beyond the local press.

Against the background of reconstruction of many iconic buildings, first and foremost the Berlin Palace, it is not astonishing that there is a call to rebuilt synagogues

---

34 Alfred Jacoby, "Synagogenbau in Deutschland nach 1945," in *Synagogen in Kassel*, ed. Stadtmuseum Kassel (Marburg, 2000), 84–88, here 87. The same article, with minor changes, was printed in 2002 in *Neue Synagoge Chemnitz*, ed. Jüdische Gemeinde Chemnitz (Chemnitz, 2002).

35 Sven Nieder, et al., *Wir freuen uns und wir weinen ...: Wiederaufbau der Herforder Synagoge* (Bielefeld, 2010), n.p. See chapter entitled "65 Jahre Wiederaufbau: Bis zur neuen Synagoge."

Fig. 20: Göttingen Synagogue, the new Torah ark, bima and other furnishings (Photograph: Katrin Keßler, Bet Tfila – Research Unit for Jewish Architecture, Braunschweig, 2020).

too. Such discussion of whether a reconstruction is the appropriate way to build new synagogues took place already during the planning process of the Dresden Synagogue (2001). Architects Wandel, Höfer and Lorch & Hirsch decided against it and instead made the site of the destroyed synagogue visible as traces in the ground. Today, these discussions are held vividly regarding the reconstructions of the Bornplatz Synagogue in Hamburg and the Berlin Synagogue Fraenkelufer, that will open a new – and special – chapter in synagogue history of post-war Germany.

In conclusion, it can be said that until the late 1970s, most synagogues had in common a lack of – and also no sought-after – connection to their surroundings.[36] Alfred Jacoby explains this "detachment from the urban fabric" with uncertainty, a lack of connection. The early post-war synagogues seem above all to satisfy a spatial, religious need. In almost all communities, synagogues are built together with other community facilities – social and school rooms, homes for the elderly, dormitories,

36 Alfred Jacoby, "Synagogenbau in Deutschland nach 1945," in *Synagogen in Kassel*, ed. Stadtmuseum Kassel (Marburg, 2000), 84–88, especially 85.

etc., sometimes also *mikvaot*. The intention to give the building a symbolic meaning seems to have been far from the minds of the architects of those years. This changed in the late 1980s; at the latest, Salomon Korn‘s furrowed tablets of the law at the Jewish home for the elderly in Frankfurt am Main clearly show that architecture now has to do more than protectively enclose the congregation. Synagogues now become more visible in the cityscape.

Synagogue buildings thus always fulfilled several functions, a) a social function as a new home, b) a religious function, c) a symbolic function, because even if this is not evident in the architecture, after the destruction of the synagogues in 1938 (as a symbol of the planned destruction of Judaism) the new synagogues are nevertheless a symbol of a new beginning and finally d) for the majority society also a political function, in that the restoration of the houses of worship is understood as a kind of "reparation." Idealistic references to the destroyed pre-war synagogues are often sought – as dates for the laying of the foundation stone or dedication, construction on the same site up to the actual reconstruction in the pre-war forms.

Future research will to be able to show whether and to what extent the synagogue buildings of the early building phase and especially those of the last thirty years were able to contribute to the "formation of tradition" in the Jewish communities. What will be the role of the synagogue within the communities, what does it represent and how is it perceived by the non-Jewish society?

The contributions

The following contributions to this volume answer several but of course not all these research questions:

Ulrich Knufinke examines the places of worship of the early and immediate post-war period, about which we still know far too little. Despite their provisional nature, the will to design can clearly be felt in the surviving examples and photographs. DP congregations that gathered in or outside the camps designed and decorated their synagogues with whatever was available to them. Knufinke examines the models they presumably had for their design on the basis of the few known examples. Due to the great difficulty of accessing sources, these investigations must remain exemplary, but they form an important foundation stone for DP research and the architectural history of post-war synagogues.

The following articles concentrate on specific features of synagogue architecture: **Katrin Keßler** looks at an aspect of the post-war synagogue that has received little attention so far: its increasing turn towards the architecture of Israel. While in the pre-war period the Holy Land played more of a symbolic role like the site of the destroyed Temple and was present in prayers, the orientation of synagogues, etc., with the founding of the State of Israel the new land became a special point of reference for Jews in Germany. This is also very clearly evident in the architecture of their synagogues and community buildings, which since the 1980s have been inscribed with greater symbolism by architects, but also by the Jewish communities and non-Jewish majority society.

The two subsequent contributions take a broader look at synagogues. In her contribution, **Beate Löffler** does not look at the architectural design of synagogues, but she examines synagogues on a meta-level – in terms of their actual and ideal "place" in the urban fabric. Beginning with a depiction of the visibility or invisibility of religion in general in German cityscape, she then examines which places are "occupied" by Jewish communities and how this Jewish topography is reflected in public perception.

Finally, **Dani Kranz** examines the synagogue space with regard to its social meaning. Her study takes us from the architectural "shell" to the community life that takes place inside, with its social and ethnological issues. Not only, but especially with the immigration of Jews from the former Soviet Union, groups appeared within the Jewish communities that from then on influenced, if not determined, community life and decisions on various fields – Liberal or traditional? And if Liberal – how Liberal exactly? Conversion and the matter of *Vaterjuden* and, of course, the relation towards Israel and Jews from Israel that immigrate to Germany are such questions that determine the virtual "spaces" of today's synagogues.

Ulrich Knufinke

Wall Paintings in Synagogues of Displaced Persons in Germany (1945–1950)

The decoration of synagogues with decorative paintings or mosaics and pictorial representations following an iconographic program has a tradition going back to antiquity, which also left traces in the synagogues and prayer rooms of Jewish survivors of the Holocaust in the immediate post-war period.[1]

Since time immemorial, certain symbols, but also images of religiously significant places and, rarely, biblical scenes, have been used in different ways in the various epochs and regions to decorate the prayer rooms and endow them with a meaning that transcends place and time. With the so-called "Jewish Renaissance" and the growing interest in traditional forms of expression of a "specifically Jewish" art and architecture, iconographic programs occasionally found their way into modern synagogue construction in Germany, for example in Görlitz (inaugurated in 1911), Essen (1913), Augsburg (1917) or Plauen (1930).[2] In parallel, synagogue painting continued or revived in Eastern Europe, where examples of fully painted synagogues were also studied by modern artists and architects such as Marc Chagall or El Lissitzky.

Only a few illustrations and material traces testify to the fact that this modern tradition of decorative and iconographic painting was also used for a few years, from 1945 to about 1950, in some synagogue rooms, which Jewish survivors of the Shoah in Germany furnished and decorated under difficult conditions.[3] While the existence of synagogues and other Jewish religious institutions in the DP communities has attracted attention in historical research as an expression of group-specific consciousness-raising, it is difficult, also due to the poor availability of visual sources, to define the institutions themselves more precisely, to describe them, and possibly to

---

1 On the furnishing and design of early post-war synagogues in Germany, see Ulrich Knufinke, "Synagogenräume der Displaced Persons und ihre Gestaltung," in *Lager – Repatriierung – Integration. Beiträge zur Displaced Persons-Forschung*, ed. Christian Pletzing, and Marcus Velke (Frankfurt am Main, 2016), 71–100. The present article examines the thoughts discussed there and focuses on the paintings of such rooms.

2 On paintings in German synagogues of the Weimar Republic period, see Harold Hammer-Schenk, *Synagogen in Deutschland. Geschichte einer Baugattung im 19. und 20. Jahrhundert (1780–1933)* (Hamburg, 1981), 524–528.

3 On the early self-organisation of Jewish survivors, see, for example, Andrea Sinn, "'Ungewöhnliche Schwierigkeiten und Situationen.' Über die Anfänge einer organisierten jüdischen Nachkriegsgemeinschaft in Deutschland," in *Überlebende des Holocaust im Bayern der Nachkriegszeit*, ed. Sybille Steinbacher (Göttingen, 2013), 166–182.

https://doi.org/10.1515/9783110750812-003

classify them in terms of architectural or art history.[4] Only a few plans, photos and descriptions survived in collections all over the world, archival material is rare and often fragmentary. Luckily some of the former DP prayer rooms survived, thus we can examine a small number of wall paintings in situ. However, the fact that the religious DPs made such great efforts to design their prayer rooms at all may testify to the great importance they also attached to them as places of identification.[5]

Art and architectural historians dealing with post-war Jewish buildings and their furnishings usually focus on the new synagogues and community centers – after all well over 100 structures were built from 1945 till the present.[6] The temporary prayer rooms established shortly after liberation have come into the view of historians and conservators in recent years, only.[7] Thus, it is only a hypothesis that in the design of post-war synagogues in Germany erected in the 1950s and 1960s we can find continuities with the brief period of the DP prayer rooms, although most of the DPs left Germany at the latest around 1950. Some DPs joined the communities that had developed outside the DP camps, mostly under the leadership of German

4 See Jim G. Tobias, "'Vertraut Gott auf ewig – schüttet ihm eure Herzen aus!' Die Wiedergeburt der jüdischen Orthodoxie in den DP-Camps," in *Religiöse Praxis in Konzentrationslagern und anderen NS-Haftstätten*, ed. Insa Eschebach, Gabriele Hammermann, and Thomas Rahe (Göttingen, 2021), 133–149; Jim G. Tobias, "'Mindestens eine Synagoge befand sich in allen Lagern.' Religiöser Neuanfang in den DP-Camps in Deutschland," *Zeitgeschichte* 47.2 (2020): 212–229; see also the projects of the Nürnberger Institut für NS-Forschung und jüdische Geschichte des 20. Jahrhunderts e.V. "Talmud Thora Schulen in Deutschland 1945–1950," www.talmud-thora.de (accessed October 18, 2021), and "Jüdische DP Lager und Gemeinden in der US Zone," www.after-the-shoah.org (accessed October 18, 2021) with lots of information about the DP camps and their religious institutions.

5 On the role of Jewish chaplains of the US Army, see Alex Grobman, *Rekindling the Flame. American Jewish Chaplains and the Survivors of European Jewry, 1944–1948* (Detroit, 1993).

6 See, for example, Alexandra Klei, *Jüdisches Bauen in Nachkriegsdeutschland. Der Architekt Hermann Zvi Guttmann* (Berlin, 2017); Ulrich Knufinke, "Architektur des Sakralen zwischen Aufbruch und Erinnerung. Zeitgenössische Synagogen im Bild deutscher Städte," in *Der sakrale Ort im Wandel*, ed. Albert Gerhards, and Kim de Wildt (Würzburg, 2015), 223–230; "Architektur und Erinnerung: Synagogenbau in Deutschland nach der Shoah," in *Geschichtsbilder und Erinnerungskultur in der Architektur des 20. und 21. Jahrhunderts*, ed. Kai Kappel, and Matthias Müller (Regensburg, 2014), 93–108.

7 On life, culture and the history of Jewish survivors a lot of research has been carried out during the last decades. See, for example, Michael Brenner, *Nach dem Holocaust. Juden in Deutschland 1945–1950* (München, 1995); Jacqueline Giere, and Rachel Salamander, ed., *Ein Leben aufs Neu. Das Robinson-Album. DP-Lager: Juden auf deutschem Boden 1945–1948* (Wien, 1995); Jim G. Tobias, *Vorübergehende Heimat im Land der Täter. Jüdische DP-Camps in Franken 1945–1949* (Nürnberg, 2002); Angelika Königseder, and Juliane Wetzel, *Lebensmut im Wartesaal. Die jüdischen DPs (displaced persons) im Nachkriegsdeutschland* (Frankfurt am Main, 2004); Nicola Schlichting, *"Öffnet die Tore von Erez Israel." Das jüdische DP-Camp Belsen 1945–1948* (Nürnberg, 2005); Peter Fassl, Markwart Herzog, and Jim G. Tobias, ed., *Nach der Shoa. Jüdische Displaced Persons in Bayerisch-Schwaben 1945–1951*, (Konstanz, 2012); Sybille Steinbacher, ed., *Überlebende des Holocaust im Bayern der Nachkriegszeit* (Göttingen, 2013).

Jewish survivors or remigrants. But, despite of the question of a "survival" of artistic traditions of the DP synagogues, for a deeper understanding of the short period of DP life and culture it may be important to shed light on the places where the religious renaissance of Jewish survivors took place. What did they look like? Who was responsible for them? What were their artistic sources? And where did the artists come from?

International Jewish aid organizations provided considerable support in establishing a religious life. Certainly, the completely destitute DPs could not establish the synagogues and prayer rooms on their own, but were dependent on help from the Allies and the aid organizations – sometimes also in dealing with hostile or delaying German authorities and the population, which had not been freed from anti-Semitism.

Different locations are documented for the synagogue rooms, depending on where and how the DPs lived and organized themselves. It can be assumed that the locations changed frequently and that it did not happen everywhere to design the rooms beyond the necessary basic equipment. DPs' synagogues existed both in camps where they were housed after liberation and where they lived in barracks and military settlements. They were not accessible to the German population. In addition, examples are known where DPs celebrated religious services in synagogues that had survived the Nazi period more or less unscathed. Here, an interaction between the population and the DPs took place, in which the role of the survivors as reminders and witnesses of the Shoah was addressed for the first time.[8]

One example of such a DP synagogue in a historic synagogue building from the British zone is the synagogue of Diepholz (Lower Saxony).[9] After the liberation of the camps the British military administration had to solve the immense problem of taking care of thousands of survivors, especially from the Bergen-Belsen camp-complex. Throughout the British zone, Jewish DP camps were established mostly in small towns not damaged by the war. One DP camp was opened in a former military airport near Diepholz in early 1946.[10] In the town, a Jewish community existed until the NS-period. Its synagogue was a tiny half-timbered building, where a prayer room was added in the nineteenth century. On Kristallnacht, the synagogue's furnishings were destroyed, but the building was not. NS-organizations used it as a workshop. As in other places, the Jewish DP community of Diepholz, organized in a "Jewish

---

8 See Tobias, *Vorübergehende Heimat im Land der Täter*, see note 7.

9 On Jews in Lower Saxony after 1945, see Herbert Obenaus, *Im Schatten des Holocaust. Jüdisches Leben in Niedersachsen nach 1945* (Hannover, 1997); Anke Quast, *Nach der Befreiung. Jüdische Gemeinden in Niedersachsen seit 1945. Das Beispiel Hannover* (Göttingen, 2001); on Diepholz, see Knufinke, "Synagogenräume der Displaced Persons und ihre Gestaltung," see note 1.

10 See www.after-the-shoah.org/diepholz-juedisches-dp-lager-und-gemeinde-jewish-dp-camp-and-community, accessed October 3, 2021.

Fig. 1: Diepholz, interior of the former synagogue, around 1946 (*Unzer Sztyme* 7 [February 20, 1946]).

committee," reclaimed the former synagogue to have services there.[11] An article in *Unzer Sztyme*, the Yiddish DP newspaper of the British zone from February 20, 1946, relates the difficulties of retrieving the building: (Fig. 1)

> In one corner of the Diepholz synagogue is a locksmith's shop, in another corner the washing is drying. This is not only blasphemy, but it is a shame for our English providers [...]. The rabbinate asked the headquarters of Diepholz to leave the place to the Jews in town. But Major Fines returned [the letter] to the rabbinate without reading it!!! [sic!] And the German washing goes on drying. And the German locksmith is satisfied, humming ‚Heil, Sieg Kameraden‘[12]

The article's sarcastic tone reveals the intentions of the DPs. They were not only in search of a place for prayer – obviously, it would have been easier to furnish a room in the barracks of their camp far outside the town. They intended to create a symbol of justice for all of the Jewish victims. The Jewish survivors in Diepholz, most of them born in Eastern Europe and, as far as we know, no one from the town,

11 See Nancy Kratochwill-Gertich, and Antje C. Naujocks, "Diepholz," in *Historisches Handbuch der jüdischen Gemeinden in Niedersachsen und Bremen*, ed. Herbert Obenaus (Göttingen, 2005), 468–478; Falk Liebezeit, and Herbert Major, *Spuren jüdischer Geschichte in Diepholz* (Diepholz, 1999).

12 Hildegard Harck, *Unzer Sztyme. Jiddische Quellen zur Geschichte der jüdischen Gemeinden in der Britischen Zone 1945–1947* (Kiel, 2004), 31 (according to *Unzer Sztyme* 7 [February 20, 1946]: 15–16).

saw themselves as the legal successors of all destroyed communities.[13] Thus, the opening of the synagogue was also a symbol of post-war German society: Jews are still alive, and they will demand the return of property robbed from the Jewish people.

The Diepholz Jewish committee succeeded finally in reclaiming the synagogue for its services. The re-inauguration took place on October 22, 1946. Chaim Aronowitz reports on it in *Unzer Sztyme* from November 2:

> On October 22nd the Jews of Diepholz celebrated the opening of the reconstructed synagogue, destroyed by the murderous hands of the Nazis in 1938. Although there are only a few Jews in Diepholz, they succeeded to furbish the splendid synagogue under the leadership of the president of the local Jewish committee, Mordechai Freudenreich.[14]

The city of Diepholz had to pay for the reconstruction of the prayer room. Thus, some plans are preserved in the city archive (Fig. 2). A local craftsman designed a new furnishing, consisting of a Torah ark, a bimah and benches. This plan obviously was not executed, otherwise the Torah ark would have had its place in front of the south wall.[15] Some other drawings in the city archive of Diepholz show colored designs for a furnishing and for wall paintings. In these plans, the Torah ark is situated correctly in front of the east wall. The papers are not dated and not signed, but it is very likely that they were drawn by a Jewish DP.

In the drawings, the ark has a vaulted top and stands in an apse-like niche. Two columns or pilasters frame the niche, two lions, holding the Tablets of the Law with Hebrew letters, and a golden crown are on the top. A red curtain, painted on the wall surrounds the ark. Right and left of it, Hebrew inscriptions are written. The lower part of the walls obviously is covered with wooden panels, while a colored frieze runs under the ceiling. We can imagine that the square fields of the frieze should be filled with figurative images. As far as is known, the Diepholz synagogue wall paintings would have been the most elaborate decor of a DP synagogue in the British zone. Whether it was carried out is as yet unknown. The post-war Diepholz Jewish community ended around 1948.

Also, in the American zone, old synagogue buildings which survived were restored as synagogues for DP communities. In most cases, the synagogues were not furnished and painted as elaborately as planned in Diepholz. The framing of the Torah ark is quite similar to a painting in a prayer room on a photo from 1948, presumably taken in Wetzlar.[16] The camp was established in the Sillhöfer Au-barracks

---

13 See Kratochwill-Gertich, and Naujoks, "Diepholz," see note 11, 476.

14 Harck, *Unzer Sztyme*, see note 12, 53 (according to *Unzer Sztyme* 14 [November 2, 1946]: 27).

15 See Kratochwill-Gertich, and Naujoks, "Diepholz," see note 11, 476. On the following, see Stadtarchiv Diepholz, Bauakte Mühlenstraße 5; the author thanks Mr. Liebezeit, Stadtarchiv Diepholz, for his support.

16 US Holocaust Memorial Museum, Nr. 82912, http://digitalassetushmm.org/photoarchives/detail.aspx?id=12549, accessed October 18, 2021. On the history of the DP camp, see Jim G. Tobias, "Eine

Fig. 2: Diepholz, design for the renewal of the synagogue of Diepholz, around 1946 (Stadtarchiv Diepholz).

in 1946 and closed in 1949. It is unclear whether the prayer room was established in the barracks or in another house of the Jewish DP community situated in Nauborner Straße 51 near the city center of Wetzlar. The room looks like a classroom with windows on one side and doors on the other and a flat ceiling (Fig. 3). A square wooden bimah stood in the center of the room and a modest cupboard-like Torah ark was situated in front of one of the walls. The ceiling was painted with ornaments. The wall around the ark was designed in a remarkable way: the neo-classical architectural framing of columns and an entablature with a curtain and a crown was for sure painted after 1945 – there was no tradition for such paintings in Germany before 1933.

In another Hessian DP camp, today the village of Trutzhain, a painted synagogue-room is still preserved. The camp was erected for prisoners of war during World War II. In 1946, the US-military government opened a camp for Jewish DPs here. In one of the barracks a prayer room was installed and painted:[17] Columns with channelings, depicted in a geometrical, abstract matter are painted between the windows. In a way they are similar with late-expressionistic or art deco-paintings of the 1920s or 1930s. On the ceiling, a Star of David is painted in different shades of blue (Fig. 4). As far as the paintings are documented, there are no other symbolic images

jüdische Stadt in Wetzlar," http://www.hagalil.com/2014/01/wetzlar, accessed October 18, 2021. Wetzlar's former community synagogue was also restored for the DPs; see Thea Altaras, *Synagogen und jüdische Rituelle Tauchbäder in Hessen. Was geschah seit 1945?* (Königstein i. T, 2007), 223.

17 See Altaras, *Synagogen und jüdische Rituelle Tauchbäder in Hessen*, see note 16, 71, and 172–173.

Fig. 3: Wetzlar, interior of the DP synagogue (United States Holocaust Memorial Museum, courtesy of National Archives and Records Administration, College Park, call no. 82912).

in the room. The barrack is private property today and not accessible for further documentation.

The region of Upper Bavaria had the most DP camps of the US zone. By chance, the paintings of a DP prayer-room in Ampfing were rediscovered during a restauration. The synagogue was established in a former catholic parochial house. This house became the center for a DP community of survivors of Dachau. In 1946, about 85 Jews lived in Ampfing. In 1947, a hall in the house was turned into a synagogue and inaugurated on December 7, 1947.[18] Since the renovation of 2010, the painted frame of the Torah ark is visible again; a red, sweeping curtain with golden braids. The vault of the hall was painted with floral ornaments and stars on a dark ground. Stylistically the paintings remind baroque traditions. On the one hand, this is typical for churches in the region, on the other hand the DPs, mostly from Poland, may be reminded the traditions of Polish synagogue paintings.[19] In the south

18 See Michael Schmidt, "Nach der Shoah: Die ehemalige Synagoge des Jüdischen Komitees Ampfing," in *das münster* 63 (2010): 135–140, here 137. According to Schmidt, this prayer hall was decorated by local painters with a "picture cycle with scenes of the emigration to Erez Israel" (139). This decoration has not been preserved.

19 Schmidt's thesis that a local painter and a church painter, who demonstrably had already done the design of the temporary prayer room in an Ampfingen inn, could have done the painting is

Fig. 4: Trutzhain, paintings in the DP prayer room in a barrack of the DP camp (Thea Altaras, *Synagogen und jüdische Rituelle Tauchbäder in Hessen. Was geschah seit 1945?*. Königstein i. T. 2007).

wall, an oriental building is depicted: in a cartouche we see a domed building in a desert landscape, in front of it a traditionally dressed praying Jew (Fig. 5). Obviously, this represents Rachel's Tomb near Bethlehem. Since the late nineteenth century, this motif from Erez Israel became popular for wall paintings in East European synagogues. Postcards with photos or etchings of Jewish places of worship in the land were distributed in European Jewish communities. Regarding the Ampfing DP community, this may give two hints for interpretation: On the one hand, it is a symbol for a longing for Erez Israel usual in Orthodox communities even without a Zionistic background. But for the DPs, it could have an additional political meaning in the sense of Zionism, too – most of them prepared for immigration to Israel, and the traditional places were witnesses to the legitimacy of settling there.[20] The Ampfing

plausible, but templates for both Rachel's grave and the Hebrew lettering must have been supplied by the Jewish community; Schmidt, "Nach der Shoah," see note 18, 139.

20 The "Eastern Jewish" tradition of symbolic-motif synagogue painting had already found resonance in Germany during the Weimar Republic. In 1928, the prayer hall of an "Eastern Jewish" Orthodox community in Remscheid was painted with corresponding motifs by the painter Heinrich Mandelbaum, himself a member of the community. However, this found resonance in the Jewish press rather as a curiosity (see *Israelitisches Familienblatt* 15.11 [1928]: 47).

Fig. 5: Ampfing, paintings in the DP prayer room, 1947 (Michael Schmidt, "Nach der Shoah: Die ehemalige Synagoge des Jüdischen Komitees Ampfing." *das münster* 63 (2010), 135–140).

Fig. 6: Gabersee, painting in the DP prayer room, late 1940s, undated photo (nurinst-archive, Nuremberg).

Fig. 7: Weiden, paintings in the synagogue by Julian Pfeiffer, 1948/49 (Photograph: Mirko Przystawik, Bet Tfila – Research Unit for Jewish Architecture, Braunschweig, 2019).

prayer room served only for a short period as a synagogue; today the building is a parochial house again.[21]

Another motif from Israel, reproduced perhaps from a postcard, was depicted in a Jewish DP prayer room in Gabersee, Bavaria (Fig. 6). It opened in a hospital for DPs. Here we see a painting of the Western Wall with prayers as a similar motif of religious and perhaps political longing for Erez Israel.[22] Clearly the motif was taken from a photo postcard or an etching.

A more comprehensive iconographic program is preserved in the synagogue of Weiden in Upper Palatinate from 1948/49. The building is still in use by the Jewish community that dates back to the DP period.[23] A painted architecture of ionic columns

---

21 Schmidt, "Nach der Shoah," see note 18, 138.

22 See Jim G. Tobias, and Nicole Grom, *Gabersee und Attel. Wartesäle zur Emigration. Die jüdischen Displaced Persons Camps in Wasserburg 1946–50* (Nürnberg, 2016), 59–73.

23 See Angela Hager, and Cornelia Berger-Dittscheid, "Weiden," in *Mehr als Steine ... Synagogen-Gedenkband Bayern vol. 1*, ed. Wolfgang Kraus, Berndt Hamm, and Meier Schwarz (Lindenberg i. A. 2007), 310–319.

Fig. 8: Weiden, paintings in the synagogue by Julian Pfeiffer, 1948/49 (Photograph: Mirko Przystawik, Bet Tfila – Research Unit for Jewish Architecture, Braunschweig, 2019).

frames several fields, some of them filled with motifs from Erez Israel (Figs. 7 and 8). Only in Weiden can we name the painter, who was Julian Pfeiffer from Będzin near Kattowice. In 1949 he immigrated to Israel.[24]

Perhaps Pfeiffer was also the painter of the wall paintings in the synagogue in Neuberghauser Straße in Munich (Fig. 9). The city had the largest Jewish population in post-war Bavaria.[25] Thus the "Central Committee of the Liberated Jews" ("Zentralkomitee der befreiten Juden") and the "Rabbinical Council of the American zone" had its domiciles here since 1945. In the former villa of an artist, Jewish services were held from autumn 1946. Here a center of religious and cultural DP institutions developed. The hall with a balcony had room for 350 persons. On the east side, the Torah ark stood in a niche. On top of it, a griffin holds the Torah scroll. Floral ornaments surrounded the ark. Other parts of the walls show musical instruments, remembering the

---

24 See Hager, and Berger-Dittscheid, "Weiden," see note 23, 316.

25 See Tobias Weger, "Die ehemalige orthodoxe Synagoge in der Neuberghauser Straße 11," in *Beth ha-Knesseth. Ort der Zusammenkunft. Zur Geschichte der Münchner Synagogen, ihrer Rabbiner und Kantoren*, ed. Stadtarchiv München (München, 1999), 201–209.

instruments of the Temple of Solomon. Perhaps painted by Pfeiffer or by another artist, the painter must have studied seriously the East European tradition of synagogue painting and its renaissance in the first third of the twentieth century.

Along with the emigration of the most of the DPs their synagogues were abandoned. DPs who decided to stay in Germany mostly became members of the German-Jewish communities. A mixture of German and East European Jewish traditions developed – here more "German" – Liberal, there more "Polish" – Orthodox. Of course, this was not without cultural, religious and social conflicts.[26] Only a few Jewish communities saw themselves explicitly continuing with the DP traditions, like in Weiden or the minyan in Possartstraße in Munich.[27]

In most cases, the synagogues built in the 1950s and 1960s respected Orthodox traditions, giving up the Liberal synagogue layout prevalent in German synagogues from the nineteenth century until 1933. Stylistically, they were designed in "modern" styles. A reflection of Eastern European traditions may be indicated by the stained-glass windows with Jewish symbols in Düsseldorf (Fig. 10). The weekday-prayer-room was designed by Hermann Zvi Guttmann.[28] He was the architect of the whole Jewish center, inaugurated in 1958. Guttmann grew up with East European Jewish traditions and became one of the most influential synagogue architects in West Germany. The warm, dark and colorful weekday-synagogue, presumably mostly used by former DPs, contrasts with the light, white main hall for the entire community. But Guttmann used modern and abstract forms to transform the traditional Jewish symbols.

As spaces of self-identification and of shaping cultural and religious self-awareness, the synagogues of the DPs and their furnishing and paintings are of high significance. It has to be stressed that all the costly work was done for, and perhaps by, persons who intended to leave the place as soon as possible. Eastern Europe Orthodox traditions and the actual political struggle for the immigration to Israel were mingled in the iconographic programs.

Nevertheless, the DP synagogues were also meant as symbols for the survival of the Jewish people and culture. Especially in the land of the persecutors it was a political signal to reconstruct and re-open synagogues that were destroyed only seven or eight years before. The visible presence of Jews and their religious and cultural

---

26 See Michael Brenner, and Norbert Frei, "Konsolidierung," in *Geschichte der Juden in Deutschland von 1945 bis zur Gegenwart. Politik, Kultur und Gesellschaft*, ed. Michael Brenner (München, 2012), 153–294, especially 163–175.

27 The Munich DP community lost many members through emigration, but it did not dissolve completely. Those who remained joined the Jewish Community in 1951. However, the group remained as a minyan, so that regular services continued to be celebrated in Neuberghauser Straße. A renovation of the synagogue hall still took place in 1961/62. In 1966, the community received a new domicile at Possartstraße 15, where the religious traditions of the DP community continue to this day; see Weger, "Die ehemalige orthodoxe Synagoge in der Neuberghauser Straße 11," see note 25, a photo is published on page 203.

28 On Guttmann, see Klei: *Jüdisches Bauen in Nachkriegsdeutschland,* see note 6.

Fig. 9: Munich, paintings in the prayer room in Neuberghauser Straße, around 1946 (Tobias Weger, "Die ehemalige orthodoxe Synagoge in der Neuberghauser Straße 11," in: *Beth ha-Knesseth. Ort der Zusammenkunft. Zur Geschichte der Münchner Synagogen, ihrer Rabbiner und Kantoren*, ed. Stadtarchiv München [München, 1999]).

institutions was part of the re-education program of the German population, especially in the US zone: In a speech held during the re-inauguration of the synagogue of Dieburg (Hesse) in the summer of 1947 the director of the military government, Dr. Newman, pointed out, that "the mission of the Americans in Germany will be fulfilled, when all men have learned to be tolerant."[29] The synagogue of Dieburg was the fourth synagogue to be re-opened in Hesse after the war. The subsequent fate of the Dieburg synagogue is comparable to that of some other synagogues from the time before 1933, which were used for Jewish services for a short time after 1945. After the

29 www.hstad-online.de/ausstellungen/online/juedisches_leben_in_suedhessen, accessed October 18, 2021; thereafter *Darmstädter Echo*, [August 2, 1947]). See also Dietrich Kohlmannslehner, and Thomas Lange, ed. *„ ... wohnen auf der verfluchten deutschen Erde". Jüdisches Leben in Südhessen nach 1945. Die DP-Lager in Lampertheim, Lindenfels, Bensheim, Dieburg und Babenhausen sowie die Anfänge der Jüdischen Gemeinde Darmstadt* (Darmstadt, 1998), 44.

dissolution of the Dieburg DP community, it was sold, rebuilt several times and finally demolished in 1965.[30] The synagogue in Diepholz was sold to a Christian and torn down in the 1950s, also without leaving any documentation. Elsewhere, the historical decorations disappeared under younger layers: The paintings in Wetzlar, Munich, and Gabersee have only been documented by historical photos.

Although only a few examples of murals in prayer rooms of Jewish DPs have been identified so far, these material testimonies of the survivors are of considerable significance for the religious and artistic ideas of the communities for which they were created. They provide evidence of an interest on the part of the DPs in designing their spaces specifically – and in doing so, drawing on traditions that can be traced far back in the history of synagogues. Iconographic sources and artistic models can so far only be described in outline, and the designing artists or the executing painters remain largely in the dark. The indications of cooperation with local craftsmen, who also produced the other furnishings of the reconstructed synagogues, should be pursued further, since a hitherto little noticed field of exchange between the Jewish survivors, the local population, the local authorities and the occupying forces is emerging here.

The DP synagogues may also be seen as places of transit of synagogue art – from East Europe to Germany, from there to Israel, the US, and to other destinations of the former DPs. The traces of transfers and the ways and ideas of transformation still have to be researched. A systematic documentation and comprehensive research of the DP synagogues and their artistic programs should bring to life this interesting period of Jewish material culture in Germany and in other countries after World War II. Such research would also help to preserve the rare remnants of these now nearly forgotten objects.

30 See Ulrich Knufinke, "Dieburg. Synagoge Am Markt," in *Synagogenarchitektur in Deutschland*, ed. Aliza Cohen-Mushlin, and Harmen H. Thies (Petersberg, 2008), 255–257.

Fig. 10: Düsseldorf, stained-glass windows of the weekdays prayer room of the Jewish community center, architect: Hermann Zvi Guttmann, 1958 (Photograph: Ulrich Knufinke, Bet Tfila – Research Unit for Jewish Architecture, Braunschweig).

Katrin Keßler

"Next Year in Jerusalem ..." – References to the Holy Land in Synagogue Architecture

The Holy Land, and especially the city of Jerusalem with the Temple, have always been an important point of reference for Judaism in Diaspora. Although an imitation of the Temple and its objects is forbidden according to Jewish religious law (*halacha*), echoes of the sanctuary can be found in synagogue architecture throughout history.[1] On one hand, the synagogue itself is a reminiscent of the Temple: its spatial division with the separation of the holy of holies – the Torah ark – and with its services three times a day, reminiscent of the Temple sacrifices, and much more.[2] On the other hand, architects have repeatedly sought to link their synagogue architecture with the Holy Land and the Jerusalem Temple. An early example is the Amsterdam Esnoga, built in 1671 to 1675 by building master Elias Bouman (1636–1686) for the Sephardi community. Its exterior buttresses, especially those of the eastern façade, are borrowed from Temple reconstructions by Juan Bautista Villalpando (1552–1608), a Spanish Jesuit Father and architect.[3]

Later, the scheme of the Temple was adapted by architect Friedrich Weinbrenner (1766–1826) for the ground plan of his Karlsruhe Synagogue (1798–1810).[4] In mid-nineteenth century Germany, the entrances of a number of synagogues were stressed by two columns reminiscent of the two pillars Jachin and Boaz, for example in Hamburg, Temple Poolstraße (1842–1844) or in Hildesheim (1848–1849). Less suspicious, two columns can already be found in the classicist synagogues of Nienburg/Weser (1823) and Rexingen (1837), although here they carried an architrave, while the pillars

1 See, for example, Harmen H. Thies, "Idee und Bild der Synagoge," in *Synagogenarchitektur in Deutschland. Dokumentation zur Ausstellung*, ed. Aliza Cohen-Mushlin, and Harmen H. Thies (Petersberg, 2008), 21–40, especially 21–26. For the simultaneous development in France, see Dominique Jarrassé, *Une histoire des synagogues francaises. Entre Occident et Orient* (Arles, 1997), 53–65, and on the use of the columns Jachin and Boaz in France, see 66–70.

2 See Carol Herselle Krinsky, *Synagogues of Europe. Architecture, History, Meaning* (New York, 1985), 5–10. Also Salomon Korn, *Geteilte Erinnerung* (Berlin, 1999), 35–39, starts his analysis of synagogues since 1945 with the Tabernacle and the Jerusalem Temple. He states that the synagogue building represents the idea of an absent almighty – as seen in the Tabernacle – in a better way than the Temple.

3 See Sergey Kravtsov, "Juan Bautista Villalpando and Sacred Architecture in the Seventeenth Century," *Journal of the Society of Architectural Historians* 64.3 (2005): 312–339.

4 Ulrich Knufinke, "Karlsruhe, Synagoge Kronenstraße," in: *Synagogenarchitektur in Deutschland. Dokumentation zur Ausstellung*, ed. Aliza Cohen-Mushlin, and Harmen H. Thies (Petersberg, 2008), 151–154.

https://doi.org/10.1515/9783110750812-004

Jachin and Boaz are assumed to be free standing.[5] Finally, the names of several Reform synagogues link these buildings directly to the Jerusalem Temple, such as the Jacobstempel in Seesen or the aforementioned Temple Poolstraße.[6]

At the turn of the twentieth century, an art-historical interest in the objects of Jewish culture developed. While initially it was the Temple and its reconstructions from written sources that inspired architects in their design of synagogues, the publication of excavation results in Palestine at the beginning of the twentieth century brought ancient synagogue buildings and their decoration into focus. Although the extensive volume of Heinrich Kohl and Carl Watzinger's *Ancient Synagogues in Galilee* did not appear until 1916 in the series of the Deutsche Orientgesellschaft,[7] there had been prior reports in various journals: As early as in 1905, the *Israelitisches Familienblatt* noted that architect Heinrich Kohl from Hanover, the private lecturer and assistant to the director of the Berlin museums Dr. Carl Watzinger and Dipl.-Ing. Hiller had left to document and research the synagogue ruins of Galilee.[8] In November 1905, that expedition was accomplished and first results were expected.[9] Two years later, Kohl and Watzinger visited the region again. A description of the situation they found on site was published in *Ost und West* in 1908.[10]

Proof that such reports indeed had a direct influence on synagogue design in Germany is given in a report in the *Israelitisches Familienblatt* of 1903 that relates the restoration of the small synagogue in Gehaus/Thuringia:

> Through these means, these two sacred places [cemetery and synagogue] soon received a better appearance. Due to a treatise on 'Jewish Decorative Arts and Synagogues' by E. Joel, the coats of arms of the twelve tribes were applied as synagogue decoration, which could be used very nicely. Other Jewish symbols also adorn the interior, and thus one feels oneself to be in a Jewish house of worship, even if it is not outwardly recognizable as such.[11]

The article by Eduard Joel to which the Gehaus congregation referred had been published in the *Israelitisches Familienblatt* barely two months earlier. There, Joel recommends on one hand a decoration of synagogue rooms in the "old Jewish style,

5 Harold Hammer-Schenk, *Synagogen in Deutschland. Geschichte einer Baugattung im 19. und 20. Jahrhundert* (Hamburg, 1981), 157 (Hamburg), 175 (Hildesheim), 171 (Rexingen).

6 On the relationship between Reform synagogues and the Temple see Harmen H. Thies, "On Typologies and Architecture of Reform Synagogues," in: *Reform Judaism and Architecture*, ed. Andreas Brämer, Mirko Przystawik, and Harmen H. Thies (Petersberg, 2016), 17–34.

7 Heinrich Kohl, and Carl Watzinger, *Antike Synagogen in Galilaea (= Wissenschaftliche Veröffentlichungen der Deutschen Orientgesellschaft 29)* (Leipzig, 1916).

8 *Israelitisches Familienblatt* 27 (July 6, 1905): 4.

9 *Israelitisches Familienblatt* 45 (November 9, 1905): 5.

10 O. Ehrhard, "Die Synagogenruinen Galiläas," *Ost und West* 11 (November, 1908): columns 665–676.

11 *Israelitisches Familienblatt* 36 (September 3, 1903): 9.

which was very similar to the Phoenician and other Near Eastern styles." Instead of the usual use of coats of arms in window decorations he suggests

> [w]hy not use the twelve tribes of Israel that are so decoratively? The Duboim plant on a red background, the coat of arms of the tribe of Reuben, the city gate on green, Simon's coat of arms, are well-known heraldic ornaments. The tribe of Levi has, like the German Empire, black-white-red horizontal stripes, in the middle the breast shield of the high priest. Judah carries the lion on a blue ground, and thus the emblems of all the twelve tribes are easily used.[12]

And further he declares, "[e]verywhere now the strive to be national is visible, even the smallest little nation of the Balkan Peninsula, for example, reflects on possessing a little peculiarity, and we with our history, glorious even in the millennia of exile, should not proudly emphasize ours?" The conclusion reads like a call for the founding of the Bezalel School: "The drawing of the designs alone would not suffice, of course; they would also have to be made in metal and glass, in leather, linen and wickerwork. The good penetrates; since there is a real need for good rituals, they would also find use, i.e., be bought, and the enterprise begun for a noble purpose would become a profitable one."

Even before that publications of the excursions and later excavation results could be found in the *Mitteilungen der Deutschen Orient-Gesellschaft* (1904), or in Jewish publications like *Ost und West*, and especially in the 1920s the topic was taken up repeatedly by art historians and also architects.[13] At the same time, applications can be found in synagogue architecture, especially in the period before World War I – in Görlitz (1909–11), Essen (1911–1913), Frankfurt am Main (1908–1910) and others.

Special elements reproduced in synagogue buildings mainly concerned stylistic choices – with regard to "ancient Jewish traditions" with their symbols recurring in synagogue construction and Jewish art – above all the Star of David, lions, tablets of the law, menorah, or echoes of the twelve tribes of Israel. As expected, these can also be found in post-war synagogues – either in the form of inscriptions, like in the Stuttgart Synagogue (built in 1952 by architect Ernst Guggenheimer), in brass symbols on the entrance door in Würzburg (Fig. 1, built in 1970 by architect Hermann Zvi Guttmann) or less clearly for the visitor as twelve windows, twelve-part domes, etc.

In the post-war period, a new way of referencing the Holy Land can be observed from the 1950s. Due to improved transport possibilities, the import of building materials and, more concretely, of stone, became fashionable. In the beginning, it was marble imported from the young state of Israel that was to be used in synagogues. Perhaps the first architect who used Israeli marble in synagogues was Hermann Zvi

12 *Israelitisches Familienblatt*. 36 (September 3, 1903): 9.

13 H. Thiersch and G. Hölscher, "Reise durch Phönizien und Palästina," *Mitteilungen der Deutschen Orient-Gesellschaft zu Berlin* 23 (September 1904): 1–51. Eberhard, "Die Synagogenruinen Galiläas," see note 10, columns 663–676. Alfred Grotte, "Die Erforschung der alten Synagogen in Galiläa," *Ost und West* 3–4 (March–April 1920): columns 88–97.

Fig. 1: Würzburg Synagogue (1970), entrance doors with symbols (Photograph: Ulrich Knufinke, Bet Tfila – Research Unit for Jewish Architecture, Braunschweig, 2006).

Guttmann (1917–1977).[14] He framed the Torah ark of the Würzburg Synagogue, inaugurated in 1970, with Peki'in marble from Israel (Fig. 2).[15] With regard to the rather restricted budget for the building, the importing of marble from Israel is astonishing; that material surely would have been available for a lower price in Europe too. Guttmann had previously used the same marble for the design of the Jewish Memorial in the former Dachau Concentration Camp, designed in 1964 and inaugurated in 1967 (Fig. 3).[16] In a dark room, a light strip of marble strives into the light at the end of which is a menorah carved from the marble.

14 On Guttmann and his oeuvre, see especially Alexandra Klei, *Jüdisches Bauen in Nachkriegsdeutschland. Der Architekt Hermann Zvi Guttmann* (Berlin, 2017).

15 Klei, *Jüdisches Bauen in Nachkriegsdeutschland*, see note 14, 215 on, and Hermann Zvi Guttmann, *Vom Tempel zum Gemeindezentrum. Synagogen im Nachkriegsdeutschland* (Frankfurt am Main, 1989), 79.

16 Klei, *Jüdisches Bauen in Nachkriegsdeutschland*, see note 14, 260–270; on the marble used in Dachau, see 266 as well as https://www.kz-gedenkstaette-dachau.de/historischer-ort/virtueller-rundgang/juedische-gedenkstaette/. Accessed July 16, 2021.

Fig. 2: Würzburg Synagogue (1970), the Torah ark with the marble wall (Photograph: Ulrich Knufinke, Bet Tfila – Research Unit for Jewish Architecture, Braunschweig, 2006).

According to Guttmann, he chose Peki'in marble "because this place – Piktin [sic] – was inhabited always, even in the heaviest times, at least by one Jew and therefore symbolizes the continuity of Judaism."[17] The town of Peki'in is located in Northern Israel, about 30 km northeast of the Sea of Galilee. According to tradition, at least one Jew or Jewish family has been living there without interruption since the Second Temple Period.[18]

It is very likely that Guttmann also used marble from Israel in other synagogues – this may suggest a drawing for the Torah ark in the Offenbach Synagogue

---

17 Guttmann in a letter to René Wander Auwera on February 23, 1962. Quoted in Klei, *Jüdisches Bauen in Nachkriegsdeutschland*, see note 14, 268.

18 On the Peki'in site, see for example https://www.jewishvirtuallibrary.org/peki-x0027-in. Accessed October 28, 2021. According to Eli Ashkenaz (*Haaretz*, July 25, 2012) "Zinati, who was born in 1931, is the last link in the chain of a Jewish community that apparently maintained a continuous presence in Peki'in since the time of the Second Temple, when three families from the ranks of the kohenim, the priestly caste that served in the Temple, moved there. Since then, the only known break in the Jewish presence was during two years in the late 1930s, when the town's Jews fled the Arab riots of 1936–39. Most of them went to what they called the Hadera diaspora. But one family, Zinati's, returned home in 1940." Cited in https://en.wikipedia.org/wiki/Peki%27in. Accessed October 16, 2021.

Fig. 3: Dachau, Concentration Camp Memorial Site, Jewish memorial of 1967 (Photograph: Ulrich Knufinke, Bet Tfila – Research Unit for Jewish Architecture, Braunschweig, 2006).

with marble in noble red and blanche; the drawing is kept in the Guttmann collection of the Jewish Museum Berlin.[19] The same is true for the use of marble at the Torah ark of his Düsseldorf Synagogue (1956–1958, Fig. 4).[20]

Israel had exported marble from Galilee and also from other parts of the country since the early 1950s, and exports to the USA are mentioned for the first time in spring 1951. This was carried out by the Israel Marble Corporation/New York and the stone was prepared by the Lime and Stone Production Company Limited in Haifa, a subsidiary of Solel Boneh Limited, which owned quarries in Nazareth and other parts of the Galilee, Carmel and Gilboa, near Jerusalem and Eilat.[21] One of the first major shipments, about three tons, went to New York to be used for a synagogue in Brooklyn – possibly the Kingsway Jewish Center.[22] A report from 1951 states that

19 Hermann Zvi Guttmann, construction drawing of the Torah ark of the Offenbach Synagogue, Frankfurt am Main. September 1955, pencil on tracing paper, 36 x 37.8 cm; Jewish Museum Berlin, inv. no. 2017/313/595, donation of Dr. Gitta Guttmann and Dr. Rosa Guttmann, Photo: Roman März (permalink https://objekte.jmberlin.de/object/jmb-obj-653595).

20 Guttmann, *Vom Tempel zum Gemeindezentrum*, see note 15, 34.

21 *Israel Digest, A Weekly Summary of News from Israel* (May 25, 1951): 8 on.

22 *Geographic School Bulletins* (1951): n.p.

Fig. 4: Düsseldorf Synagogue (1958), Torah ark made from marble (Photograph: Ulrich Knufinke, Bet Tfila – Research Unit for Jewish Architecture, Braunschweig, 2007).

> [s]hipments of the Israel marble in four different basic colors – white, gold, grey and pink – have already been sold to several American construction, architectural, and monument firms. Great interest in Israel marble comes from houses of worship, both Jewish and Christian. The sentiment attached to Israel marble makes it a natural for use in synagogues and churches,' Mr. Doeh asserted. He said that his firm will shortly bring to the United States shipments of Israel granite from the Negev.[23]

It can be assumed that the exports did not last long, as the deposits were soon exhausted. While in 1967, they were still mentioned,[24] in 1999, the occurrence of marble was already forgotten: the journal of the German Palestine Association claims that Israel is particularly suitable for examining marble artefacts, as there are no marble deposits in the country and it can therefore be assumed that all the marble

23 *Israel Digest, A weekly Summary of News from Israel* 2.24 (June 29, 1951).

24 Erika Spiegel, *New Towns in Israel: Urban and Regional Planning and Development* (New York, 1967), 169.

Fig. 5: Darmstadt Synagogue (1988), façade from west (Photograph: Ulrich Knufinke, Bet Tfila – Research Unit for Jewish Architecture, Braunschweig, 2007).

pieces found were imported.[25] At that time, the deposits had already fallen into oblivion – or had not become widely known at all.

Instead of marble, another fashion entered synagogue architecture in the years that followed. Some architects refer to the Holy City by deliberate use of a light-coloured sand-lime stone, reminiscent of the golden Jerusalem Stone. According to British Mandatory law, introduced in 1918 under the governorship of Sir Ronald Storrs, buildings of the city of Jerusalem had to use the local – yellowish and sometimes even pink – limestone on their exteriors in order to "preserve the character of Jerusalem."[26] This most typical element of Jerusalem architecture was adapted by German architects for Jewish buildings. As early as 1988, German-Jewish architect Alfred Jacoby (* 1950) mentions such an intention for his Darmstadt Synagogue (Fig. 5):

25 *Zeitschrift des Deutschen Palästina-Vereins.* (Wiesbaden: Harrassowitz, 1999), 91.

26 Ruth Kark, and Michal Oren-Nordheim, *Jerusalem and its Environs: Quarters, Neighborhoods, Villages. 1800–1948* (Jerusalem, 2001), 187. And on modern Jerusalem architecture, see Ulrich Knufinke, *Bauhaus: Jerusalem. A Guide Book to Modern Architecture* (Tel Aviv, 2012).

Fig. 6: Jerusalem, Great Synagogue (Photograph: Martin Vines, 2009, Montreal, Wikipedia, CC BY-SA 3.0).

> The memory of Jerusalem and the Holy Temple is also kept alive by another building detail: the yellow-gold natural stone, which the Jerusalem building law prescribes for all buildings in the Holy City. It symbolically connects Darmstadt's synagogue with Jerusalem and the Holy Temple.[27]

The architect of the Wuppertal synagogue (2001–02), for which Seeberger sandstone from Thuringia was used, explains that the stone "can be reminiscent of walls in Jerusalem."[28] Often the exterior of the Dresden Synagogue too is associated with Jerusalem stone, but in fact, the intention here was instead to incorporate the building into the cityscape of Dresden, with its light sand stone used for many public buildings.[29]

Anyhow, the use of light-yellow stone was not new and surely not restricted to Jewish architecture. In his Stuttgart Synagogue (1952), Ernst Guggenheimer (1880–1973) used Kehlheim shell limestones – the building and the material also

---

27 Alfred Jacoby, "Solitär und Mittelpunkt jüdischen Lebens – Entwurfsbeschreibung," in *Das Darmstädter Synagogenbuch*, ed. Eva Reinhold-Postina, and Moritz Neumann (Darmstadt, 1988), 60–68, here 64 on.

28 Hans-Christof Goedeking, "Zur Architektur der neuen Synagoge in Wuppertal," in *Dies soll ein Haus des Gebets sein für alle Völker. Festschrift zur Einweihung der neuen Bergischen Synagoge in Wuppertal*, ed. Freundeskreis Neue Synagoge e.V. (Wuppertal, 2002), 36 on.

29 Interview with the architect Andrea Wandel in Hamburg on July 1, 2021.

referred to the Temple Oberstraße in Hamburg (1931, Felix Aschmann and Robert Friedmann).[30] The Synagogue Trier (1957, Alfons Leitl) used quarry stone masonry made of Eifel sandstone and the façade of the synagogue in Hagen (1960) by Karl Gerle was made from a beige natural stone too. However, it seems that at this point, the use of local stone was chosen for other reasons.

In a certain sense, those synagogue buildings that today use the original Jerusalem Stone – the light-coloured limestone from quarries in Israel – are following such exports or imports. Probably the earliest example can be found in the Duisburg Synagogue, built in 1999 by the Polish-Israeli architect Zvi Hecker (* 1931). On the exterior, the building is an exposed concrete structure that stretches out into the landscape like fingers. Jerusalem Stone was only used in the synagogue interior for the Torah ark and the women's gallery – applied in a way that can be found in Jerusalem, for example, in parks as flooring. According to the architect, he aimed to create a "biblical landscape" through the simplicity of the space and the materials (Fig. 7).[31]

In the Bochum Synagogue (2005–2007), Jerusalem Stone is used on the façade.[32] In Munich, the façades of the Jacobsplatz Synagogue, designed by Wandel, Höfer and Lorch (2003–2006), clearly refer to the Jerusalem Western Wall, although the stone (travertine) did not come from Jerusalem, but from Gauingen/Baden-Württemberg. On the other hand, upon the special wish of the Jewish community, stone imported from Jerusalem is used in the interior of the synagogue (Figs. 8 and 9).

Not directly imported from Israel, but at least from the Middle East and referring to the Temple building material, is the reddish cedar wood used for example in Stuttgart (1952) or in Munich (2006). In the Kassel Synagogue (2000, Fig. 10), cedar wood was used for the bimah and the lectern of the cantor: "While the adjoining structures are characterized by exposed concrete and plaster, the sacred space received a cladding of cedar wood, which corresponds to the requirement from the Torah to build a 'temple of the cedar of Lebanon.'"[33]

Along with the use of building material from Israel, symbolism seems to have played a greater role in synagogue construction only since the 1980s. In 1999, Salomon Korn refers to the verticality of the eastern part with the Torah ark with windows of Danzig cameo glass (*Überfangglas*) above the Torah ark of the 1963 inaugurated Hanover Synagogue. He describes it as

30 On Stuttgart, see, for example, Korn, *Geteilte Erinnerungen*, see note 2, 47. On Hamburg, see Knufinke, "Hamburg, Synagoge (Tempel) Oberstraße,", see note 1, 265–268.

31 Nicole Rinza, "Synagogenneubauten nach 1945 in Deutschland. Von den Anfängen bis zur Gegenwart," [unpublished manuskript], ca. 2007, 55.

32 Regina Meleusencova, "Die neue Synagoge der Jüdischen Gemeinde Bochum-Herne-Hattingen," in *Synagogen in Nordrhein-Westfalen. Architektur und Erinnerung*, ed. Alexandra Klei (Berlin, 2019), 130.

33 *Baunetz*, May 26, 2000: „Aus der Mitte heraus. Einweihung eines Synagogen-Neubaus in Kassel," Accessed on July 10, 2021).

Fig. 7: Duisburg Synagogue (1999), interior towards east (Photograph: Ulrich Knufinke, Bet Tfila – Research Unit for Jewish Architecture, Braunschweig, 2007).

> part of the stylised burning thorn bush, which through its emphasized verticality could also represent the pillar of fire pointing the way at night during the desert wanderings of the children of Israel. The symbolic light of fire refers to the interpretation of the Holy Scriptures kept in the Aron hakodesh as the light, teaching and guide of Judaism. This message, translated into architectural art, seems to have been Guttmann's central concern in the synagogue in Hanover.[34]

In contrast to Korn's review, Hermann Guttmann did not charge his synagogue with any symbolism in his description of 1963 – and the same can be said for his contemporary synagogue architects. He stresses the choice of material, the practicability and the division of the room. Only one sentence gives an idea of a symbolic meaning: "The purpose of this type of construction is to keep the element of fear away from a place of worship in our time, in which destruction is present almost

34 Korn, *Geteilte Erinnerungen*, see note 2, 51.

Fig. 8: Munich Synagogue (2006), façade reminding of the Jerusalem wailing wall (Photograph: Katrin Keßler, 2017).

daily, and instead to bring in the closeness to nature and great hope."[35] Light and hope seem to constitute the most important elements of his architecture.

In contrast, the 1980s buildings were full of symbols: Salomon Korn's Frankfurt Community Center (1986) strikingly shows the crack that went through German Jewry and that was still to remain palpable. On the window wall of the synagogue in Kassel (Jacoby) cracks and fractures are painted, which should be reminders of the cracks and fractures in the life of man.[36] The outer wall of the Wuppertal Synagogue shows nine narrow window slits with elevated lintels, which are supposed to be reminiscent of the

35 Hermann Guttmann, "Das Gemeindezentrum in Hannover," in *Leben und Schicksal. Zur Einweihung der Synagoge in Hannover*, ed. city of Hannover and Jewish community of Hannover (Hannover, 1963), 199–207, here 205.

36 Esther Haß, "Eine neue Synagoge für Kassels Jüdische Gemeinde," in *Synagogen in Kassel*, ed. Stadtmuseum Kassel (Marburg, 2000), 89–98, here 98.

Fig. 9: Munich Synagogue (2006), interior towards east (Photograph: Ulrich Knufinke, Bet Tfila – Research Unit for Jewish Architecture, Braunschweig, 2007).

Hanukkah candles – in memory of the re-dedication of the Jerusalem Temple after its destruction.[37] The Darmstadt synagogue, designed by Alfred Jacoby in 1988, is reminiscent of Jerusalem buildings in its cubic design with flat roofs from which domes rise, e.g. the Great Synagogue in Jerusalem built by Alexander Friedman in 1982 (Figs. 5 and 6).

Domes that were regularly found in synagogue architecture since the nineteenth century were given an additional meaning in the twenty-first century. Usually symbolizing the canopy of heaven, they were now seen as the heaven over Jerusalem. The Mannheim tapestry-lined dome, designed by artists Peter and Paul Stask, is meant to evoke the sky over Jerusalem.[38] In the small Herford Synagogue,

37 Goedeking, "Zur Architektur der neuen Synagoge in Wuppertal," see note 28, 36 on.
38 Rinza, "Synagogenneubauten nach 1945 in Deutschland," see note 31, 100.

Fig. 10: Kassel Synagogue (2000), interior with walls covered with cedar wood (Photograph: Ulrich Knufinke, Bet Tfila – Research Unit for Jewish Architecture, Braunschweig, 2007).

there was even an elaborate arrangement of 248 lights – indicating the number of commandments – in the form of the starry sky over Jerusalem on the night of Rosh Hashanah 5770 (September 19, 2009).[39]

The tent motive – remembrance of the Tabernacle in the desert – was not a new symbol in architecture. It returned to synagogue and church buildings in the early 1950s and saw a revival with the Dresden Synagogue (2006, Fig. 12). Tent constructions can already be found in the mid-1950s, for example in the buildings of Helmut Goldschmidt (Dortmund, 1956, Fig. 11) and were often applied to church buildings, for example the Protestant Apostle Church in Bonn (1955/56 by the Bonn architects

39 Tabea Schüler, "Die Herforder Synagoge," in *Synagogen in Nordrhein-Westfalen. Architektur und Erinnerung*, ed. Alexandra Klei (Berlin, 2019), 164.

Fig. 11: Dortmund Synagogue (1956), interior forming a tent-like structure (Photograph: Ulrich Knufinke, Bet Tfila – Research Unit for Jewish Architecture, Braunschweig, 2007).

H.A. Rolffs and W. Orzol). In the Münster Synagogue (1961), Goldschmidt himself describes the interior as a

> concrete frame construction (exposed concrete) and lined with red clinker bricks. In form and color, the building blends in with the local building style that is generally used today. With this new synagogue, the Jewish community in Münster has probably created a dignified and modern house of worship of which it can be proud [...].[40]

And again, there is no reference here to any symbolism. The synagogue in Dresden, with its twisting massive structure, is intended to reflect the permanence of the Temple, while in the interior a filigree light metal mesh symbolizes the provisional tabernacle (Fig. 12). These two echoes were also used by the same architects for the Munich Synagogue.

---

40 Rinza, "Synagogenneubauten nach 1945 in Deutschland," see note 31, 111; there after *Festschrift zur Weihe der neuen Synagoge in Münster/Westf. 12. März 1961* (Münster, 1961).

Fig. 12: Dresden Synagogue (2006), a tent-like curtain separates the women (Photograph: Ulrich Knufinke, Bet Tfila – Research Unit for Jewish Architecture, Braunschweig, 2007).

The idea was already conceived in 1988 by Salomon Korn for the design of the synagogue in Darmstadt. Korn was defeated in the competition by Alfred Jacoby, whose design was implemented. Instead, Korn published his design in the Frankfurt catalogue for the exhibition "Synagogues in Germany." His design was to be a "synagogal antinomy" of "permanent temple walls" and "provisional tabernacle canopy." However, he implemented the tent as a curved concrete ceiling.[41] Then, the jury judged Korn's design in 1986: "The monumental character and the choice of hard, forbidding materials seem out of place."[42]

The idea of firm and light structures was applied in the Regensburg Synagogue, built by architect Volker Staab (* 1957) and inaugurated in 2019, using wooden planking:

> With the firmly fixed wall at the bottom and the shimmering arcade of light with the almost textile-looking dome shell at the top, the architecture connects the two images of remembrance that are so important for Judaism: Solomon's Temple in Jerusalem and the tabernacle that served as the central meeting place during the Israelites' exodus from Egypt.[43]

41 "Kritik an Darmstadts Synagoge, eine Abrechnung unter Kollegen. Peinliches in einem Frankfurter Ausstellungskatalog," (December 3, 1988) (unclear in which newspaper it was published), in: Archives of Alfred Diamant.

42 Jury protocol of May 12, 1986, quoted in "Kritik an Darmstadts Synagoge" see note 41.

43 *db deutsche bauzeitung* 8 (2019): 33.

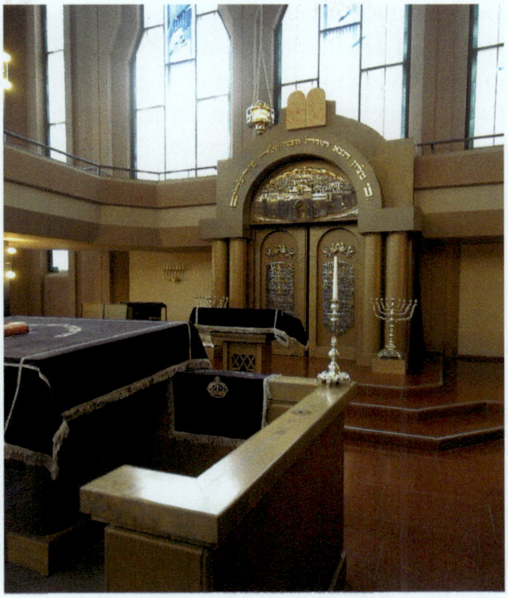

Fig. 13: Mannheim Synagoge (1987), Torah ark designed by an Israeli artist (Photograph: Ulrich Knufinke, Bet Tfila – Research Unit for Jewish Architecture, Braunschweig, 2007).

Sometimes it was not building materials that were imported from Israel, but the "software" in the form of artists or architects who were commissioned to design synagogues or furnish them. The choice was usually up to the congregations and in many cases personal contacts played a large part in it. For example, the fountain of the new Essen synagogue (1959, Dieter Knoblauch and Heinz Heise) was designed by the Israeli artist Eva Samuel, the daughter of the former Essen rabbi Salomon Samuel.[44] Kurt Lewy (1898 Essen–1963 Freiburg), an artist who emigrated to Brussels but was eventually interned in the Gurs camp and escaped from there, designed the glass surfaces in the dome.[45] Other artists commissioned for this building, however, were again not Jewish, such as Joseph Albert Sögtrop (1926–1980) from Menden, who designed the mosaic surfaces.

In Bad Nauheim, it was the artist Yehuda Azulay, who immigrated from Israel a few years earlier, who did the painting of the windows. Artist and goldsmith Alice Bloch, a Jew from Saarbrücken who emigrated to Switzerland in 1935, designed the

44 Rinza, "Synagogenneubauten nach 1945 in Deutschland," see note 31, 62.

45 Rudolf Vierhaus, *Deutsche biographische Enzyklopädie (DBE)* 6 (München, 2006), 412.

parochet of the Stuttgart Synagogue (1952, Guggenheimer).[46] The Ner Tamid as well as the Torah ark in Mannheim (1987, Fig. 13) is a work by the artist Frank Meisler from Tel Aviv, made of silver-grey glazed bird's eye maple.[47] Also, Israeli ambassador's presence at synagogue dedication ceremonies or words of greeting in commemorative publications show the close relationship to Israel.[48]

On the whole, it can be noted that although most of the commissioned artists came from Germany and were not necessarily Jewish, especially special objects – the Torah ark, its curtain (*parochet*), candelabra, etc. – were certainly more frequently given as commissions to Jewish and/or Israeli artists.

With these references or direct imports, sometimes obvious or – like the use of materials from Israel – only known to the community members, the synagogue building is charged with a special meaning, and its symbolism serves as a kind of connecting element between the Holy Land and the German communities.

46 Rinza, "Synagogenneubauten nach 1945 in Deutschland," see note 31, 130.

47 Rinza, "Synagogenneubauten nach 1945 in Deutschland," see note 31, 100.

48 For example, in *Festschrift zur Weihe der Synagoge und des jüdischen Kulturzentrums in Osnabrück 15. Siwan 5729–1. Juni 1969*, ed. Stadt Osnabrück (Osnabrück, 1969). The inauguration of the Wuppertal Synagogue (see Goedeking, "Zur Architektur der neuen Synagoge in Wuppertal," see note 28, even took place in the presence of the Israeli President Moshe Katzav. See Rinza, "Synagogenneubauten nach 1945 in Deutschland," see note 31, 135.

Beate Löffler

Impressive and Invisible. Reflections on the Urban Disposition of Synagogue Buildings in Germany Since 1990

Introduction: Religion in Central European urban space

The city is a human habitat of the highest complexity and non-simultaneity. Here, society asserts and perpetuates historical patterns on the one hand, and articulates and negotiates demands for change, on the other. This is particularly evident in the realm of religious practices, where the supra-temporal perspectives of religions, the persistence of rituals, beliefs, and built form, and the sometimes fast-moving everyday realities of today collide.

Yet, the religious topography of our Central European cities seems to be an unambiguous matter. After more than a millennium, in which society, the dominance of Christian practice of faith and the built environment mutually influence(d) each other, quite stable spatial and symbolic dispositions have developed. In 1970, French sociologist Roland Barthes summed this up and described the center of a European city as a place of abundant social interaction, "a marked site, it is here that the values of civilization are gathered and condensed: spirituality (churches), power (offices), money (banks), merchandise (department stores), language (agoras: café: and promenades)."[1]

From the architectural standpoint, his summary is expressive and apt. It foreshadows, however, the challenges that arise when the multi-religious modern society wants to express itself and become present in an urban space that is conceived and contextualized as mono-religious. The historical presence of Jewish communities, the intra-Christian diversity that began with the Reformation at the latest, and the religious heterogeneity of modern times still hardly play a role when we talk about the structural and symbolic dimensions of our cities. This contrasts evidently with the rising architectural and urban visibility of synagogues and mosques in Germany, as observed by religious studies and architectural research. It raises the question of how these communities manage to rewrite the traditional urban dispositions in their own sense and to shape their own spaces in the juxtaposition of architectural signs. Moreover, it remains unclear how this development relates to the likewise stated deconstruction of Christian architecture and institutional infrastructure.

In order to gain new insights, the project *Transformations of Sacredness* uses the example of the three Abrahamic religions to examine the interplay of socio-

1 Roland Barthes, *Empire of Signs* (New York, 1989), 30.

https://doi.org/10.1515/9783110750812-005

economic change, religious architecture and the city in Germany since the unification in 1990. In close cooperation between religious studies and architectural history, we apply a combination of quantitative and qualitative approaches to look at places of worship that have been newly built or subjected to significant structural or functional changes, including demolition, during the last thirty years. This essay outlines the observations from the quantitative surveys of synagogues and discusses them in the context of the overall study.

The data basis

The total numbers of Abrahamic believers and places of worship in Germany are unknown, but some data is known: The two main churches currently list a total of 44,400 churches, plus approximately 130 synagogues and Jewish prayer houses, 2,500 to 3,000 Muslim prayer rooms and mosques, as well as a large number of churches of various Christian denominations.[2] Even in view of this vague information, it is evident that the buildings recorded in the database so far can only represent a tiny section of the religious topography and its recent change. We mainly recorded processes that have been noticed and discussed by experts and the public, especially if they have been communicated supra-regionally.[3] As a result, the data with regard to churches and mosques is rather discourse-oriented, while the small number of Jewish congregations as well as the extensive and easily accessible basic research in this area promoted a very balanced nationwide survey.[4]

Our database lists 1,517 buildings with worship spaces that have been significantly altered, rebuilt, converted, abandoned or demolished since 1990. They are located in 771 places, have links to 392 organisations and 548 people, mostly planners and commissioners (as of August 31, 2021). Churches clearly dominate (1,122 entries) and show a wide range of occurrences between new construction and demolition and a

2 See regarding numbers, for example, Sekretariat der Deutschen Bischofskonferenz, ed. *Katholische Kirche in Deutschland. Zahlen und Fakten 2019/20* (Bonn, 2020), 72–73. For further reading about the number of mosques, see Doris Kleilein, "Knowhow im Moscheebau," *Bauwelt* 3 (2017): 6; Armin Käfer, "Bund finanziert Imamausbildung mit," *Badische Zeitung* (October 15, 2010), https://www.badische-zeitung.de/bund-finanziert-imamausbildung-mit--36598241.html, accessed September 12, 2021; Christoph Strack, "Islam made in Germany – ein einzigartiges Ausbildungsprojekt," (June 14, 2021), https://www.dw.com/de/ausbildungsprojekt-islamische-imame-made-in-germany/a-57879191, accessed September 12, 2021; Ulrich Pick, "Moscheen in Deutschland. Fromm, unauffällig – und gefährlich?," (August 3, 2016), https://www.deutschlandfunk.de/moscheen-in-deutschland-fromm-unauffaellig-und-gefaehrlich.724.de.html?dram:article_id=361983; Thomas Schmitt, and Jonas Klein, "Moscheen – islamische Sakralbauten in Deutschland," *N aktuell* 13 (September 2019): 6, s.p.

3 The church-related survey profited from a data corpus from the Wüstenrot Foundation (Dr. Stefan Krämer, Dr. Tino Mager, Dr. René Hartmann), which was created as preliminary research for the competition "Kirchengebäude und ihre Zukunft. Sanierung – Umbau – Umnutzung" (Church Buildings and their Future. Redevelopment – Reconstruction – Conversion). It combined objects from publications and specialist journals as well as findings from a larger online search, especially on the projects of relevant architectural firms.

4 Here, only cemeteries and mourning halls are conceptually and informationally difficult to grasp for a quantitative analysis and the assignment of relevance.

regional focus in the federal state of North Rhine-Westphalia. The mosques (317) mainly comprise architecturally significant facilities in the old Federal States, while the so-called backyard mosques, which have already been the subject of much discussion and represent more than eighty percent of Islamic places of worship in Germany, were not the focus. However, they must always be considered in the analysis of urban change. The 77 synagogues and prayer houses surveyed include buildings of the most diverse types with an evenly distribution throughout Germany.

Synagogue buildings in Germany

The urban and architectural reality of synagogues in Germany proves to be more diverse in the overview than the literature seems to have depicted so far. Although the data on congregations and synagogues is readily available, it is difficult to form an overall picture in the synthesis of historical observations, architectural-historical analyses of the pre- and post-war situation and the publications on the more recent buildings by Alfred Jacoby and other planners. For example, the project proposal initially formulated the thesis that "synagogues experience a special public perception and are characterized by experimental architecture, often in city centers," an assumption that needs to be taken with a pinch of salt.[5] The quantitative survey led to a series of observations, which we briefly present here. Subsequently, we will discuss the direction in which questions for further research arose over time.

The enormously high building-related activity of the Jewish communities during the past three decades was perhaps the most significant result of the survey in the overall context. In a sense, this was to be expected, as the growth of the communities due to the influx of so-called contingent refugees from the successor states of the Soviet Union was a central impetus for the present research project. Nevertheless, these activities affected a good half of the communities, an order of magnitude that is still noticeable in the comparison of the overall survey even when all biases in the coverage are taken into account.

Significant building and conversion activity is also evident, for example, in the New Apostolic Church (NAC), which is adapting its congregational structures and worship spaces to declining membership, and various Muslim umbrella organisations, but in each case against the background of larger institutional structures and/or numbers of congregations and worshippers. Therefore, the question arises as to how Jewish

5 Concerning the project and database, see https://sawa.ceres.rub.de/en/, as well as the outline of the project at an early stage in Kim De Wildt, et al., "Transformations of 'Sacredness in Stone': Religious Architecture in Urban Space in 21st Century Germany – New Perspectives in the Study of Religious Architecture," *Religions* 10.11 (2019):, 602, especially 11/16; https://doi.org/10.3390/rel10110602. Accessed September 3, 2021.

communities managed to realise their projects in the midst of the internal integration process. It might be worthwhile to do further research in order to derive experiences or even guidelines that will make it easier for other religious minorities to anchor themselves in the German religious topography. For it became apparent in many cases during the surveys how demanding it can be to deal with the real estate market, building and planning law and the companies carrying out the work. So far, we can only assume that the anchoring of Jew citizens in the center of society, the unequivocal recognition as a religious body and the explicitly formulated political will to support and promote Jewish communities could have a certain influence on success.

The entirety of the building-related activities of Jewish communities splits into three groups of roughly the same size. They include new buildings and conversions as well as other activities such as building maintenance, renovation, extensions and re-consecration. Maintenance, restoration and small modifications are a matter of course in every building's life story. In case of religious buildings, such measures, like the practices of worship or the rite de passage of each member of the community, strengthen the congregation within and add to its relationship with the building and the neighborhood. In our study, they played but a minor role since they do not usually intend to change the community's impact on its built environment. Yet, such activities get attention by the neighbourhood and contribute to the social visibility of the community. It might be valuable to study its impact on the urban religious landscape in detail to gain insight in the role of overlapping and mingling social networks for urban stability.

The other building-related activities recorded are more obvious in their influence on public discourse and urban space. A specific case are the re-consecrations after extensive renovations, restoration or after the translocation of a historic building. Here, different processes mix to a degree that complicates analysis. The celebrations of the completion of the construction work on the synagogues in Görlitz and Lübeck made national news in 2021 (Figs. 1 and 2). In Lübeck, a congregation re-appropriated its established synagogue. In Görlitz, however, the festivity addressed a building of architectural value but currently without congregation.[6]

6 The congregation is in the process of institutionalisation and will use side rooms of the reconstructed building in the near future. Concerning the building, see, for example, the entry on the homepage of Deutsche Stiftung Denkmalschutz (German Foundation for Monument Protection), https://www.denkmalschutz.de/denkmal/ehem-synagoge-goerlitz.html, accessed September 10, 2021. Concerning Jewish life in the city, see, for example, media coverage such as Karin Schuld-Vogelsberg, "Die Synagoge wird 100 Jahre alt. Doch als Gotteshaus wird sie nicht genutzt," *Jüdische Allgemeine* (March 14, 2011), https://www.juedische-allgemeine.de/unsere-woche/die-perle-der-lausitz/, accessed September 12, 2021; Silke Schröder, "Will die Görlitzer Stadtverwaltung jüdische Geschichte tilgen?," *Jüdische Rundschau* 10.74 (October 2020), https://juedischerundschau.de/article.2020-10.will-die-goerlitzer-stadtverwaltung-juedische-geschichte-tilgen.html and "Wächst eine jüdische Gemeinde?," *mdr* (June 13, 2021), https://www.mdr.de/religion/juedisches-leben/synagoge-goerlitz-juedische-gemeinde-100.html, both accessed September 10, 2021.

Fig. 1: Lübeck, Carlebach Synagoge, 1880, Ferdinand Münzenberger (1846–1924) (Photograph: Phasus, 2021, Wikipedia, CC BY-SA 4.0).

Fig. 2: Görlitz, former synagogue, 1911, Lossow & Kühne (Photograph: H. J. Janßen, 2019, Wikimedia, CC BY-SA 4.0).

Here, past and present, religious topography, liturgical practice, *memoria* and monument protection are inextricably intermingled and embodied in the materiality of a single building. The cultural narrative might even overlay the reality of religious life.

The situation with conversions is different. Here, the synagogues seem to dissolve in the city space since they largely disappear behind the building typology of the adopted structures. They cover a wide range of structural and urban conditions that the congregations have to cope with in each case. The thirty conversions of existing buildings affect residential buildings, buildings previously used for commercial or social purposes, and churches. In some cases, the congregation uses the entire property, in others only parts of it. The reasons for choosing a particular building also vary. The community *Adass Jisroel* in Berlin moved into rooms of a historic residential building in 1990, which the community had already used before the Shoah; others occupy Jewish-connoted places anew, as in Bamberg, or set up in rooms to which there are no historical connections, as in Marburg (Figs. 3 and 4).

Fig. 3: Bamberg Synagogue, former Sewing Silk Factory Kupfer und Hesslein (Photograph: Ulrich Knufinke, Bet Tfila – Research Unit for Jewish Architecture, Braunschweig, 2006).

Fig. 4: Marburg Synagogue, 1931, Emil H. Schweizer, former AOK Health Insurance Fund offices (Photograph: Hydro, 2016, Wikipedia, CC BY-SA 4.0).

Often, conversions remain hidden inside; occasionally, they become visible to the outside and give passers-by a hint as to the shift in function.

The impact of re-use on the religious topography are most evident with the adoption of churches. The majority of cases involve modest buildings embedded in everyday environments, where but a ridge turret and the high windows of a hall hint at the specific function. Yet, some go along with a privileged urban disposition and/or a significant building. There is, for example, the heritage protected church building of the early eighteenth century in Cottbus or the community center *Etz Chaim* in Hanover. In Cottbus, urban disposition and architectural typology fit the expectations in Roland Barthes's summary while the new use adds a level of ambiguity that has been present for centuries but remains discussed only occasionally.[7]

7 The discussion concerning the building typology of a synagogue was very present following the Jewish emancipation in Germany, both within the congregations and in public. The Shoah interrupted the fruitful discussion about the interrelation of form, faith, belonging and modern society that similarly involved and still involves church architecture. Concerning the Synagogues, see for example Ulrich Knufinke, *Synagogen im 19. und 20. Jahrhundert. Bauwerke einer Minderheit im Spannungsfeld widerstreitender Wahrnehmungen und Deutungen, in: Gideon Botsch et al. ed.: Islamophobie und Antisemitismus – ein umstrittener Vergleich* (Berlin/Potsdam, 2012), 201–226, and Aliza Cohen-Mushlin, and Harmen H. Thies, ed. *Synagogenarchitektur in Deutschland. Dokumentation zur Ausstellung* (Petersberg, 2008).

Fig. 5: Cottbus Synagogue, 1714 (tower 1870) [former Schlosskirche] (Photograph: Clemensfranz, 2010, Wikipedia, CC BY-SA 3.0).

Fig. 6: Hanover, Community center *Etz Chaim*, 2009, Ahrens & Grabenhorst, former Gustav Adolf Church, 1971, Fritz Eggeling (1913–1966), (Photograph: Beate Löffler, 2019).

Fig. 7: Dresden Synagogue, 2001, Wandel, Hoefer und Lorch + Hirsch (Photograph: Maros Mraz, 2009, Wikipedia, CC BY-SA 3.0).

The conversion of the post-war church in Hanover created a structure whose urban position suggests the dominant religion, but in its expression develops a new form of architectural dignity that inspires further research concerning the contemporary expression of faith and transcendence (Figs. 5 and 6).

These observations invite us to understand the change in religious topography not just as a change in the use of urban space alone. They ask us to involve religious buildings in a comprehensive discussion of the communication of power created by the building typologies of our cities once more and to question the understanding of religious space in modern society in general. This background might also explain some of the architectural interest or disinterest in new synagogue buildings in Germany.

There are 23 newly built synagogues and at least four projects in different states of realisation in Germany since 1990. In an architectural sense, most share what might be described as non-typological expressions of architectural dignity: stereometric bodies, balanced proportions, a precise handling of surfaces and a conscious attribution of spaces and volumes (Figs. 7–11).

While these are characteristics shared with smaller museums or other cultural institutions, it would be interesting to investigate to what extent the models of Hermann Zvi Guttmann's (1917–1977) post-war buildings proved to be formative and how some of Alfred Jacoby's (*1950) designs relate to that as well.[8]

8 Unfortunately, this is one of the moments when quantitative recording raises questions that it cannot answer itself. The literature for answering them is at least partially available. To realise it, however, the focus must be shifted to such a degree as to be impossible in the current project. For work in this regard, see, for example, Elisabeth Rees-Dessauer, *Zwischen Provisorium und Prachtbau – Die Synagogen der jüdischen Gemeinden in Deutschland von 1945 bis zur Gegenwart* (Göttingen, 2019).

Fig. 8: Chemnitz Synagogue, 2002, Alfred Jacoby (*1950) (Photograph: Sandro Schmalfuß, 2015, Wikipedia, CC BY-SA 3.0, edited).

There are two or three observations, however, that might denote a shift concerning the architecture of synagogues in Germany. Firstly, but for Alfred Jacoby, the commissions involved small and mid-sized offices, often without a background in religious architecture. This is in contrast to the strong role of Jewish architects since the post-war reconstruction. Second, synagogue projects in Germany and publications related to the past and present of synagogue architecture gained attention in architectural media such as BauNetz.de or Bauwelt.[9] While the reports favour known architects and significant buildings, there is some indication that the topic itself became more visible among planners by now. This might be due to, thirdly, the two new synagogues in Dresden, 2001 and Munich, 2006. The office Wandel, Hoefer and Lorch (+ Hirsch) realized both buildings, which gained extensive attention in the media (Fig. 7 and 9).

What distinguishes these two buildings from other new synagogues in Germany, however, is that this discussion seems to have ultimately left the subject area of synagogue construction: the buildings were finally understood as religious architecture and as examples of contemporary form finding in a broader sense. This is arguably not only due to the space-creating qualities of the two buildings but also the professional networks of architects and the architectural zeitgeist, but it is also significant for the understanding of our religious environment.

9 This is relevant, since architectural discourse does not really discuss mosques in Germany apart from the Cologne Central Mosque by Paul and Gottfried Böhm or the Islamic Forum in Penzberg by Alen Jasarevic, while a number of such buildings abroad gain attention.

Fig. 9: Munich, Ohel Jakob Synagogue, 2006, Wandel, Hoefer and Lorch (Photograph: Katrin Keßler, 2017).

Fig. 10: Bochum Synagogue, 2007, Peter Schmitz and Ulrike Beuter (Photograph: Maschinenjunge, 2008, Wikipedia, CC BY-SA 3.0).

Fig. 11: Konstanz Synagogue, Wilhelm und Hovenbitzer/Prof. Fritz Wilhelm 2019 (Photograph: Waithamai, 2019, Wikipedia, CC BY-SA 4.0).

On the one hand, the buildings in Dresden and Munich can serve as representatives of other synagogues, prayer houses and community centers in Germany, referring to the Jewish sacral topography in Germany. Many synagogues gained attention as part of the congregation's history, needs and aspiration but despite the works of many colleagues, architectural writings are still of limited supply. On the other hand, the two buildings tie Jewish architecture into the challenging search for religious architecture in modern societies. As such, they connect to a contemporary 'rediscovery' of the sacred building as an architectural subject, whereby the structures, which are not infrequently discussed across all religions and borders, are considered largely independently of their liturgical function or historical significance.[10] Parallel to this, the various intra-religious negotiations on the appropriate form of the worship space proceeded and

---

10 Phyllis Richardson, *Neue sakrale Architektur. Kirchen und Synagogen, Tempel und Moscheen* (München, 2004); Robert Klanten, and Lukas Feireiss, *Closer to God: Religious Architecture and Sacred Spaces* (Berlin, 2010); Karla Cavarra Britton, ed. *Constructing the Ineffable. Contemporary Sacred Architecture* (New Haven, 2010); Chris van Uffelen, *Sacred Architecture + Design. Churches, Synagogues & Mosques* (Salenstein, 2014); James Pallister, *Sacred Spaces. Contemporary Religious Architecture* (London, 2015). See also the planning-related publications such as Nicholas W. Roberts, *Building Type Basics for Places of Worship* (Hoboken, 2004); Rudolf Stegers, Dorothea Baumann, Negar Hakim, *Entwurfsatlas Sakralbau* (Basel, 2008).

continue to proceed,[11] occasionally tying back once more into a more general question of how to 'house' the experience of transcendence.

Church and mosque rub up against the historical subtexts of their architecture in the present: their building typologies reproduce, in order to remain legible in urban communication, with towers and domes, halls and building decoration, also a claim to power that was inscribed in the historical form and is often still thought of today. The absence of an unambiguous building typology of the synagogue, sometimes perceived as problematic in architectural design, is a strength here, because it allows the congregations to renegotiate the link between religion-related space and community-related space with each new conception and to re-define the building's relationship with its environment anew whenever they undertake building-related action. As such, the congregation does not have to fulfil or deconstruct typological expectations. Thus, their solutions for understanding and organising spaces might contribute to an understanding of a contemporary interlinking of religion, modern society, historical profundity and concepts of the future beyond the Jewish communities themselves.[12]

Changes in religious topography: Synagogues and further contexts

The synagogues, prayer houses and community centers were and are a sometimes visible, sometimes invisible part of German cities. While their spatial development during the last decades is specific and tightly linked to the Jewish history in Central Europe, it is part of the negotiation of religious heterogeneity in modern society. As such, it allows tracing and understanding public discourses and architectural shifts as well as gaining insights in the processes of 'place keeping' and 'place making.'[13] Reading the recent developments of Christian, Jewish and Muslim communities in Germany in parallel, it becomes apparent that their participation in urban space

11 E.g., Wolfgang Jean Stock, and Walter Zahner, *Der sakrale Raum der Moderne: Meisterwerke des europäischen Kirchenbaus im 20. Jahrhundert* (Berlin, 2010); Edwin Heathcote, and Laura Moffatt, *Contemporary Church Architecture* (New York, 2007).

12 The issue of security is arguably of relevance as well. While this awareness was in the background of the evaluation of a building and its urban situation, it would need specific research to understand the extent of its influence on the design process.

13 See Irene Becci, "New religious diversity in Potsdam: keeping, making and seeking place," in *Religion in der Stadt. Räumliche Konfigurationen und theologische Deutungen*, ed. Christopher Zarnow, Birgit Klostermeier, and Rüdiger Sachau (Berlin, 2018), 101–118. Compare as well Nina Clara Tiesler, *Muslime in Europa. Religion und Identitätspolitiken unter veränderten gesellschaftlichen Verhältnissen* (Berlin, 2006).

varies significantly. Here, the different historic, legal and social backgrounds have an impact and create intrinsic developments.

However, it is obvious that the discourses that accompany the emergence or disappearance of emblematic religious architecture reflect a social reality. The architecture, its forms and its use of space express the inner reality of the religion in question, which is already an integral part of our cities. The discourses are therefore not concerned with their existence per se, but with their specific role in society today. Even if synagogues will probably remain special cases in Germany's sacred topography, not least because of the comparatively small number of worshippers, they are a normal part of the urban structure at the same time. The solutions they found for this structural accommodation are an important contribution to the negotiation of the architectural-symbolic coexistence of religions. They show both the organisational-financial challenges of a minority religion and an active participation in the design of the built environment, with all the visibility or invisibility that the communities choose for themselves.

Dani Kranz

The Dynamics of Jewish Space(s): Jewish Agency, Individual, Collective and the Creating, Maintenance or Discarding of Jewish Dominated Jewish Spaces

Jews, Jewish structures, places of worship and places for social and cultural gatherings in Cologne in the present must be understood against their historical backdrop. The historical backdrop must not be limited to the current borders of Germany: the majority of all Jews[1] who live in Germany have either immigrated themselves, or they have at least one parent who immigrated to Germany. Migration underpins the heterogeneity of the Jewish population, its diverse religious and cultural praxes, the on-going negotiations and power struggles about issues ranging from who is a Jew, to what *nussach* (religious ritual) should be followed in the synagogue, which *minhag* (religious custom), or more like, which *minhagim* (religious customs) is/are deemed relevant, if the praxis should be Eastern European style Orthodox, German style Liberal, if Israeli components can be included, what features of the praxes of Jews from the countries of the former Soviet Union can be included, how and if styles can be mixed and blended – and how to negotiate the boundary to the non-Jewish surroundings.

This heterogeneity and the resulting negotiations are not limited to the religious arena: for this reason, this chapter seeks to reappraise the notion 'Jewish space' and shift the attention to a Jewish space, or more like intersecting Jewish spaces, which Jews created or co-created, in which they are power holders, and where they control the boundaries. This can lead to the discarding of a Jewish space if the boundary cannot be fixed, and that what is within the boundary became too unattractive.[2] Negotiations about the boundary are underpinned by politics of belonging, differences in political opinion, different emphases in terms of engagement within the Jewish sphere and socio-political activism beyond it, different takes on the State of Israel and, in broad terms, the Middle East conflict, and, last but not least issues of living in Germany. In other words, Jews in Germany are a 'mixed bunch,' and Cologne, which is central in this case study is no exemption. The situation in Cologne can be seen as offering trends, which occur in variations across the country. The essay is set up chronologically, moving from the post-Shoah period to the present: or, one could say, it moves from utter destruction and frail beginnings to a flourishing, self-confident, and well-established present.

1 In terms of Jews by way of self-definition.

2 Fredrik Barth, "Introduction," in *Ethnic Groups and Boundaries: The Social Organization of Cultural Difference*, ed. Fredrik Barth (Long Grove, 1998 [1969]), 9–38.

https://doi.org/10.1515/9783110750812-006

What's up with the Jewish space?

This attempt wishes to reappraise the concept of 'Jewish space.'[3] Diana Pinto conceptualized the Jewish space (in Europe) as an arena for all things Jewish, in which Jews, and non-Jews, meet and create 'things Jewish.'[4] Whatever that means in praxis is contentious: Ian Levenson and Sandra H. Lustig agree with Pinto's flexible notion and see the Jewish space as a space for all things Jewish, while Y. Michal Bodemann cautions against this flexibility.[5] Bodemann stressed in *In den Wogen der Erinnerung* (In the Drift of Memories) how the (official) Jewish community in post-war West Germany constitutes an invention of the German, non-Jewish imagination; he emphasizes how German non-Jews created 'Judaizing milieus' and Jewish spaces, which were about Jews but without Jews. Ruth Ellen Gruber argued along similar lines in *Virtually Jewish.*[6] She locates similar structures across Europe, which Bodemann's emphasizes in his German case study – and which Geneviève Zubrzycki uncovered in her case study of philosemitism in Poland, as well as Magdalena Waligorska regarding *Klezmer's Afterlife.*[7] Specific aspects of Jewish heritage have been reappropriated by the non-Jewish majority post-Shoah, they serve specific political purposes, and, I would argue, they mitigate the feelings of loss, guilt, and mourning concerning the murdered Jews: the loss is not total if one keeps *this* – *their* – heritage alive. In this case the Jewish space is a space where Jews are being revalorized as having been desirable (now dead) carriers of culture, and as part of a desirable national culture, which is incomplete without Jews and yet, which functions just fine without living Jews. If the latter are visible, it is for specific events, and in specific roles.[8] This not to say that Jews were unaware of their purpose, yet, due to their tiny numbers, negotiations, not to say rebellions, remain unduly complicated.

---

3 Part of this chapter is based on the presentation "The Dynamics of the Jewish Space," given at the German Studies Association annual conference, 2007, and on chapter 1 of my PhD dissertation, "Shades of Jewishness: The Creation and Maintenance of a Liberal Jewish Community in Post-Shoah Germany," University of St. Andrews, 2009. However, the research work has been on-going so dynamics that occurred after 2009 have been amended. https://research-repository.st-andrews.ac.uk/handle/10023/872.

4 Diana Pinto, "The Jewish Space in Europe," in *Turning the Kaleidoscope. Perspectives on European Jewry*, ed. Sandra Lustig, and Ian Leveson (New York/Oxford, 2006), 179–188.

5 Y. Michal Bodemann, *In den Wogen der Erinnerung: Jüdische Existenz in Deutschland* (München, 2002). Y. Michal Bodemann, "A Jewish Cultural Renascence in Germany?," in *Turning the Kaleidoscope: Perspectives on European Jewry*, ed. S. Lustig, and I. Levenson (New York/Oxford, 2006), 164–175.

6 Ruth Ellen Gruber, *Virtually Jewish: Reinventing Jewish Culture in Europe* (Los Angeles, 2002).

7 See Genevieve Zubrzycki, "Nationalism, 'Philosemitism,' and Symbolic Boundary-Making in Contemporary Poland," *Comparative Studies in Society and History* 58.1 (2015): 66–98; and in Magdalena Waligorska, *Klezmer's Afterlife: An Ethnography of the Jewish Music Revival in Poland and Germany* (Oxford, 2013).

8 Y. Michal Bodemann, *Gedächtnistheater: Die jüdische Gemeinschaft und ihre Deutsche Erfindung* (Hamburg, 1996); and Anthony D. Kauders, *Unmögliche Heimat: Eine deutsch-jüdische Geschichte der Bundesrepublik* (München, 2007).

At present, living Jews demand a reappraisal of the Jewish space in the widest sense, and furthermore, they demand a discussion of the figure of the Jew,[9] which serves as a smoke screen for wishes, desires, and nightmares at the same time,[10] and which turns 'the Jew' into a perpetual other who is never genuinely local.[11] The current demand of living Jews (in Germany and beyond) must be seen in historical perspective, and in relations to their increased amount. Counterintuitively, Jews have been immigrating to Germany since 1945, the increase of the Jewish population owes to immigration and not to natural increase. It holds true that Jews were – and often remain – at the receiving end of a lop-sided power relationship because they are a small minority in any European country. Yet, they showed a vitality that is surprising in the face of the destruction of European Jewry in the 1930s and 1940s.[12] Bodemann,[13] Anthony D. Kauders,[14] and Jeffrey M. Peck[15] underlined that Jews in Germany were initially pre-occupied with economic survival, and more so, that 'making money' served as a morally pertinent reason to remain in Germany.[16] Yet, with time passing by, and the Second Generation coming of age a dynamic manifested that had been kept behind doors as early empirical research by Harry Maor and Alphons Silbermann reveals:[17]

> [...] the Jews of Germany and the Jewish displaced persons in particular, had begun to form an armoured cocoon shielding themselves against an alien and hostile world, the world of their murders and tormentors, a world that they had rejected, and that had initially rejected them. Within that cocoon, Jews married and raised children, established nursing homes and schools and a large web of personal, social, and economic relations, and more complex communal structures. It is my contention that this armoured cocoon was the precondition for a renascence of communal Jewish

9 Elad Lapidot, and Hannah Tzuberi, "Jewish Friends: Contemporary Figures of the Jew," *Jewish Studies Quarterly* 27.2 (2020): 103–107.

10 Dani Kranz, "Ein Plädoyer für den Alloismus: Historische Kontinuitäten, Zeitgeist und transkultureller Antisemitismus," in *Flucht ins Autoritäre – Rechtsextreme Dynamiken in der Mitte der Gesellschaft*, ed. Oliver Decker, and Elmar Brähler (Leipzig, 2018), 177–192.

11 Zygmunt Bauman, "Allosemitism. Premodern, Modern, Postmodern," in *Modernity, Culture, and "the Jew,"* ed. Bryan Cheyette, and Laura Marcus (Cambridge, 1998), 143–156.

12 Raul Hillberg, *The Destruction of the European Jews* (Eastford, 2019 [1961]).

13 Bodemann, *Gedächtnistheater*, see note 8, and Bodemann, *In den Wogen der Erinnerung*, see note 5.

14 Kauders, *Unmögliche Heimat*, see note 8, and Kauders, "West German Jewry: Guilt, Power, and Pluralism. Quest. Issues in Contemporary Jewish History," *Journal of Fondazione CDEC* 1 (2010): 15–33.

15 Jeffrey M. Peck, *Being Jewish in the New Germany* (Piscataway, 2006).

16 Kauders, "West German Jewry," see note 14.

17 Alphons Silbermann, "Zur sozial-kulturellen Situation der jüdischen Gemeinden in Deutschland: Bemerkungen und Fragen der geistigen Wiedergutmachung," *Kölner Zeitschrift für Soziologie und Sozialpsychologie* 12 (1960): 204–223. Harry Maor, "Über den Wiederaufbau der jüdischen Gemeinden in Deutschland seit 1945," unpublished PhD dissertation, Philosophy Department, University of Mainz, 1961. Available at http://harrymaor.com/download.htm#item1, accessed October 23, 2006.

> life in Germany; when the cocoon began to burst in the mid-1980s, it had created the preconditions for a new vitality of Jewish life beyond the stagnation of the previous forty years.[18]

This chapter will stress that Jews have been agentic throughout, despite an unequal power relationship that went/goes against them, and which, as Bodemann argued turned them into actors in the German theatre of memories (*Gedächtnistheater*).[19] In the same vein, while an increase of the number of Jews, and a Jewish renaissance is politically wanted by the German, non-Jewish side it is too simplistic to talk about a "reforestation"[20] of Jews by way of immigration from countries of the former Soviet Union (FSU). Soviet, and post-Soviet Jews did take active decisions to migrate, and they did have at least some choice in their destination country: Israel would have been an option for all of them, based on the Israeli Law of Return (1950/1970).[21] Agency is also clearly expressed with Israelis: they chose to leave the only Jewish majority country to immigrate to Germany; their motivation to immigrate might be positively impacted by exchange programs and cultural diplomacy.[22] By this token, and considering Jews as active actors and agents, this essay will chronicle the Jewish spaces – that is Jewish founded, driven, and dominate spaces – that emerged in Cologne post-1945 as a case study at city scale. In other words, my concerns are Jewish spaces for and by Jews, and not Jewish spaces or Judaizing milieus:[23] these exist in Cologne too. One might talk of parallel Jewish spaces vs. Jewish themed spaces; but, again, my concern lies with Jewish space(s).

Beginnings after the destruction

About 500,000 Jews lived on German territories at the beginning of the Nazi rule.[24] Antisemitism intensified after the Nazis rose to power, it was enshrined in Nazi policy and law (*Nürnberger Gesetze*), and acted upon. In 1945, about 2,000 German Jews[25] returned to Berlin from concentration camps; others had survived by way of

18 Bodemann, *In den Wogen der Erinnerung*, see note 5, 166.

19 Bodemann, *Gedächtnistheater*, see note 8.

20 Hannah Tzuberi, "'Reforesting' Jews: The German State and the Construction of 'New German Judaism,'" *Jewish Studies Quarterly* 27.3 (2020): 199–224.

21 Yvonne Schütze, "Warum Deutschland und nicht Israel? " *BIOS* 2 (1997): 186–208.

22 Dani Kranz, "Towards an Emerging Distinction between State and People: Israeli Diasporas between Self-Management and Coveted Citizens," *Migration Letters* 17.1 (2020): 91–101.

23 Bodemann, *In den Wogen der Erinnerung*, see note 5.

24 Bodemann, *Gedächtnistheater*, see note 8; Erica Burgauer, "Jüdisches Leben in Deutschland (BRD und DDR) 1945–1990," unpublished PhD dissertation. Faculty of Philosophy, University of Zurich, 1992; Maor, "Über den Wiederaufbau," see note 17.

25 Peck, *Being Jewish*, see note 15, 9.

intermarriage, and in hiding. Sixty to seventy Jews had survived in Cologne.[26] The estimate for the American and British zones lies at 10,000 to 20,000 surviving German Jews;[27] Cologne was part of the British zone. These German Jews were joined by a substantially higher number of survivors from Eastern Europe of between 200,000[28] to 250,000,[29] who had become Jewish Displaced Persons (DPs); they did not come with the intention to settle, they wanted to transit through Germany as quickly as possible to leave for the US and Palestine/Israel.

For the most part, the DPs lived in (transit) camps until their emigration; some slipped away to the cities and started making a living there.[30] With the foundation of the State of Israel and changes in US immigration policy the camps emptied out quickly.[31] The number of DPs had dropped to 20,000 upon closure of the last camp.[32] The first statistics of the *Zentralwohlfahrstelle der Juden in Deutschland* (*ZWST*, Central Welfare Offices of the Jews in Germany) bear witness to two specifics: only a 15,952 Jews had remained in West Germany and West Berlin, and the age structure indicated mainly elderly Jews had stayed,[33] evidencing that the increase of Jews in West Germany owed to immigration throughout.

Cilly Kugelmann, herself a child of Eastern European Shoah survivors, outlines that the identity and ideology of DPs and German Jews differed.[34] The identity of DPs was defined by their experience as survivors, and the complete destruction of their communities in Eastern Europe. These communities were often Orthodox in practice, and differed from those of their German counterparts, which were oftentimes

---

26 Günther B. Ginzel, and Sonja Güntner, *"Zu Hause in Köln ... "* (Vienna, 1998), 95.

27 Jael Geis, *Übrig sein: Leben danach, Deutsche Juden in der Britischen und Amerikanischen Zone* (Berlin, 2000), 15.

28 Peck, *Being Jewish*, see note 15, 9.

29 Geis, *Übrig sein*, see note 27, 16.

30 Geis, *Übrig sein*, see note 27, and Jay H. Geller, *Jews in Post-Holocaust Germany*, 1945–1953 (Cambridge, 2005). The film *Shalom Peter Schwartz* (Dir. Yael Reuveny, 2013) reconstructs the life-history of Peter Schwartz who slipped away and blended into the (East) German mainstream, while *Aida's Secrets* (Dir. Alon, and Shaul Schwarz, 2017) shows the complicated intergroup relations between Jewish DPs, and non-Jewish DPs in the camps.

31 Angelika Königseder, and Juliane Wetzel, *Lebensmut im Wartesaal: Die jüdischen DPs (Displaced Persons) im Nachkriegsdeutschland* (Frankfurt am Main, 1994).

32 Königseder, and Wetzel, *Lebensmut im Wartesaal*, see note 31.

33 Zentralwohlfahrtsstelle der Juden in Deutschland. N.d. Mitgliederstatistik (ZWST) 1955–1985 (Überblick), https://www.zwst.org/medialibrary/pdf/ZWST_Mitgliederstatistik_1955-1985.pdf.

34 Cilly Kugelmann, "Die Identität osteuropäischer Juden in der Bundesrepublik," in *Jüdisches Leben in Deutschland seit 1945*, ed. Micha Brumlik, et al. (Frankfurt am Main, 1988), 177–181; Cilly Kugelmann, "The Identity and Ideology of Jewish Displaces Persons," in *Germans, Jews and Memory: Reconstructions of Jewish Life in Germany*, ed. Y. Michal Bodemann (Ann Arbor, 1996), 65–76.

Liberal.[35] Yet, these existing variations need to be treated with caution, because perceptions, power structures, and judgement played into the intergroup relation: Bodemann mentions a secular Yiddish speaking culture of Polish Jews,[36] while Samuel J. Spinner analyzed *Jewish Primitivism*[37] that is the zeitgeist perception of "primitive" Jews as savage tribesmen from the point of view of Jewish intellectuals, of whom a significant amount were German Jews or German-speaking Jews. The sociologist Alphons Silbermann, himself a German Jew who returned to Germany, asked as early as 1960 what Jewish cultural heritage in Germany means in these circumstances, what role Israel, the imagined Israel, plays[38] – and what form of religious service can be established. Eventually, the Orthodox form of practice won out. The idea was that any Jews could attend the service, as a Liberally practicing Jew can attend an Orthodox service, but not vice versa. In practice that meant that not every Jew – by way of self-definition – could attend as some Jews lacked papers, others had converted to Christianity to survive, yet others had Jewish fathers and non-Jewish mothers, or their conversions to Judaism were not recognized.[39] Besides this difference in the interpretation of the *Halacha*, the Jewish religious law, intermarriage caused frictions throughout:[40] my research participants in Cologne held different opinions on this as on various matters across all generations, indicating that the heterogeneity ranged from intimacy to macro levels.

Structuring the Jewish community

The differences within the Jewish in-group led to a two-tier system in terms of organisations. DPs founded different institutions from German Jews.[41] It took until 1950 to form the Central Council of the Jews of Germany (*Zentralrat der Juden in Deutschland*); the structure prevails to date but has lost power since the mid-1970s.[42] The Central Council represents the member communities of the *Einheitsgemeinde* (Unified Community): in most cases these communities follow the interpretations of Orthodox Judaism. In some cases, Liberal or Reform communities are also members

35 The pre-*Shoah* Liberal practice differed from the current practice in Germany or the US. In Cologne, men and women sat separately in the Liberal synagogue.

36 Bodemann, *Gedächtnistheater*, see note 8.

37 Samuel J. Spinner, *Jewish Primitivism* (Stanford, 2021).

38 Silbermann, "Zur sozial-kulturellen Situation," see note 17; Kauders, *Unmögliche Heimat*, see note 8.

39 Barbara Steiner, *Die Inszenierung des Jüdischen: Konversion von Deutschen zum Judentum nach 1945* (Göttingen, 2015).

40 Kauders, *Unmögliche Heimat*, see note 8.

41 Geller, *Jews in Post-Holocaust Germany*, see note 30.

42 Kauders, "West German Jewry," see note 14.

of the *Einheitsgemeinde*. As it stands, two rabbinical conferences, the Orthodox (founded in 2003) and the General Rabbinical Conference (founded 2005) exist, indicating the present, and public heterogeneity of Jewish practices. Cologne, and its Jewish structures is part of these dynamics, as the graphic of the Jewish spaces of the city, which I composed as part of my PhD dissertation in 2009, indicates (Fig. 1).[43]

The *Synagogengemeinde Köln* (*SGK*) remains an important Jewish space in Cologne, it is part of the *Einheitsgemeinde*. The Jewish groups that created spaces beyond the *SGK* offer insights into the dynamics of the Jewish space of the city. These Jewish groups and their Jewish spaces allow unravelling creation, maintenance, and decay functions, and the fixation of boundaries in the process of negotiating "the stuff within the boundary" of the groups.[44] I will chronicle the groups in situ starting in the early 1980s with the *Jüdische Gruppe* (Jewish Group, founded late-1970s, discarded), and move on to the *Jüdisches Forum* (Jewish Forum, founded in 1991, discarded), the Liberal Jewish community (founded in 1996) and then sketch some of later developments, *A Groisse Liebe* (A Big Love, founded in 2005, discarded), and move to current dynamics, which are driven by Jews of the Third Generation as well as their co-generationalists.[45] Owing to a higher mobility but more so the structures of mobile communication and social media that intersected with their coming of age, paired with national connection points that support the existing difference and dynamic the third generation – as an age cohort – has not founded any new fixed groups and/or religious Jewish community or permanent Jewish spaces. Typically, things moved online and then to social media that is available 24/7 via mobile internet. Alongside the groups in Cologne, I will introduce some of the key characters who are or have been active in the Jewish social groups for the Second Generation, and offer clues as to why Jews of the third generation-age cohort have not founded fixed groups like Second Generations.

---

43 Kranz, Dani. *Shades of Jewishness: The Creation and Maintenance of a Jewish Community in Post-Shoah Germany* (St Andrews, 2009). Open Access, https://research-repository.st-andrews.ac.uk/handle/10023/872.

44 Barth, "Introduction," in *Ethnic Groups and Boundaries*, see note 2, 15.

45 Third Generation Jews are grandchildren of survivors, their co-generationalists are Jews of the same age groups, who might, or might not be grandchildren of survivors. They can be FSU Jews who immigrated to Germany with their families or Israelis who came to Germany, for example. While the biographical differences exist between members of this generation, the barriers between them are not as insurmountable as with their parents' generation. If third generation is not capitalized, I refer to the age cohort in general, if capitalized it is limited to Third Generation as in the grandchildren of survivors who were born and raised in Germany.

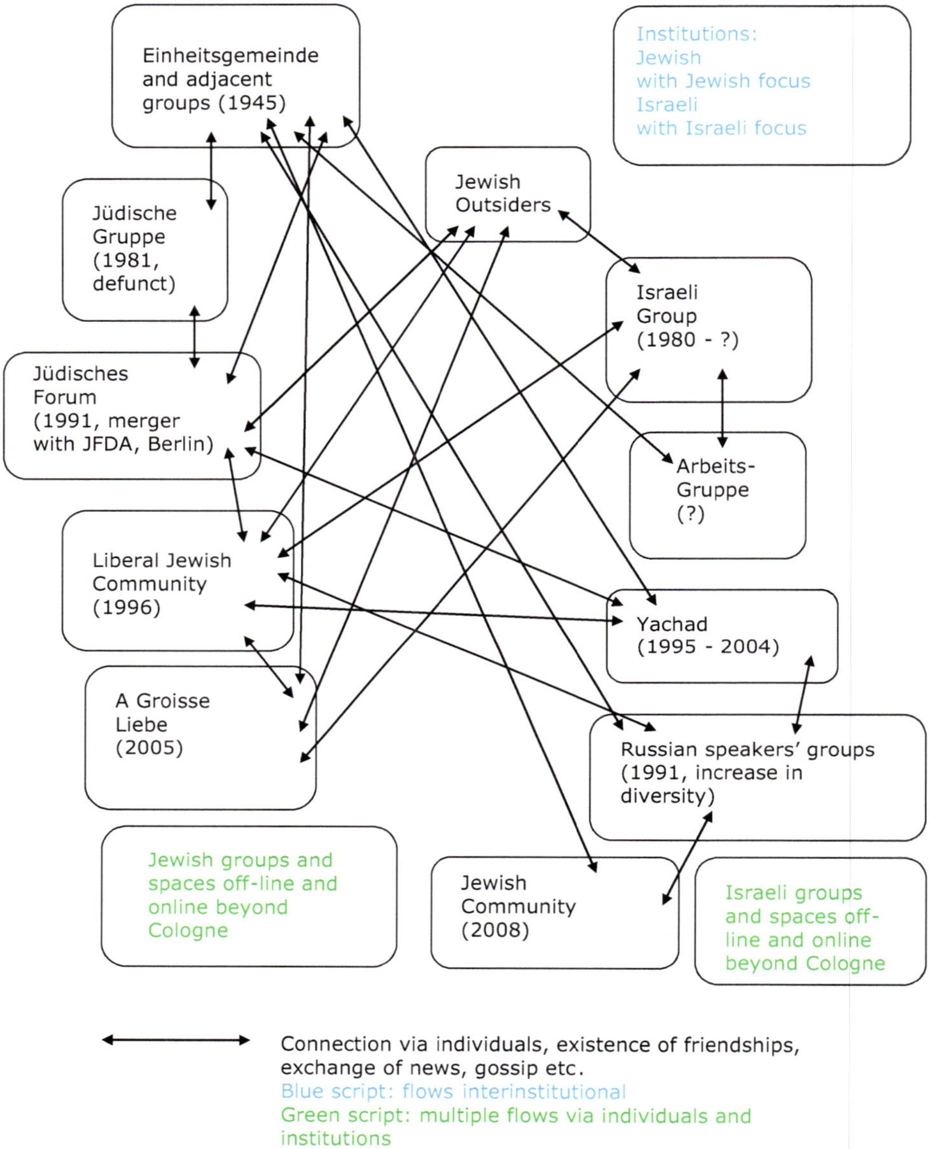

Fig. 1: The Jewish spaces in Cologne, 2009.

Cracks in the façade

The increasing number of publications since the 1990s indicate that the Jewish space (in terms of the Jewish dominated spaces in focus here, and in terms of Jewish spaces where non-Jews do Jewish) gained in a dynamic not seen since 1933.[46] With time, publications became more diverse and varied in scope, in particular scholars of the Jewish present – Jewish and non-Jewish alike – allowed for an appreciation of existing Jewish diversity:[47] the diversity that the sociologists Alphons Silbermann[48] and Harry Maor[49] had found behind closed doors, was now out in the open, and differences in religious practice, political opinion, or social mores found their way into broad daylight.

In the fieldwork amongst Jews in Cologne, the aftermaths of one specific event changed the Jewish space. This event was the first Lebanon War in 1982. Its justification was rejected by parts of the German left and left-wing Jews of the Second Generation. The massacres perpetrated by the Lebanese Phalangist Militia on Palestinian refugees without the IDF (Israel Defense Forces) intervening caused uproar against the conduct of the IDF in Israel,[50] and sent shockwaves through Germany's official Jewish community. The *Einheitsgemeinde* had always been supportive of Israel; left-wing Second Generations criticised Israeli conduct publicly: the façade cracked. However, these Jewish left-wingers had to realize that their public criticism of Israel fed into antisemitic propaganda as voiced by non-Jewish left-wingers in Germany:[51] secondary antisemitism with an Israel focus gained in prominence.

The cracks in the Jewish façade had repercussions on a local level. The formation of the groups of the Second Generation indicates the shift to an extended Jewish space because the singular Jewish space of the *Einheitsgemeinde* and its auxiliaries did not suffice anymore. According to Jews in Cologne, different opinions about the Lebanon war, and being Jewish in Germany, were voiced. The opinions diverged to an extent that those critical of the *Einheitsgemeinde*, the war, and concerned about

46 These sources are typically not part of the canon of Judaic or Jewish Studies in Germany. These remain past-centered (Kranz and Ross 2022). Dani Kranz, and Sarah M. Ross, „Jüdische Selbstermächtigung in der deutschen Wissenschaftslandschaft: Tektonische Verschiebungen in der Judaistik und Jüdische Studien nach 1990“, in *Weitergaben und Wirkungen der Shoah in Erziehungs- und Bildungsverhältnissen der Gegenwartsgesellschaft* ed. Marina Chernivsky, and Friederike Lorenz (Leverkusen, 2022), 1–22.

47 Dani Kranz, "The Quest for Jewish Anthropology in Germany post-1945," *Journal of Modern Jewish Studies*. Forthcoming.

48 Silbermann, "Zur sozial-kulturellen Situation," see note 17.

49 Maor, "Über den Wiederaufbau," see note 17.

50 The Kahan Commission was formed to inquire into the massacres. The IDF was found "indirectly responsible" for the massacres, because they had had knowledge of the Phalangists entering the refugee camps (MFA 1984).

51 Shila Khasani, "Eine Minderheit in der Minderheit: Das Engagement der linksorientierten Juden in der Frankfurter Jüdischen Gruppe," *Trumah* 14 (2005): 55–74.

living in Germany (as opposed to just sojourning in Germany) formed a group with like-minded Jews. This was the first group outside of the *Einheitsgemeinde*, and for Jewish Cologne it was a harbinger of things to come.

Mayan, who was at that point in time in her early thirties, still narrated the events vividly more than twenty years later, when I met her during my PhD fieldwork in the early and mid-2000s. She recounts how she went to protest against the war in Lebanon with her best friend, a non-Jewish German. The protest took place after Sabra and Shatila. She heard members of the German left shout: "Israel perpetrates a Holocaust against the Palestinians," and: "Sharon is Israel's Hitler." A stout left-winger herself, Mayan felt unable to stay in the protest, and went home with her friend to explain what upset her. "I talked to her the whole night. I explained to her how this is not a Holocaust, how Sharon is not Hitler. I talked and talked. She did not understand me. By the end of the night, I had lost my best friend." She and other left-wing Jews in Germany felt that they needed a (Jewish) space where "we can be amongst ourselves," a space where she felt she did not need to explain herself, a space based on similarities. These similarities can be summarised as the experience of being Jewish in Germany, and more precisely as being secular, left-wing, and Jewish in the Second Generation in Germany, and not in sync with the *Einheitsgemeinde*. The Jewish space that came into being, the *Jewish Group* was – nearly – exclusively Jewish, with boundaries that were strictly policed. Individuals with a left political view and a critical acceptance of Israel and its politics were allowed in. Similar groups existed in all major cities in West Germany, with Frankfurt am Main and Berlin having the most influential of these *Jewish Groups*; owing to the small number of Jews in Germany the group members knew each other across West Germany.[52] The *Jüdischen Gruppen* (plural: Jewish Groups) can be defined as the first expressions of Jewish identity praxes that lay beyond the hegemony of the *Einheitsgemeinde*: These Jews were critical, but supportive of Israel, and these Jews did not count matrilineal descent, and/or conversion of children as Jewish fathers as the sole criteria for being Jewish , but considered being Jewish as an act of self-definition; their definition of Jewishness lay beyond Jewish religious law.

The Jewish group in Cologne was small: prior to the immigration from countries of the FSU in the 1990s and early 2000s the *SGK* had about 1,500 members. The development from the *Jüdische Gruppe* to the Liberal Jewish community took about fifteen years, and it happened via Jewish spaces that were discarded on the way. The developments of the 1980s and 1990s indicated a new dynamic of Jewish life in Germany, which prefigured the arrival of Jews from the FSU.[53] Membership of the

52 Lynn Rapaport, *Jews in Germany after the Holocaust* (Cambridge, 1997).
53 Bodemann, "A Jewish Cultural Renascence in Germany?", see note 5; for a case study of Berlin, see Alexander Jungmann, *Jüdisches Leben in Berlin: Der aktuelle Wandel in einer metropolitanen Diasporagemeinschaft* (Bielefeld, 2007).

Einheitsgemeinde remained at 30,000 members nationally. Bodemann estimates that only forty percent to sixty percent of all Jews in Berlin were members (personal communication, 2005). In Cologne it might have been seventy percent of all those who could be members, because the *SGK* and its adjacent structures was the only permanent Jewish space, turning it into a meeting point of Jews beyond religion. The dynamic that had developed in the 1980s, changed with the large-scale arrival of Jews from countries of the FSU: these Jews had yet a different relationship to Germany, the Shoah, and their Jewishness than the existing Jewish fractions in Germany.[54] Also, they had a different idea about what a Jewish community should be, and what it should be there for.

The breakdown of the communist bloc and its effects on the Jewish community in Germany

In 1989, the communist bloc collapsed and with it the Berlin wall. Within a year Germany would be reunited, and the law of the Federal Republic of Germany applied now to both parts of the country. Before formal reunification, a number of Jews from the collapsing USSR had left for the GDR, which had invited them to immigrate due to increasing antisemitism that went hand in hand with the collapse of organisational structures.[55] The last resolution of the parliament of the GDR was to ensure that Jewish immigration would not be stopped with the reunification of the two Germanies. The West German government had initially rejected this proposal but relented after a huge public outcry.[56]

The number of immigrants by far exceeded the expectations of the German state, and the *Einheitsgemeinde*. The total of the 'Russian Jews' or 'Russian speaking Jews' stood at 219,604 in 2004,[57] when the legal framework was changed.[58] The *Einheitsgemeinde* reached more than 100,000 members at its height in the late 2000s. Its membership has been declining since, as the growth of the Jewish population hinges on immigration: the Jewish community, like German society in general, is aging. The disparity between the number of *Kontingentflüchtlinge*, and the membership

---

54 Franziska Becker, *Ankommen in Deutschland* (Berlin, 2001).

55 Becker, *Ankommen in Deutschland*, see note 54, 44.

56 Becker, *Ankommen in Deutschland*, see note 54, 45–46.

57 Sonja Haug, and Peter Schimany, (2005). *Jüdische Zuwanderer in Deutschland: ein Überblick über den Stand der Forschung*. Working Paper, 3 (Nürnberg: Bundesamt für Migration und Flüchtlinge [BAMF] Forschungszentrum Migration, Integration und Asyl [FZ], 2005), https://nbn-resolving.org/urn:nbn:de:0168-ssoar-352438.

58 Joseph Cronin, Russian Speaking Jewish in Germany's Jewish Communities, 1990–2005 (Cham, 2019).

of the *Einheitsgemeinde* bases on three factors. First, USSR law treated Jews as a nationality, and it did not follow matrilineality. This runs contrary to the *Einheitsgemeinde*, which applies the halachic rule of matrilineality to define Jewish status, and thus eligibility for membership. Second, not all individuals who were included in the total were Jews: non-Jewish spouses are also included in the total. Third, not all of those who were eligible wanted to be members. Beyond these issues, not all Jews had papers to prove they were Jews: Jews were discriminated against in the USSR, leading to the obliteration of proof of Jewishness.[59]

The strict application of the *Halacha* led to exclusions from the *Einheitsgemeinde*, and bitterness amongst some FSU incomers. They had experienced antisemitism in their native country, upon immigration to Germany they did not qualify as Jews. Anette Vesper, and Alphons Silbermann engage exclusively with Russian Jews in Cologne.[60] Vesper found that the approaches to being Jewish were influenced by two factors: being *halachically* Jewish, and the state-favoured atheism of the USSR. *Halachic* Jews and those with two Jewish parents had a stronger attachment to being Jewish. These Jews had been recognized as Jews by the Jewish communities in their native countries too. Children of intermarriages indicated a lesser attachment to religious Judaism.[61] Given the small size of Vesper‘s sample and her access through the *SGK*,[62] a bias prevails: Jewishness in the social sphere, or self-definitions of non-*SGK*-FSU-Jews are beyond her study. Children of intermarriage had[63] and have[64] a difficult standing in the *Einheitsgemeinde* in general, and the treatment of the non-Jewish parent did not help to make them feel homely. Alienation could occur: these Jews (of self-definition) were immigrants to German and wanted as Jews, but not as Russians, and they were strangers in the Jewish communities.

Ivan, a Russian Jewish incomer who lived in Cologne in the 1990s and 2000s, terminated his membership of the *SGK* in Cologne. He recounted that his children

---

59 Becker, *Ankommen in Deutschland*, see note 54.

60 Annette Vesper, “Migrationsmotive und Selbstverständnis russischer Juden und ihrer Familien in Köln: Eine ethnologische Fallstudie,” unpublished Master’s thesis, Department of Ethnology, University of Cologne, 1995; and Annette Vesper, “Das Ringen und Selbstverständnis und Identität: Russische Juden in Köln,” in *“Zuhause in Köln ...* ” ed. Günther B. Ginzel, and Sonja Güntner (Vienna, 1998), 75–82. Alphons Silbermann, “Partizipation und Integration von Jüdischen Immigranten aus der ehemaligen Sowjetunion – eine Fallstudie aus der Synagogen-Gemeinde Köln,” *Menorah* (1999): 61–73.

61 I do not agree with Vesper‘s findings on this matter. From my research it seems that non-*halachic* Jews had been turned away by the *Einheitsgemeinde* and this led to a rejection of the *Einheitsgemeinde*. The result was a withdrawal into a private Judaism, (Liberal) conversion, or political activism. Complete detachment from Judaism as a religion might have occurred, but I have not come across a detachment from Jewishness.

62 Vesper, “Migrationsmotive und Selbstverständnis,” see note 59, 20.

63 Kauders, *Unmögliche Heimat*, see note 8.

64 Lea Wohl-von Haselberg, ed. *Hybride juedische Identitaeten: Gemischte Familien und patrilineare Juden* (Berlin, 2015). Ruth Zeifert, *Nicht ganz koscher: Vaterjuden in Deutschland* (Berlin, 2017).

who are non-*halachic* Jews were told by the leader of the youth group that they were not wanted because "you are not Jews." The local *Chabad* rabbi mentioned he believes that some of the "Russians will learn proper [Orthodox] practising" and that some of them showed a huge interest in Jewish religion, and a Jewish way of life regardless of if they had a Jewish mother or a Jewish father. The main rabbi of the community only answered vaguely with "this [community] is a living organism" to the question how the integration of FSU Jews. In other words, when I conducted my PhD fieldwork between 2004 and 2006, the topic was still so hot, that rabbis, and community officials, remained opaque to foreclose potential misgivings.

Silbermann remained true to his empirical finds throughout his career, however inconvenient those were. His study on participation of FSU incomers in the *SGK* was published in 1999. He found that the majority had emigrated for two reasons. Elderly people left for fear of antisemitism, younger ones for economic reasons.[65] The option to practice their religion freely ranked only fifth amongst the reasons for immigration to Germany at the time of Silbermann's research.[66] Overall, the official Jewish community was needed as a bridge to German authorities, and a means to integrate. This attitude resembles the attitude of Jews in Germany in the early post-Shoah period. Günther Ginzel as well as Monika Grübel and Georg Mölich outline that the *SGK* initially had the key function to provide help to Jews in a non-Jewish surrounding.[67] By the time the FSU Jews arrived, the community had redefined itself as a religious community primarily. The members were settled in Germany, they did not require attention from the office of social affairs. Silbermann outlines that the different perception of what the Jewish community should be led to problems amongst those who had been in residence and the FSU incomers, he argued that a consensus would only be reached "if both groups accept each other [in their difference]".[68] Internal sources indicate that the two groups existed at a distance to each other at the time of my initial fieldwork, but approximated each other over time, and certainly with the third generation since the 2010s.[69]

---

65 Silbermann, "Partizipation und Integration," see note 59, 67.

66 Published twenty years later, the research of Maja Vataman underlines the generational change that occurred across generations, and the quest for Jewish religion of post-Soviet Jews (Maja Vataman, *Migration – Adoleszenz – Identität: Fallstudien zur Identitätskonstruktion jüdischer Jugendlicher aus der ehemaligen Sowjetunion in Deutschland* (Baden-Baden, 2020)).

67 Günther B. Ginzel, "Phase der Etablierung einer Jüdischen Gemeinde in der Kölner Trümmer Landschaft 1945–1949," in *Köln und das Rheinische Judentum: Festschrift Germania Judaica 1959–1984*, ed. J. Bohnke-Kollwitz, et al. (Cologne, 1984), 445–461. Monika Grübel, and Georg Mölich, "Jüdisches Leben im Rheinland," in *Jüdisches Leben im Rheinland: Vom Mittelalter bis zur Gegenwart*, ed. Monika Grübel, and Georg Mölich (Vienna, 2005), IX–XX.

68 Silbermann, "Partizipation und Integration," see note 59, 63.

69 Dani Kranz, "(Friendly) Strangers in Their Own Land No More: Third Generation Jews and Socio-Political Activism in the Present in Germany," in *The Stranger in Jewish Thought, History and Fiction*, ed. Catherine Bartlett, and Joachim Schlör (Amsterdam, 2021), 113–138.

Jews from the FSU constitute the majority of the members of the *SGK* in Cologne, and in a number of Liberal communities. This means that on a macro-structural level the majority membership has changed for a third time since 1933. Before 1933, German Jews had the majority position, between 1945 and 1991, DPs and their descendants formed the majority, now FSU/post-Soviet Jews make up the majority of all Jews in Germany.

From the *Jüdische Gruppe* to *Jüdisches Forum* to the bridge to tradition

It would be deceiving to relate the foundation of the Liberal Jewish community in Cologne to the influx of FSU Jews. Its key drivers consisted of birth Jews of the Second Generation who felt in need of a space of their own, where they could talk and engage openly. These Jews had to come to the realisation that their opinions about being Jewish in Germany, and about Israel, could be taken out of context, feeding into what they experienced as antisemitic and anti-Israeli discourses in Germany.[70] This overarching problem led to those Jews looking for like-minded people, as Mayan and Ron told me. This like-mindedness was based on individual opinions regarding politics, but at the same time underpinned by biographical similarities. This biographical background was lived out and interpreted differently by the participants of the group, though for all participants their Jewishness lay beyond the confines of the *Halacha* – matrilineality was not then issue.

On an individual level, a significant number of the founding members of the Liberal community were non-*halachic* Jews who had no access to the Orthodox community or Jews, matrilineal and patrilineal, who had non-Jewish partners. These had a difficult standing in the Orthodox practicing *Einheitsgemeinden*,[71] which was made up of survivors and their descendants, and which implemented the *Halacha* also as a boundary measure: interestingly, this implementation, although slightly softened, was going to be replicated in the foundation process of the Liberal community. Ron, a founding member of the *Jüdisches Forum* (Jewish Forum) and the Liberal Jewish community repeatedly described the *Einheitsgemeinde* as insular, as unwilling to engage with its German surrounding. Mayan, a patrilineal Jew, found the non-acceptance of children of Jewish fathers, and the rejection of the non-Jewish spouses, appalling. She, like some others, would undergo conversion in the process

70 Khasani, "Eine Minderheit in der Minderheit," see note 51.

71 Kauders, *Unmögliche Heimat*, see note 8; Rapaport, *Jews in Germany after the Holocaust*, see note 52.

of creating a Liberal Jewish community, which is to say her community of like-minded Jews would also implement the *Halacha* as a boundary.

The issue of descent spans wider than mere matrilineal descent, it extends to issues of kinship, which in turn relates to dealing with the German, non-Jewish, surrounding. This resonates in the acceptance of non-Jewish spouses, and the encouragement to bring non-*halachically* Jewish children along and acquaint them with Jewish religion in the Liberal Jewish community. This does not mean that the engagement with the German, non-Jewish surrounding is free of tensions. Despite the problems the members of the Liberal community seek for a future orientated approach to being Jewish in Germany, they deemed the approach of the *Einheitsgemeinde* as backward looking during my initial fieldwork: with generational changes the *Einheitsgemeinde* changed too, and it has become more inclusive.

The differences in approaches to being Jewish in Germany had been manifesting in the creation of new Jewish groups that occupied the Jewish space since the late 1970s. As outlined before, the reason underlying the exclusive Jewish setting were based on misgivings between Jews and non-Jews concerning politics, and in particular concerning Israel and being taken out of context. As mentioned earlier, Mayan lost her best friend over a protest in 1982. The *Jüdische Gruppe* in Cologne was small, and after a couple of years in the mid-1980s changed in focus. Mayan described this change of focus as a fizzling out, whereas Ron described it as a change in the nature of the group. Politics were now only one issue, while the leaning of the group was more towards Jewish culture in its widest sense. However, this change in focus came with a change of the participants of the group, individuals who had been in it for mere political reasons left, while others joined: this Jewish space changed in content.

Then, in 1991 the first Gulf War occurred. Significant parts of the German left opposed this war. The (officials of the) *Einheitsgemeinde* saw it as justified, as Israel was under threat. As in 1982, the 1991 war had consequences. It deepened existing rifts within the *Einheitsgemeinden*. In Cologne it would lead to the momentum that was needed to re-create the energy that had led to the initial foundation of the *Jüdische Gruppe*. This time around the momentum culminated in the creation of a more durable Jewish space outside of the *Einheitsgemeinde* in Cologne. This space was called *Jüdisches Forum* (Jewish Forum) or short *Forum*. The first event of the *Forum* ran two days after the war in Iraq had started, it attracted an audience too big to accommodate all attendees. Both this event and the *Forum* had been the brainchild of Ron, who had been part of the *Jüdische Gruppe*. Ron had tried his luck as the Head of Cultural Affairs in the *SGK*. His agenda had been too open for the *SGK* "at that point in time." Over the years I heard him repeatedly rage about the *SGK*, although he conceded (in the mid-2000s), nearly twenty years after the first Gulf War: "they've changed. There are other people in power now."

The 1991 foundation of the *Forum* was another attempt to create a space for like-minded Jews to discuss politics, and beyond that engage with the non-Jewish surrounding. The key to the idea of the *Forum* lies in Ron's stance to seek interaction with his non-Jewish surrounding, and to demand understanding for his own – unapologetic – positionality as an Israeli Jew in Cologne: "I don't hide that I am a Jew or an Israeli." But it was not only Ron who sought this kind of dialogue. Mayan who had been active in the Jewish Group did too, as did Jonathan and James, who are respectively the first head of the Liberal community to be, and its founding father. Besides these four and some more Jews, the *Forum* attracted a following of non-Jews, who sought for a dialogue with Jews. These non-Jews were politically leaning to the left and they embraced an Israel supportive stance too. The common ground, and the wish to interact across the German/Jewish divide, made for an instant success of the *Forum*. The success was rather short-lived, however. An unbridgeable divide between Jews and German non-Jews opened up, which led in turn to the foundation of *Gescher LaMassoret*, the Liberal Jewish community. What had happened in the *Forum* to cause this development?

James felt that the *Forum* was becoming anti-Israeli in its focus, and that again misunderstandings between Jews and non-Jews were unbridgeable. Discussions about politics could become so heated that members walked out. Jewish members felt in the same predicament as they had felt before. Furthermore, the wish for a religious service arose amongst some of the birth Jewish[72] members, and some of the non-Jewish members. These religious services ran initially once a month. They followed the idea of a Liberal service: men and women were equals, vernacular (German) language was included in the service, and the services were short. Some of the Jewish members were appalled by this religious turn. One elderly lady, Sarah,[73] mentioned: "I stopped going when it [the religious turn] started. That wasn't for me anymore, I'm not religious." Sarah was a long-term member of the *SGK* where she does not attend services either. Another synagogue was of no interest to her. A non-Jewish member, Monika,[74] opined: "[I]t turned more and more religious, that wasn't for me anymore. It was like some people wanted to be Jews, and some of the Jews wanted a service, the intellectual debate died at that point." What bothered Monika most was that "it really annoyed me that I was treated differently because I am very good friend with one of the Israelis [Ron]. That was really sick." Monika felt that her friend's Israeliness made him essentially desirable to others in the group, and that his Israeliness rubbed off on her.

What was going on in this *Forum*, a presumably secular intellectual gathering ground for dissenting Jews and non-Jews alike? James claimed it became anti-Israeli, Sarah complained it became too religious, and Monika felt that besides its religious leaning, the *Forum* favoured Israelis. All three hint at a development that

---

72 I use the term birth Jew to refer to a person who has at least one Jewish parent, although some individuals with only one Jewish grandparent I met in Cologne self-identified as Jews.

73 Sarah died in the mid-2010s.

74 Monika died in 2009.

was taking place in the *Forum*, which was that it became more religious in its outlook, and that especially the Jewish members were feeling they were in a minority situation similar to that in the German left again. The 'religious' turn was to become a means of creating a boundary, by imperatively invoking the *Halacha* to create certainty.

James expressed this wish openly. He wanted a Liberal Jewish community where only Jews could be members, and where subsequently those non-Jews who felt Jewish enough would need to convert. James wished for a community where boundaries were clearly defined, with non-Jews on the outside and Jews on the inside but that with a Liberal form of service. He wanted what Mayan had described as "a Jewish home," which neither of them could realise in the *Jüdisches Forum*. The sociologist Lynn Rapaport[75] and the psychoanalyst Kurt Grünberg demonstrated in their research work on Jews of the Second Generation in Germany that reactions like these could not be understood without reference to the Shoah. The loss of family and trauma were constantly present, as were unsettling moves between countries, and multiple break points in one's own biography.[76]

The more pronounced openness towards the non-Jewish surrounding led the dissenting Jews to seek out like-minded people to form their own Jewish dominated Jewish space. It turned out that the like-mindedness and similarities between Jews and non-Jews, and moderately religious Jews and Jewish atheists was not enough. The internal differences disabled a clear focus of the *Forum*. The members were simply too different on too many levels, which led to the disintegration of the *Forum* and the creation of a more focussed, and bordered Jewish space in form of the Liberal Jewish community.

While Mayan, Ron, James, and some others went on to create a Liberal Jewish community, and thus deprive the *Forum* of its key drivers, a substantial number of non-religious Jews did not join the Liberal community. They either remained non-practicing members of the *SGK*, or refused to be members of any *Verein* (club), such as Stefan who declared that: "I don't want to be member of any German club." A club, including the *SGK*, or a Jewish space based on definite entry criteria and a rigid boundary was not to his liking.

Despite its internal problems from its foundation in 1991 until the foundation of the Liberal Jewish community in 1996 the *Jüdisches Forum* offered a space to birth Jews and interested non-Jews to gather, discuss, exchange ideas, and find a space for the Jewish parts of their identities. For Jews, *halachic* or not, the interest in the *Forum* already indicated that they had an interest in satisfying their need for a Jewish space with other, like-minded Jews. For the non-Jews, the involvement had different reasons.

---

75 Rapaport, *Jews in Germany after the Holocaust*, see note 52; Rapaport, "The Difficulties of Being Jewish in Germany Today," *Trumah* 3 (1992): 189–215.

76 Kurt Grünberg, *Liebe nach Auschwitz: Die Zweite Generation* (Frankfurt am Main, 2000).

According to a long-term observer of Jewish life in Cologne a number of the non-Jews in the *Forum* wanted "to do Jewish on occasion. They wanted to be Jewish without actually being Jews." This observation resonates with Y. Michal Bodemann[77] and Alexander Jungmann's[78] analyses of non-Jews doing Jewish without being Jewish as a means to position themselves as 'different' Germans. In this local case, some of the early non-Jewish members of the *Forum* had developed such a strong connection to being Jewish that they converted. Simone was amongst those who converted. She made *Aliyah*[79] during my PhD fieldwork and has been living in Israel since the late 2000s. Heinz and Rachel who had spent time in Israel with *Aktion Sühnezeichen Friedensdienste* (Action Reconciliation Service for Peace)[80] converted too. They became members of the Liberal community.[81]

Within two years the wish of the Jewish members to introduce religious components into the intellectually biased *Forum* had grown to the point that an *Erev Shabbat* service was run once a month. The introduction of a regular religious component into the previously secular *Forum* led to a first construction of a social boundary within the *Forum*. The majority of the Jewish members aligned themselves with the idea of introducing a service, and to establishing more religious activities beyond the most important holidays. However, Jews and non-Jews could participate in the religious service. Non-Jews were allowed to read psalms, an issue which would become one of the strongest boundaries between Jews and non-Jews in the Liberal Jewish community: only *halachically* recognized Jews are allowed to take an active role in the service. In other words, one cannot do Jewish without being Jewish in *Gescher LaMassoret*.

Gescher LaMassoret – Bridge to tradition

James is widely acknowledged as the founding father of *Gescher*, as the Liberal Jewish community is commonly known. He employed the *Halacha* in the foundation although he privately rejects the idea that only a child of a Jewish mother is Jewish.

---

77 Bodemann, *In den Wogen der Erinnerung*, see note 5.
78 Jungmann, *Jüdisches Leben in Berlin*, see note 53.
79 Hebrew: ascend. The immigration of Jews to Israel is referred to as *Aliyah*.
80 *Aktion Sühnezeichen Friedensdienste* was founded in 1959. In 1958, Lothar Kreyssing of the Protestant church had called for an organization that would help to undo the hurt that the Nazis had caused, in particular in Russia, Poland and to Jews. (http://www.asf-ev.de/ueber_uns/asf_geschichte/gruendungsaufruf/, accessed February 3, 2007). Since then, the organization has sent volunteers to these countries and to Israel. It has furthermore been active in the peace movement in Germany, and pushed for a civic service (http://www.asf-ev.de/ueber_uns/asf_geschichte/die_aktion_suehnezeichen_im_westen_von_1959_bis_1991/, accessed February 3, 2007).
81 Heinz and Rachel both died in the late 2010s.

James's motives to push for the creation of the Liberal Jewish community were not religious: "I'm an atheist. I found the conversion was a very negative experience." James recounted that he pushed for *Gescher* in order "to destroy the *Forum*," which he felt "had become antisemitic and especially anti-Israeli." He felt that the criticism of Israeli foreign policy eerily echoed the arguments "often heard in Germany, which are more in favour of Palestinian suffering than of Israel." Israel, and the safety of the state of Israel is a matter close to his heart. To him Israel is the secular home for Jews beyond Jewish religion, it is the anchoring point for his Jewish identity. In the *Jüdisches Forum* he felt that not only was this part of his identity under threat but that the State of Israel was vilified. James identifies himself as part of the Jewish people: "I am part of the *B'nei Yisrael* (sons of Israel)." Within the highly charged *Forum* he, a patrilineal Jew, found himself – again- out of a space that could function as a Jewish home. With this impending threat he decided to become active, he wrote a pamphlet lobbying for the foundation of a Liberal Jewish community. This community would be Liberal in practice and allow for an intellectual exchange about Israel, but it would be strictly regulated in its membership, and only allow recognized Jews to be members.

James had been careful to set up boundaries for membership in the community he had lobbied for. The membership would include Jews only. However, James learned quickly that to set up a Jewish community, an affiliation to a Jewish umbrella organisation was needed to obtain infrastructural help. The organisation of choice was the *World Union of Progressive Judaism* (*WUPJ*), which helps with the building of communities, development of leadership, youth work,[82] and various other issues that arise; it helps as well with international ties, and runs conferences and workshops. This organisation would grant the nascent Liberal Jewish community official recognition, and let it appear as more than just a loose gathering such as the *Jüdische Gruppe* or the *Jüdisches Forum*; the *WUPJ* would link it to the wider Jewish world. Yet, it demanded matrilineal descent or conversion, which Mayan and James had resisted so far. The incentive to create their own community led them to do just that. In the process of the creation of *Gescher LaMassoret*, the Bridge to Tradition as James named the community, James, Mayan, and James's late wife underwent *Giyur*. These three, plus Jonathan, Ron, and ten or so others set up *Gescher LaMassoret* in 1996 when "twenty-five members [...] was our dream!"

By 2008, when the chapter concerning the creation of *Gescher* for my PhD was written, the community has grown to nearly 100 members; in 2021 it has grown to more than 100. Its services attract guests, Jewish and non-Jewish alike. While the policy of the community is one of openness towards the non-Jewish visitors, their

82 As with the *SGK*, *Gescher* also offers activities for young members. These activities are not independent of its communities, but run on a national level as the actual number of young Jews in each community remains small.

presence challenges boundaries, it leads to constant tensions as *Gescher* members see their community as a closed Jewish space, a space for Jews, where Jews are in the majority and power holders. Calls to limit the amount of guests, or to keep events internal have been accompanying my fieldwork since day one in 2002. An underlying problem is that any event of *Gescher* is characterised by transience, only a very limited number of individuals are regulars. This means that it is difficult to figure out who is a Jew and who is a non-Jew at the service because any non-member only needs to submit a request to attend a service, and undergo to a security check but they are not checked for Jewish status. In consequence the similarity of biographical backgrounds and values, which was supposed to underpin this setting cannot be taken for granted in praxis. The presence of non-Jews and the issue of conversion of individuals from completely non-Jewish families have been creating problems that resurface in members' meetings, and that have been hotly and vitriolically debated. The ordinary members' meetings are held annually, but in case of urgent matters a meeting can be called at any time. Decisions are taken by democratic majority vote in the meetings. In order to ensure the smooth running of the community and deal with the regular affairs the board meets monthly. In the spirit of the democratic nature of the Liberal community the board, which consists of five members who are elected at the ordinary annual meeting, cannot make 'policies' for the community. All policies need to be decided by majority vote in the members' meetings. For urgent matters extraordinary members' meetings or *Diskussionsrunden* (discussion rounds) are summoned.

Recurrent issues which are discussed at the members' meeting center around the management of the boundary to the non-Jewish surrounding on two levels. On a first level, it is the boundary to non-Jewish Germans in general. On a second level it is the boundary to how much Germanness is allowed into the Jewish space through the conversion of individuals with completely non-Jewish families who bring with them different experiences to being in Germany and life-stories, which have no similarities to those of birth Jews (even if the similarities of the life-stories of the latter are rather tenuous).

Other Jewish spaces

With the creation of *Gescher*, the *Forum* withered away recounted Yitzhak, who served as one of the chairpersons of the *Forum* in the mid-2000s: "the people who pushed went into *Gescher*." The *Forum* had become reduced to "a mailing list and a monthly newsletter," which was also discarded in the summer of 2007. The *Forum* does not have a webpage, nor does it seek to recruit members, it just lingered when I finished my PhD fieldwork in early 2006; I have not received any information of its existence since 2009. Some of the last remaining members of the *Forum* had refused to join *Gescher* as they are non-religious, others lost any interest in Jewish matters after the infighting that accompanied the creation of *Gescher*, yet others set up new Jewish spaces that were more to their liking: the dynamic of the Jewish space also meant that spaces were discarded on the way. Sheer goodwill and 'a moment of interest' did not suffice to keep them active.

A Jewish space that followed the *Forum*, but that had a different focus was *A Groisse Liebe* (Yiddish: A Big Love). Set up in May 2005, it sought to attract Jews, and interested non-Jews, who cherish a debate about Israel, Judaism, films, or music in a secular setting: it is less political in focus than the *Forum*, which owes to its initiators. The location of *A Groisse Liebe* moved several times, it always took place in a freely accessibly bistro pub in the center of Cologne. Information about *A Groisse Liebe* could be accessed via its webpage, and any person who wished to do so can join the mailing list via the webpage; neither of these remain, and the big love died away although its initiators stayed in Cologne.

Upon arriving at *A Groisse Liebe* in the summer of 2005, I learned that the attendance was made up of Second Generation Jews who were often members of the *Einheitsgemeinde*. Hardly any First and no Third Generation Jews were around; FSU Jews were not part of this Jewish space, the lingua franca was German even though most of the attendees had immigrated to Germany as children or teenagers. Some of the non-Jewish spouses were present: "most of us are married to non-Jews." Besides the experience of intermarriage, most attendees were non-religious or little religious, the founders of *A Groisse Liebe* attest to being "Jewish atheists." However, unlike James, who felt that a boundary to non-Jews was needed, Stefan and Roland were interested in creating an "open space, where any Jew can come and bring their non-Jewish spouses and mixed children." The majority of the non-practising attendees were members of the *SGK*, they had grown up in this community, and they were children of survivors. They had known each other from childhood and sought the proximity to other Jews with similar experiences in a social space. Non-practicing as they were, they wanted their membership in the *SGK*, to maintain at least some connection to the Jewishness they had grown up with in a symbolic form.[83] This could take curious turns such as with one British born attendee who refuses to obtain German citizenship by way of German descent: "I bought a grave. [...] I want to be buried with my people." I asked what would happen with his non-Jewish wife: "She will be buried on the other sides of the wall" meaning that his wife would be buried on the adjacent, non-Jewish cemetery.

83 Herbert Gans, "Symbolic Ethnicity: The Future of Ethnic Groups in America," *Ethnic and Racial Studies* 2.1 (1979): 1–20; Herbert Gans, "Symbolic Ethnicity and Symbolic Religiosity: Towards a Comparison of Ethnic and Religious Acculturation," *Ethnic and Racial Studies* 17.4 (1994): 577–592; Kurt Grünberg, "Szenische Erinnerung der Shoah." Paper presented at "Szenische Erinnerungen der Shoah," Siegmund Freud Institut and University of Frankfurt, Frankfurt am Main, November 16 and 17, 2008.

In the opinion of these members of the *SGK* overstepping the *Halacha*, marrying a non-Jew, or eating non-kosher food was permissible. Publicly opposing the *Einheitsgemeinde* in general and *SGK* specifically was a step too far though; the same went for public criticism of Israel. This was deemed to weaken the Jewish community, undermining the unwritten law of categorical Jewish cohesion and erode the boundary to the categorical 'other.' Non-Jewish spouses and intimate friends were degoyified, they entered a special category.[84] Problematically, this strategy brought these members of the *SGK* in close a proximity with their German non-Jewish surrounding: if they did not practice, and did not care actively about "the community", how did they construct the boundary to non-Jews? Their membership in a religious community, where also their parents had been members and that distinguishes clearly between Jews and non-Jews supported the construction of an ethnic Jewish identity, without betraying Jewish belonging.[85] Furthermore, it ensured a symbolic Jewish continuity to the living and the dead,[86] which is key to descendants of survivors. It was indeed this categorical belonging that enabled them to overstep the *Halacha* and sustain their Jewishness.

Whereas the foundation of *Gescher* was about setting a boundary, *A Groisse Liebe* was about breaking it down. This worked briefly, although the pressure that was on the *Forum* did not apply to *A Groisse Liebe* because of the existence of *Gescher*. Those Jews who wished for an alternative to the *Einheitsgemeinde* had their own (religious) community. Adjacent groups to either community offered additional Jewish spaces: the *Forum* if they were closer to *Gescher*, or in the shape of *A Groisse Liebe*, if they were closer to the *Einheitsgemeinde*. Neither of the two lasted though, which is also owing to individuals moving away, or in some cases passing away.

Despite its openness neither *A Groisse Liebe* nor the *Forum* attract third generation Jews, nor FSU Jews. The FSU immigrants founded their own Jewish spaces, the prominent were the *Jüdische Gemeinde* (Jewish community), a religious community, and the *Nash Dom* (Our House) a gathering of Russian-speaking pensioners. Younger Russian speakers have been gathering privately in Cologne, a pattern the ethnologist Alina Gromova evidenced for Berlin.[87] The same applies to third generation Jews as an age cohort. These Jews set up loose Jewish spaces, but not lasting ones that resemble physical communities.

During my initial fieldwork, Israelis in Cologne formed a loose Israeli Group, which gathers in private spaces. Although the Israeli population in and around

---

84 Rapaport, *Jews in Germany after the Holocaust*, see note 52; Rapaport, "The Difficulties of Being Jewish," see note 74.

85 Rapaport, *Jews in Germany after the Holocaust*, see note 52.

86 Grünberg, "Szenische Erinnerung der Shoah," see note 82.

87 Alina Gromova, *Generation »koscher light«. Urbane Räume und Praxen junger russischsprachiger Juden in Berlin* (Bielefeld, 2013).

Cologne remains small, and much interaction takes place via social media, the *Israeli community North Rhine-Westphalia (NRW)*, which counts about 20 families as their core members (personal communication, November 2021) took shape from 2018 onwards; by 2021 it was a legally registered *eingetragener Verein* (registered club), which means it has statutes, a board, it can charge a membership fees – and it can regulate who is in, and who is out. Beyond the mere legal regulation: as with Russian speakers' gatherings, the *Israeli community NRW* is inaccessible to non-Israelis/non-Hebrew speakers: lingua franca is Hebrew. Yet, generational changes also resonate in these groups. During my PhD fieldwork, I was told that the point of the Israeli gathering is "to be less homesick for Israel." During return visits this had changed: while some Israelis who are long-term Cologne residents maintain this notion, younger, and more recent arrivals meet for social gatherings, for Israeli style Purim, or to acquaint their children with spoken Hebrew beyond the confines of their homes. Tellingly, the Israeli long-term residents, and the newer residents hardly intersect in the Israeli/Hebrew spaces.

Yet other Jewish spaces I encountered during my initial fieldwork collapsed completely: *Yachad* (Hebrew: together), the gathering of gay and lesbian Jews became dysfunctional. Social media contacts, and national groups such as *Keshet* took its place; LGBTQI* Jews as well as other third, and maybe forth, generation Jews are more mobile than previous generations. Owing to a higher mobility, but in particular to mobile communication and social media they set up Jewish spaces online, or they set up a temporary physical space, but they do not set up fixed, local communities like the generations before.

Conclusion: Jewish spaces in Cologne post-Shoah

Since its reopening the Orthodox synagogue of the *Einheitsgemeinde*, the *SGK*, was the center point of Jewish life in Cologne, loved by some, ignored by others, derided by yet others. In the 1980s, with the coming of age the Second Generation of post-Shoah Jews in Germany, this community became too small to accommodate the existing diversity. Break away members and non-members met with like-minded *halachic* and non-*halachic* Jews to form the politically informed *Jüdische Gruppen*. In Cologne the *Jüdische Gruppe* developed into the *Jüdische Forum*, and from the *Forum* grew *Gescher LaMassoret*. As adjacent Jewish spaces, the *Forum* and *A Groisse Liebe* filled in for specific parameters beyond the communities. These developments show that the boundaries to the non-Jewish surrounding are constantly being negotiated by Jews in Cologne, and that Jewish spaces are wanted and needed that are Jewish dominated. In particular, this dynamic indicates that the different experiences that individual Jews bring with them, lead to the creation of new Jewish spaces. For a group to sustain itself the overlaps need to be significant enough; they need to amount to a critical mass of like-mindedness/homophilous qualities – and they need to provide the members with rights, which they can exercise,[88] and which they can implement to regulate membership and to sustain a boundary to individuals on the outside, and to other groups.

At the point of revisiting output written in 2007 and 2008, some of the developments feel historical, as so much more dynamic, cacophony, but also self-confidence defines Jewish life in Germany: one is not shy anymore to show differences, and the issues that led to the set up and collapse of Jewish spaces seem normal now. The nuances depicted in ethnographic details for this period seem small to an outside observer were crucial within Jewish Cologne, and they have a lasting impact. Being Jewish in Cologne as in Germany as a whole remains anything but neutral despite changes, and different expressions of Jewishness need to be (carefully) negotiated.

Closed spaces with strong boundaries such as the *Einheitsgemeinde* and *Gescher* remain focal points; Jewish spaces that cater to a specific language community came into existence, but they do not challenge the power structures. Jews beyond the Second Generation and FSU Jews of the same generation do not seem to feel the need for more fixed communities. The third generation grew up with more Jewish diversity than the generation before them, a diversity that was public, as the façade had already been cracked. Any of their efforts are temporary in spatial dimension and benefit strongly from digital infrastructures. These changes can be seen in another graphic, for which I would need a tool that allows me to show dynamics and movement on a sheet of paper. The local Jewish space in Cologne is connected to other Jewish spaces at regional, national, and transnational levels; the speed of the connections between the spaces and the flows have accelerated.

On a city scale, the dynamics of the Jewish space in Cologne indicate some threads that run through its different communities, groups, and gatherings. Individuals attend more than one Jewish space within the overall Jewish space, and express different parts of their Jewish identities in each. The major drivers of the Jewish spaces are age, intra-ethnic subcategory, native language, country of birth and youth, as well as life-style choices such as preference for a specific form of Jewish practice, marriage/partnership choices, and *halachic* or non-*halachic* descent. This means that features of homogeneity and homophily run through the groups that maintain themselves. The homogeneity refers to intra-ethnic subcategory, native language, and country of birth and youth. The homophily refers to life-style choices and the attitudes that underpin them. All of these feed into the identity of each of the individuals I have met over the years. These create a matrix from which unique identities are formed. It is here where the social and personal component of the Jewish identity of each individual intersect, and where collective and individual Jewish agency are expressed to create, maintain, and discard Jewish (dominated) spaces.

88 Don Handelman, "The Organization of Ethnicity," *Ethnic Groups* 3.3 (1977): 187–200.

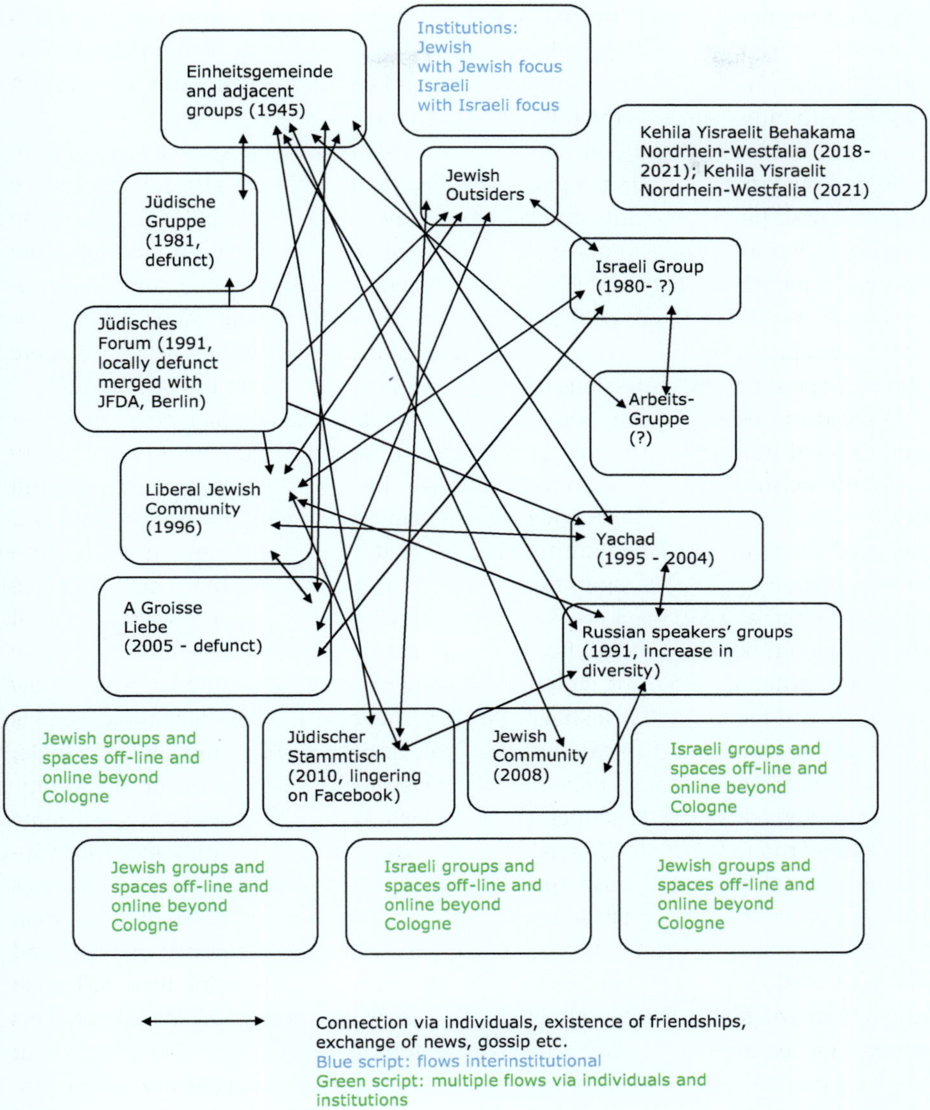

Fig. 2: The Jewish space in Cologne, 2021.

Part 2: **Ritual Objects**

Barbara Staudinger

Introduction to Part 2: Objects of Religious Practice in the Jewish Communities of Germany after 1945

The Shoah marked the deepest rupture in the history of Germany's Jewish communities. After 1945, only a few German Jews returned from exile or from the National Socialist concentration camps. Thus, it was mainly the Displaced Persons who, coming from all over Europe, formed new Jewish communities in the "Land of the Perpetrators."

At first, these communities were not intended to be permanent and had not yet become institutionalized. The survivors primarily sought emigration and sat on packed suitcases, ready to leave Germany as soon as possible. However, the desire to be able to lead a self-determined life again eventually caused Jewish communities to form, despite all reservations about continuing to live in Germany. These communities were first established in temporary facilities within the DP camps or even outside the camps in assigned houses or synagogues that had not been completely destroyed in 1938.

Fig. 1: Leipheim, Jewish service in the DP camp Leipheim, undated photo (Photograph: Breslawski Schneiderman, Yad Vashem Photo Archive, ID 1486_651).

https://doi.org/10.1515/9783110750812-007

Torah scrolls, prayer books, prayer shawls, tefillin and other ceremonial objects needed for religious practice were missing. Approximately ninety percent of all cult and ritual objects owned by Jewish communities, individuals or even Jewish museums in Germany had been looted by the National Socialists. In addition, there also existed looted ceremonial objects in Germany that had been stolen from all over Europe by National Socialist organizations for the Institute for the Study of the Jewish Question (*Institut für die Erforschung der Judenfrage*).[1]

In addition to the American Jewish Joint Distribution Committee (JOINT), the Jewish Restitution Successor Organization (JRSO) and the Jewish Cultural Reconstruction (JCR) for the American occupation zone, as well as the British Jewish Committee for Relief Abroad (JCRA) and its operative arm, the Jewish Relief Unit (JRU) for the British occupation zone, organized, with the help of the Western Allies, the tracing and return of Jewish property and, in particular, Jewish ceremonial objects. If the former owners of Jewish cult and ritual objects had survived and could be found, they were returned to them. Where this was not possible, the objects defined as heirless property were distributed to Jewish institutions: To the newly forming Jewish communities in Germany, but also to Jewish institutions in Israel and other states. However, the majority of the cult and ritual objects looted by the National Socialists remained lost.[2] Since the confiscated looted property was not sufficient to enable a religious life in the newly emerging communities, prayer books and Judaica had to be procured from other countries as well and brought to Germany.

In 1949, Hannah Arendt wrote a report for the JCR in which she described the situation in the British occupation zone.[3] Although the JCR, as trustee of heirless Jewish cultural property, was at that time only responsible for the American zone of occupation, it was already able to distribute more than half a million heirless properties to Jewish communities and institutions worldwide. For the British zone, the Jewish Trust Organization (JTC) was not assigned this task until 1950. According to Arendt, apart from other reasons, the delay was due to the differing interests of the newly forming Jewish communities, which were fighting for the legal succession of the pre-1933 communities and thus for legal recognition, on the one hand, and the

1 Julie-Marthe Cohen, Felicitas Heimann-Jelinek, and Ruth Jolanda Weinberger, *Handbuch zur Judaica Provenienzforschung: Zeremonialobjekte* [Looted Art and Jewish Cultural Property Initiative] (Claims Conference and WJRO, 2019).

2 See the databasis provided by Claims Conference and World Jewish Restitution Organization (WJRO), https://art.claimscon.org/resources/overview-of-worldwide-looted-art-and-provenance-research-databases/. Accessed November 2021.

3 Elisabeth Gallas, "Jüdische Kulturgüter in der Nachkriegszeit. Hannah Arendts Bericht zur Situation in Hamburg," in *Hamburger Schlüsseldokumente zur deutsch-jüdischen Geschichte* (January 30, 2017), https://dx.doi.org/10.23691/jgo:article-89.de.v1. Accessed November 2021. For the report, see "Hannah Arendt, Jewish Cultural Reconstruction Field Reports, 1948–1951," *Tätigkeitsbericht* 18 (February 15 – March 10, 1950). Trans. Insa Kummer. Available in *Hamburger Schlüsseldokumente zur deutsch-jüdischen Geschichte*, https://dx.doi.org/10.23691/jgo:source-126.de.v1. Accessed November 2021.

Fig. 2: Augsburg, Rally against the British Palestine policy in the fountain courtyard of the Augsburg Synagogue, March 24, 1947 (Jewish Museum Augsburg Swabia/Esther Fritsch, JKMB-006582).

international Jewish representatives, who saw no future for Jewish life in Germany, on the other. However, a look at the effects of legal succession shows that this was not a dispute about principles: With legal succession, claims could be made both to the property of the former Jewish communities and to property that had been declared heirless. The international aid organizations pursued their own interests just as much as the Jewish communities themselves.

The National Socialist looting of cultural objects had led to collections being torn apart and hardly remaining in their original places. Throughout Germany, Jewish ceremonial objects were found in non-Jewish municipal museums or depots. Initially, they were handed over to local Jewish community representatives, without any consideration of whether these objects had also previously been in the possession of that community. However, the Jewish welfare organizations, on the one hand, did not believe that the artefacts were safe in the possession of fragile and financially strapped new Jewish communities in Germany and, on the other hand, also understood themselves to be representing the interests of the emigrated German Jews, who also laid claim to the ceremonial objects that had been found. Largely for this reason, many of the rescued objects eventually ended up in educational institutions and communities in the United States and Israel and were therefore lost to the new Jewish communities in Germany in the long term.

It seems difficult to summarize the problematic situation regarding Jewish ceremonial objects and community development in Germany after 1945. Too many parameters need to be taken into account. On the one hand, the partly very differing situation in the various occupation zones must be mentioned, but also regional differences (large and small DP camps, connection to pre-war communities or not, etc.)[4] played a role regarding the distribution of resources to the Jewish communities as well as their self-confidence and possibilities for action. This situation did not become simpler later on, as there were then two German states that had different political views regarding their handling of the National Socialist past, regarding the continued existence of Jewish communities in Germany, as well as regarding claims to Jewish property that had been declared heirless.

Nevertheless, if we want to start defining the questions that outline the research field of "Jewish Ceremonial Objects in the Jewish Communities after 1945," we could focus on the following: A scholarly examination of Jewish ceremonial objects in post-war communities in Germany has to, in order to draw a preliminary conclusion, look at the subject matter from several perspectives: First, what ceremonial objects are involved, for what religious actions are they used, and to what extent is their possession a reflection of the communities' self-image? Secondly, we need to focus on the people involved: Who was active in the Jewish communities and who in the Jewish aid organizations? What goals did the individual players pursue? Third, the focus must be placed not only on where the ceremonial objects that were given to the Jewish communities came from, but also from which contexts they were torn. And fourth, it is necessary to ask about the subsequent whereabouts of the ceremonial objects: Were they only used in the communities for a short time and soon replaced by others, did the objects remain in the communities or were they transferred to a museum?

These ceremonial objects, their history and their significance for the present and the future of the Jewish communities, will be the focus of the following chapters. For, in contrast to the institutional development of the camp communities and early community building outside the camps, they have so far hardly been studied.

4 For an overview, see after-the-shoah.org, a project of the Nuremberg Institute for Holocaust Studies: https://www.after-the-shoah.org. There you can find an example of a small DP camp in Swabia: https://www.after-the-shoah.org/saulgau-ein-wartesaal-in-der-schwaebischen-provinz-a-waiting-room-in-the-swabian-province/. Accessed November 2021.

Fig. 3–4: Prayer book of Sche'erit Hapleta, cover, printed on behalf of the American Joint Distribution 1946 (Jewish Museum Augsburg Swabia, JKMB-007768).

The contributions

In her chapter, **Ayleen Winkler** takes a first look at what was left of Germany's Jewish communities after the Shoah. On behalf of the Jewish Scientific Institute (YIVO), Mordechai Bernstein, who had survived the Nazi era in Soviet prisons, traveled through former Jewish communities in Germany starting in 1948, searching for remnants of their history. Often religious objects were the only things he could still find. These objects were used in different ways: they were ignored, hidden, repurposed or exhibited.

Mordechai Bernstein recorded the status quo: he inventoried still existing possessions of the Jewish communities, researched their history and went in search of looted cultural property. He later summarized his findings in three volumes published in Yiddish. In 2020, the Jewish Museum Munich dedicated the exhibition "In the Labyrinth of Times. With Mordechai W. Bernstein through 1700 years of German-Jewish history." In her contribution, Winkler discusses how communities continue to deal with their history: From breaking with traditions to the musealization of history.

While Mordechai Bernstein was dealing with the history of the former Jewish communities, new communities slowly began to establish themselves in the occupied zones. In her contribution, **Lea Weik** takes a closer look at the British occupation zone. There, the majority of the Displaced Persons were housed in the former Bergen-Belsen concentration camp, where terrible conditions prevailed and the survivors were still dying months after their liberation. It was up to the Jewish relief organizations to provide not only food, clothing and shelter, but also everything needed for religious practice. In the process, they faced procurement difficulties due to the large number of items needed, which had to be solved. In addition to the Jews in DP camps, the relief organizations also took care of survivors outside the camps, especially German Jews who were trying to rebuild their communities. In order to strengthen them, they were provided with ceremonial objects from the destroyed communities of Germany. Weik not only shows the work and tasks of the Jewish relief organizations in these first years after the liberation. She also shows how objects of religious practice were important for the survivors' self-confidence and their will to live.

Around 1950, the DP camps were closed. Help was now provided to the Jewish communities, which slowly built up more and more steady structures. As a result, new community centers and synagogues were built, and old communities were now formally re-established and their representatives elected. Religious differences and the resulting conflicts accompanied this process, as it became necessary to find a new self-conception as a Jewish community in a Germany in which one now wanted to remain. The consolidation of Jewish life in Germany thus went hand in hand with the expansion of the communities' infrastructure, the renovation or new construction of synagogues and other facilities – and finally also with a new attitude toward their ceremonial objects. Whereas cult and ritual objects had initially been distributed by the Jewish help organizations out of necessity and taken over by the Jewish communities, the new communities had to come to terms with which traditions they wanted to continue and which they did not. As a result, new ceremonial objects were acquired in some cases, while old ones went into storage or, as in the case of Augsburg, into a Jewish museum.

Sarah König's contribution is also devoted to the relationship between the Jewish community and the museum. However, this time the focus is not on the immediate post-war period, but on the period between 1960 and 1985, the year in which the Jewish Museum Augsburg was founded as the oldest Jewish museum in the Federal Republic of Germany, and at the same time the period that can be described as a phase of consolidation of the Jewish communities in Germany. Unlike in other cities, it was not possible to fall back on older holdings of Judaica that had already been included into a museum, but a completely new collection had to be set up.

The founder of the museum and at the same time chairman of the Jewish community, Julius Spokojny, was able to include ceremonial objects from the Jewish community as well as his private collection in the museum. In addition, the Bavarian National Museum was persuaded to lend its Judaica collection to the Jewish Museum on a permanent basis. In addition, however, Judaica made by the Israeli artist Yehoshua Freiman were acquired for the museum. When it was founded, the museum did not see its task as presenting regional Jewish traditions in Bavarian Swabia, but in showing the "beauty of Jewish tradition." Therefore, the question must be asked whether other museums' ceremonial objects apart from the newly purchased ones had been used at all before they came to the museum.

Both the origin and the subsequent use of ceremonial objects in Jewish communities or museums thus open up a deeper view into the development of Jewish communities after 1945. They tell of new beginnings and the preservation of memory, but they also speak of forgetting and the search for a new identity. Thus, based on the stories behind the religious objects and the motives of the people involved, we can approach the topic of religious life in the DP camps and subsequent Jewish communities from different perspectives. The respective stories behind the ceremonial objects therefore also reflect the transformation of Judaism after the Shoah.

While it was initially the Jewish relief organizations that supplied the Jewish communities inside and outside the DP camps with religious objects, it later became the Jewish communities themselves that procured Judaica from various sources. Differences in religious traditions played as much a role in the selection of objects as did the means of procurement. The histories behind the objects refer both to the attempt to reconnect with the former communities and to the attempt to forget and allow new traditions. Essential in this context seems to be the need for those who returned and survived to regain a new self-consciousness through religious practice. This self-consciousness was subsequently reflected not only in the ceremonial objects used by the Jewish communities, but also in the newly established Jewish museums.

Ayleen Winkler

Locating and Relocating: Mordechai W. Bernstein, Jewish Successor Organizations and the Musealization of Jewish Cultural Heritage Objects

"In the Labyrinth of the Times. With Mordechai W. Bernstein through 1700 years of German-Jewish History" is the title of an exhibition by the Jewish Museum Munich. It is based on the work of Mordechai W. Bernstein, who had been involved in the attempts of successor organizations to locate and relocate Nazi-confiscated cultural heritage. In three books Bernstein published his findings and thus created an imaginary museum of the destroyed German-Jewish culture. Yet, the placement of Jewish cultural heritage objects in physical museums is regarded more critically by Bernstein. The following chapter analyzes some of Bernstein's texts, in order to determine factors influencing his opinion on the musealization of Jewish cultural heritage objects, in light of his work for successor organizations.

Successor organizations and Mordechai W. Bernstein

At the end of World War II, a vast number of books and ritual objects were piled in so-called collecting points in the American occupation zone in Germany.[1] Two successor organizations were responsible for handling the Nazi-confiscated cultural heritage: the Jewish Restitution Successor Organization (JRSO) and the Jewish Cultural Reconstruction Inc. (JCR). The JRSO had been acknowledged as successor organization for Jewish property on June 23, 1948, the JCR followed as agent of the JRSO on February 15, 1949.[2]

---

1 In Bamberg, Celle, Marbach, Munich, Nuremberg, Offenbach and Wiesbaden: Elisabeth Gallas, *"Das Leichenhaus der Bücher" Kulturrestitution und jüdisches Geschichtsdenken nach 1945* (Göttingen, 2016), 29.

2 Elisabeth Gallas, "Fragmente einer verlorenen Welt. Zur Rettung und Restitution Jüdischer Kulturgüter in der Nachkriegszeit," in *Unser Mut. Juden in Europa 1945–48*, ed. Kata Bohus, et al. (Berlin/Boston, 2020), 224–243, especially 235; Bilha Shilo, "When YIVO was defined by territory: Two perspectives on the restitution of YIVO's collections," in *Contested Heritage. Jewish Cultural Property after 1945*, ed. Elisabeth Gallas, et al. (Göttingen, 2020), 79–89, especially 80; Dana Herman, "'A Brand Plucked Out of the Fire': The Distribution of Heirless Jewish Cultural Property by Jewish Cultural Reconstruction, Inc., 1947–1952," in *Neglected Witnesses: The Fate of Jewish Ceremonial*

https://doi.org/10.1515/9783110750812-008

Together, JCR and JRSO tried to locate the original owners of the cultural objects or their heirs. Where this was unsuccessful, the objects were handed over to Jewish communities and institutions,[3] some of them newly founded communities and DP camps in Germany. Most objects though were transferred abroad, mainly to Israel and the USA,[4] since the representatives of JRSO and JCR did not believe there would be permanent Jewish life in Germany ever again.[5] The objects, however, were supposed to be used in thriving communities and their traditions and histories preserved in Jewish institutions.[6]

One of the numerous staff members of JCR was Mordechai W. Bernstein (born June 14, 1905, in Bytén, died April 4, 1966, in New York),[7] a Polish librarian and journalist.[8] During the Shoah, he was incarcerated in various Soviet prisons due to his political activities for the General Jewish Labour Bund (henceforth, Bund).[9] At the end of the war, he tried to be reunited with his wife and his daughter in the USA, but was unable to obtain the necessary papers.[10] Since in Poland he was again threatened with imprisonment due to his continued work for the Bund,[11] he left for Germany in 1948, where he first arrived in a DP camp before moving to Stuttgart.[12]

Objects During the Second World War and After, ed. Julie-Marthe Cohen, and Felicitas Heimann-Jelinek (Amsterdam, 2011), 29–62, especially 29; Gallas, "*Das Leichenhaus der Bücher*," see note 1, 15, 66, 85, 129, and 134; The precondition for the nomination of non-governmental successor organizations was military law no. 59, which was ratified in 1947: see Gallas, "*Das Leichenhaus der Bücher*,", 66, and 124.

3 Shilo, "When YIVO was defined by territory," see note 2, 80.

4 Herman, "'A Brand Plucked Out of the Fire,'" see note 2, 32, 34; Gallas, "*Das Leichenhaus der Bücher*," see note 1, 143, 148, and 174.

5 Gallas, "Fragmente einer verlorenen Welt," see note 2, 236; Herman, "'A Brand Plucked Out of the Fire,'" see note 2, 30–31; Gallas, "*Das Leichenhaus der Bücher*," see note 1, 114, 149–150; the American military government was of the same opinion: Gallas, "*Das Leichenhaus der Bücher*," 63.

6 Herman, "'A Brand Plucked Out of the Fire,'" see note 2, 31–32, 33, and 56; Gallas, "*Das Leichenhaus der Bücher*," see note 1, 248.

7 Roger S. Kohn, *An Inventory to the Mordechai Bernstein Collection 1905–1965* (New York, 1986), 5 and 10.

8 Kohn, *An Inventory to the Mordechai Bernstein Collection 1905–1965*, see note 7, 7; Marie Luise Knott, ed., *Hannah Arendt – Gershom Scholem. Der Briefwechsel. Unter Mitarbeit von David Heredia* (Berlin, 2010), 206.

9 Martyna Rusiniak-Karwat, "Bundists under the Soviet Occupation: The Case of Matwiej Bernstein," *Studia Polityczne* 45.3 (2017): 141–151, especially 141, and 147–148; Kohn, *An Inventory to the Mordechai Bernstein Collection 1905–1965*, see note 7, 6.

10 Interview by the Jewish Museum Munich with Karen Leon (granddaughter of Mordechai W. Bernstein) on February 19, 2021.

11 Interview by the Jewish Museum Munich with Karen Leon (granddaughter of Mordechai W. Bernstein) on February 19, 2021.

12 Rusiniak-Karwat, "Bundists under the Soviet Occupation," see note 9, 150; Kohn, *An Inventory to the Mordechai Bernstein Collection 1905–1965*, see note 7, 7; Masha Leon: "Eli Zborowski Center

In Germany, Bernstein worked for the YIVO (*yiddisher visnshaftlikher organisatsye*), where he had already been employed before and during World War II in Warsaw and Vilnius as a librarian and historian.[13] Now he collected various materials for the YIVO, like pamphlets from DP camps, publications regarding German Judaica but also Antisemitica.[14] Moreover, he compiled inventories of the vast archives of German Jewish communities.[15] As mentioned, Bernstein also worked for the JCR,[16] and thus had contacts with the JRSO as well.[17] In the JCR he was part of a small team of scientists, which had been assembled by Hannah Arendt,[18] executive director of JCR.[19] Arendt strove to find Nazi-confiscated cultural heritage specifically in German museums, archives and libraries.[20] In theory, these institutions were obliged to notify the Allied authorities of such assets in their collections. They were, however, mostly hesitant to comply with this demand.[21] Also, the refund law only applied to goods worth 1,000 DM or more. Cultural heritage objects, especially private property, often did not amount to this sum.[22]

On behalf of the JCR, Bernstein visited hundreds of (former) Jewish communities in Germany.[23] He didn't stop at tracking down Nazi-confiscated cultural heritage though. Instead, he researched the extensive history of these communities, sometimes as far back as to their beginnings in late antiquity. He published his findings in the 1950s and 1960s in Buenos Aires, where he had emigrated to in

Stage at American Society for Yad Vashem Luncheon," *Forward* (June 1, 2012), https://forward.com/articles/157206/eli-zborowski-center-stage-at-american-society-for/.

13 Kohn, *An Inventory to the Mordechai Bernstein Collection 1905–1965*, see note 7, 5–6; Rusiniak-Karwat, "Bundists under the Soviet Occupation," see note 9, 142–143; Peter Honigmann, "Die Akten des Exils. Betrachtungen zu den mehr als hundertjährigen Bemühungen um die Inventarisierung von Quellen zur Geschichte der Juden in Deutschland," *Der Archivar* 54.1 (2001): 23–31, especially 27–29; Knott, *Hannah Arendt – Gershom Scholem*, see note 8, 306.

14 Honigmann, "Die Akten des Exils," see note 13, 27–29; Kohn, *An Inventory to the Mordechai Bernstein Collection 1905–1965*, see note 7, 7.

15 Honigmann, "Die Akten des Exils," see note 13, 27–29; Kohn, *An Inventory to the Mordechai Bernstein Collection 1905–1965*, see note 7, 7.

16 Gallas, "*Das Leichenhaus der Bücher*," see note 1, 165.

17 I.e., Mordechai Wolf Bernstein, "Die 'Gottesmutter' im Schnaittacher Tora-Schrein," in *Im Labyrinth der Zeiten. Mit Mordechai W. Bernstein durch 1700 Jahre deutsch-jüdische Geschichte. Mit Übersetzungen aus dem Jiddischen von Lilian Harlander und Lara Theobalt*, ed. Bernhard Purin, Ayleen Winkler (Berlin/Leipzig, 2021), 276–283, especially 280.

18 Gallas, "*Das Leichenhaus der Bücher*," see note 1, 165.

19 Herman, "'A Brand Plucked Out of the Fire,'" see note 2, 30; Gallas, "*Das Leichenhaus der Bücher*," see note 1, 140.

20 Gallas, "*Das Leichenhaus der Bücher*," see note 1, 165.

21 Gallas, "*Das Leichenhaus der Bücher*," see note 1, 165.

22 Gallas, "*Das Leichenhaus der Bücher*," see note 1, 165; Knott, *Hannah Arendt – Gershom Scholem*, see note 8, 486–487.

23 Mordechai Wolf Bernstein, *In labirintn fun tkufes* (Buenos Aires, 1955, Yiddish), 17, and 395; Kohn, *An Inventory to the Mordechai Bernstein Collection 1905–1965*, see note 7, 7–8.

1952.[24] These three Yiddish books on German Jewish communities are: *In labirintn fun tkufes* (1955), *Nisht derbrente shaytn* (1956) and *Doz iz geven nusekh ashkenaz* (1960). With these publications he curated a *musée imaginaire*[25] of Jewish culture in the territory of modern-day Germany. The exhibition "In the Labyrinth of the Times. With Mordechai W. Bernstein through 1700 years of German-Jewish History" in the Jewish Museum Munich transformed this into a "real museum." It showed eighteen objects from different places, which Bernstein had tracked down during his research travels. Some of the objects shown are among those, Bernstein was looking for on behalf of JCR.

The question of musealization

While Bernstein may have created a *musée imaginaire*, some comments in his books indicate that Bernstein did not always approve of the placement of Jewish cultural heritage objects in museums. For example, in Laupheim he questioned whether visitors of a museum properly appreciated the displayed Torah finials.[26] In other cases, though, his remarks on objects in museums are more favorable, as in the case of *mizrachim*. Some of these he considers to be of such artistry, they should be on display in a museum.[27] This raised the question, which factors in the musealization of objects affected Bernstein's evaluation of this process and whether working for the JCR might have influenced his opinion on the matter. The following chapter focuses on the latter part of the question. Since the evaluation of the musealization of objects was not Bernstein's primary concern when writing his texts, his opinion

24 Kohn, *An Inventory to the Mordechai Bernstein Collection 1905–1965*, see note 7, 8; Knott, *Hannah Arendt – Gershom Scholem*, see note 8, 653; Rusiniak-Karwat, "Bundists under the Soviet Occupation," see note 9, 150.

25 The term *musée imaginaire* describes the idea that every person has access to an imaginary museum, shaped by their experiences and viewing habits. These imaginary museums are able to contain more and more diverse objects, than physical museums could. Derek Allan, *Art and the Human Adventure: André Malraux's Theory of Art* (Amsterdam, 2009), 255–274; Dennis Niewerth, *Dinge – Nutzer – Netze: Von der Virtualisierung des Musealen zur Musealisierung des Virtuellen* (Bielefeld, 2018), 210–222.

26 Mordechai Wolf Bernstein, "Die verbrannte Tora-Krone in Laupheim," in *Im Labyrinth der Zeiten. Mit Mordechai W. Bernstein durch 1700 Jahre deutsch-jüdische Geschichte. Mit Übersetzungen aus dem Jiddischen von Lilian Harlander und Lara Theobalt*, ed. Bernhard Purin, and Ayleen Winkler (Berlin/Leipzig, 2021), 250–257, especially. 254–255.

27 Mordechai Wolf Bernstein, "'Zwei Misrachim' im Fürstlichen Museum Amorbach," in *Im Labyrinth der Zeiten. Mit Mordechai W. Bernstein durch 1700 Jahre deutsch-jüdische Geschichte. Mit Übersetzungen aus dem Jiddischen von Lilian Harlander und Lara Theobalt*, ed. Bernhard Purin, and Ayleen Winkler (Berlin/Leipzig, 2021), 130–137, especially 131.

on this must be regarded as latent meaning which can be examined through qualitative content analysis.[28]

In what follows, the approach to qualitative content analysis by Philipp Mayring[29] has been used to examine the eighteen articles by Bernstein, translated, researched and published in the exhibition catalogue of the Jewish Museum Munich. This ensured a reasonable scope for a preliminary study,[30] based on which further inquiries can be undertaken. The qualitative content analysis allows to structure the material based on predetermined classification criteria, which are presented in a category system. In this way, distinctive characteristics can be determined and evaluated,[31] and, in this case, characteristics regarding Jewish cultural objects in museums were filtered and evaluated according to Bernstein's assessment. Additional historical material has been used to construct a category system: Since Bernstein worked and wrote in light of the JCR's attitude toward the further placement of Jewish cultural objects, the category system has been developed using aspects of both the JCR's attitude and Bernstein's texts.

Jewish Cultural Reconstruction, Inc.

> The Jewish people succeeded in salvaging some 500,000 volumes, 1,200 scrolls of law, 7,000 artistic and ceremonial objects. These were distributed to institutions throughout the world. Far beyond their monetary value, these collections symbolize the continuity of the heritage of the Jewish people. This way they are likely to fructify all aspects of Jewish culture for generations to come.[32]

This is how Salo W. Baron, president of the JCR,[33] described the JCR's work in retrospect in an article of 1955. He mentions two central aspects: First, the focus on Jewish life outside of Germany, "throughout the world." Hence, the JCR tried to restitute

---

28 Chad Nelson, and Robert H. Jr. Woods, "Content Analysis," in *The Routledge Handbook of Research Methods in the Study of Religion*, ed. Michael Stausberg, and Steven Engler (London/New York, 2011), 109–121, especially 110; Siegfried Lamnek, *Qualitative Sozialforschung* (Weinheim, 2010), 439.

29 Philipp Mayring, *Qualitative Inhaltsanalyse. Grundlagen und Techniken* (Weinheim/Basel, 2003).

30 On the necessity of defining ultimately analyzed material, see Mayring, *Qualitative Inhaltsanalyse*, see note 29, 47.

31 Mayring, *Qualitative Inhaltsanalyse*, see note 29, 58–59, 92; Philipp Mayring, "Qualitative Content Analysis: Demarcation, Varieties, Developments," *Forum Qualitative Sozialforschung/Forum: Qualitative Social Research* 20.3 (2019), https://doi.org/10.17169/fqs-20.3.3343.

32 Salo W. Baron, "Communal Responsibility for Jewish Social Research," *Jewish Social Studies. Papers and Proceedings of the Tercentenary Conference on American Jewish Sociology* 17.3 (1955), 242–245, especially 243.

33 Knott, *Hannah Arendt – Gershom Scholem*, see note 8, 651; Gallas, "*Das Leichenhaus der Bücher*," see note 1, 17.

objects or give them to Jewish communities and institutions outside of Germany. Second, Baron mentions the aspect of continuity. The objects were meant to "fructify" Jewish life "for generations to come." They were supposed to be used in their original function or as educational objects and thus continue Jewish culture.

Category system

While the aspect of continuity has proved difficult to determine through a category system and will be discussed when examining the finds, the question of location turned out rather useful in a first test run[34] of the category system. During the test run, all mentions of museums in Bernstein's texts were marked and according to the goals of the JCR categorized into museums in Germany and museums in other countries. It became apparent, though, that in addition a further category for "unspecified museums" was necessary. In these cases, Bernstein does not speak of a specific museum, but of museums in general. Also, Bernstein not only writes about Nazi-confiscated cultural heritage, but also about the whole history of certain German Jewish communities. The category system, therefore, had to differentiate between objects or collections in museums, that had been acquired in a NS-context and those, that had been acquired prior to the Shoah. At the same time, Bernstein's evaluation of these cases was supposed to be included. The category system used to analyze the material is presented in Table 1:

Tab. 1: Category system.

	Pre-war collections/ objects in German museums	**Collections/ objects with a NS-context in German museums**	**Pre-war collections/ objects in non-German museums**	**Collections/ objects with a NS-context in non-German museums**	**Pre-war collections/ objects in unspecified museums**	**Collections/ objects with a NS-context in unspecified museums**
Positive evaluation	A1	B1	C1	D1	E1	F1
Negative evaluation	A2	B2	C2	D2	E2	F2
Neutral evaluation	A3	B3	C3	D3	E3	F3

34 On the necessity of test runs, see Mayring, *Qualitative Inhaltsanalyse*, see note 29, 44.

Tab. 2: Extraction of finds.

Category	Number of finds	Percentage
A1	9	64,29
A2	3	21,43
A3	2	14,29
A total	**14**	**46,67**
B1	0	0
B2	4	80
B3	1	20
B total	**5**	**16,67**
C1	0	0
C2	1	33,33
C3	2	66,67
C total	**3**	**10**
D1	0	0
D2	1	50
D3	1	50
D total	**2**	**6,67**
E1	3	75
E2	0	0
E3	1	25
E total	**4**	**13,33**
F1	0	0
F2	2	100
F3	0	0
F total	**2**	**6,67**
Number of finds total	30	100

The smallest component analyzed was a sentence, but whenever possible it was one or more paragraphs.[35] This way each mentioned museum is counted as one find and connected with one evaluation by Bernstein.[36] Table 2 shows the overall findings, coding the eighteen articles:

At first glance, Tab. 2 indicates that Bernstein generally regarded the musealization of objects with a NS-context as negative, with most cases belonging to either B2, D2 or F2. The categorization of pre-war collections, however, appears to be more divers, containing multiple positive evaluations as in A1. To determine factors which might have influenced Bernstein's evaluation, the categorized cases have to be examined more closely and contrasted with one another. However, since not all finds can be discussed at length within the scope of this chapter, a case of restitution will be presented and contrasted with one exemplary find regarding an object with a NS-context in a German museum (category B). This way the specific differences in Bernstein's evaluation of Nazi-confiscated cultural heritage in museums and objects given into restitution can be highlighted. The overall findings, as presented in the above table, will be used to raise further questions and to look at more detailed aspects.

Restitution in Gunzenhausen

In the Middle Franconian small town of Gunzenhausen, Bernstein was looking, among other things, for two Torah shields, one of them can be seen in Fig. 1. He had been continuously asked about their fate, probably by former residents of Gunzenhausen.[37] He impressively describes his joy on turning some of the found objects over to the Nuremberg Palace of Justice, where he usually reported on the progress of his research.[38] Not always, but sometimes, he was able to also hand over objects which were then prepared for restitution. This positive evaluation of delivering the Gunzenhausen objects already indicates Bernstein's commitment to either restitution or else an alternative

35 Mayring, *Qualitative Inhaltsanalyse*, see note 29, 53.

36 At times, Bernstein uses sarcasm or irony in his texts, indicated for example by quotation marks. This had to be considered when categorizing the text passages.

37 Mordechai Wolf Bernstein, "Die Gunzenhäuser Tora-Schilder," in *Im Labyrinth der Zeiten. Mit Mordechai W. Bernstein durch 1700 Jahre deutsch-jüdische Geschichte. Mit Übersetzungen aus dem Jiddischen von Lilian Harlander und Lara Theobalt*, ed. Bernhard Purin, and Ayleen Winkler (Berlin/Leipzig, 2021), 264–269, especially 264; Bernstein believed, he had successfully located both of the shields, but was mistaken regarding one shield, which was given to the Jewish Museum Franconia only in the 1990s: Bernhard Purin, "Das Tora-Schild aus Gunzenhausen," in *Koordinierungsstelle für Kulturgutverluste Magdeburg*, ed. Beiträge öffentlicher Einrichtungen der Bundesrepublik Deutschland zum Umgang mit Kulturgütern aus ehemaligem jüdischen Besitz (Magdeburg, 2001), 107–117, especially 107.

38 Bernstein, "Die Gunzenhäuser Tora-Schilder," see note 37, 269.

Fig. 1: Torah crown, silver, gilded, master's marks: Magnus Unsin, born 1819 in Unterammingen/Unterallgäu, master 1847, died 1889 in Augsburg, assayer's mark: Augsburg 1867–1868, Augsburg (Museum for the History of Christians and Jews, Laupheim, Inv. No. 1994/0904).

placement of the objects outside of Germany. Finally, Bernstein writes about the two Torah shields: "After years of wandering and desecration, they returned to their rightful place – two more rescued 'non-burnt' logs."[39] Regarding the history of the objects, he here differentiates clearly between the time of National Socialism ("wandering" and "desecration") and handing the objects to the JCR, which he characterizes as returning them to their rightful place. Restitution of the Nazi-confiscated cultural heritage objects or placing them with Jewish communities or institutions, is therefore positively connoted for Bernstein.

Musealization in Laupheim

Bernstein's article on the city of Laupheim in Württemberg shows that the musealization of Nazi-confiscated heritage objects in German museums is regarded quite differently by Bernstein. The synagogue of the Jewish community in Laupheim had been burned down during the November pogroms in 1938,[40] and by the end of 1942 not a single Jewish person still lived in Laupheim.[41] Only some Judaica had survived the destruction of the community and the synagogue;[42] they had been transferred to a municipal museum by the time Bernstein visited Laupheim.[43] The museum's employees, apparently, were not trained to handle Jewish ritual objects and, for example, presented a Torah crown (Fig. 2) as headdress for a bridal couple.[44] Regarding this, Bernstein writes: "He [a museum employee] meant the crumpled Torah crowns that had undergone a transformation in the museum."[45] The term "transformation" certainly

---

39 Bernstein, "Die Gunzenhäuser Tora-Schilder," see note 37, 269; translated from German to English by AW.

40 Stadt Laupheim, ed., *Miteinander. Nebeneinander. Gegeneinander. Museum zur Geschichte von Christen und Juden in Laupheim. Ein Museumsbegleiter zur und durch die Ausstellung* (Stuttgart, 2006), 84; Paul Sauer, *Die jüdischen Gemeinden in Württemberg und Hohenzollern. Denkmale, Geschichte, Schicksale. Mit einem Beitrag von Julius Wissmann. Zur Geschichte der Juden in Württemberg 1924–1939. Herausgegeben von der Archivdirektion Stuttgart* (Stuttgart, 1966), 18 and 120; Georg Schenk, "Die Juden in Laupheim," in *Laupheim. Herausgegeben von der Stadt Laupheim in Rückschau auf 1200 Jahre Laupheimer Geschichte 778–1978*, ed. Kurt Diemer (Weißenhorn, 1979), 286–305, especially 300.

41 Stadt Laupheim, *Miteinander. Nebeneinander*, see note 40, 85; Schenk, "Die Juden in Laupheim," see note 40, 300; Michael Niemetz, "Arisierung" in Laupheim – ein Forschungsstand," in *Ausplünderung der Juden in Schwaben während des Nationalsozialismus und der Kampf um Entschädigung*, ed. Peter Fassl (Konstanz, 2020), 109–112, especially 111.

42 Stadt Laupheim, ed. *Miteinander. Nebeneinander*, see note 40, 84.

43 Bernstein, "Die verbrannte Tora-Krone in Laupheim," see note 26, 254.

44 Bernstein, "Die verbrannte Tora-Krone in Laupheim," see note 26, 254.

45 Bernstein, "Die verbrannte Tora-Krone in Laupheim," see note 26, 254; translated from German to English by AW.

Fig. 2: Torah shield, silver, partially gilt, maker's mark: missing, probably Thomas Ringler, born 1638, master 1661, died 1709, assayer's mark: missing, c. 1661–1670, Nuremberg (Dottheim Brooks Family, New York).

relates to the misinterpretation of the Torah crown by the museum's employee. However, when talking about panels of wooden synagogues Bernstein uses the term to describe the musealization process (categorized as A1).[46]

Therefore, in the case of Laupheim, the term might as well at least partially relate to the musealization of the object. While in this passage a negative connotation of musealization is merely indicated, it becomes much more obvious a few passages further down, when Bernstein writes about the Judaica in the museum: "How much longer will they wander without salvation?"[47] This clearly negative description of the object history is striking, especially in comparison with the description of the objects in Gunzenhausen. While handing the objects over to the JCR – and thus starting the process of restitution or placement in Jewish communities outside of Germany – is described as returning them to their rightful place, the musealization of the objects in Laupheim is portrayed as a lack of salvation. Similarly, in his foreword

46 Mordechai Wolf Bernstein, "Die Wandmalereien in den Synagogen," in *Im Labyrinth der Zeiten. Mit Mordechai W. Bernstein durch 1700 Jahre deutsch-jüdische Geschichte. Mit Übersetzungen aus dem Jiddischen von Lilian Harlander und Lara Theobalt*, ed. Bernhard Purin, and Ayleen Winkler (Berlin/Leipzig, 2021), 116–123, especially, 116.

47 Bernstein, "Die verbrannte Tora-Krone in Laupheim," see note 26, 255; translated from German to English by AW.

to *Nisht derbrente shaytn* Bernstein describes objects held in museums, archives or libraries as asking to be transferred to a place of rest.[48] The rupture, which National Socialism caused and which is experienced as "wandering" or "desecration," as described in the text about Gunzenhausen, appears not to be fixed or healed by the musealization but rather to be sustained or even continued.

Conclusion

The example of Laupheim in comparison with Gunzenhausen strongly indicates that Bernstein regarded the musealization of objects with a NS-context in German museums as negative. The other finds of category B confirm this assessment.

This could indicate that in accordance with the JCR's attitude toward placement of Nazi-confiscated cultural heritage, Bernstein is troubled by the location of the objects in German museums and would have preferred them to be handed to Jewish institutions outside of Germany. This is contradicted, however, by the cases found in category D, objects with an NS-context in museums outside of Germany. While one is not evaluated by Bernstein, one is regarded as negative. In this case Torah scrolls had been reused by National Socialists as everyday objects and transferred to various museums outside of Germany.[49] Hence, it seems less likely that the location of the museum is the defining aspect in Bernstein's evaluation.

This leaves another aspect that Salo W. Baron mentioned about the work of the JCR, which might be considered as relevant in Bernstein's evaluation: The wish for continuity. While, as mentioned above, this aspect was hard to grasp using qualitative content analysis on the eighteen articles, in Bernstein's fore- and afterwords, continuity appears as a central aspect of his work.[50] For example, in accordance with A.J. Herschel he writes: "*Lomir nisht fartakhleven di yerushe fun ashkenaz.*"[51] He does not, however, connect this idea of continuity explicitly with the placement of objects in museums. Here, the analysis of his articles may shed some light on the role museums play in producing continuity for Bernstein. For, as Tab. 2 shows, not only are objects with NS-context in museums negatively evaluated, but some pre-war collections as well (categories A, C and E), which might indicate a general dislike of

48 Mordechai Wolf Bernstein, *Nisht derbrente shaytn* (Buenos Aires, 1956, Yiddish), 10.

49 Mordechai Wolf Bernstein, "Verbrannte Tora-Rollen und geschändete Pergamentblätter," in *Im Labyrinth der Zeiten. Mit Mordechai W. Bernstein durch 1700 Jahre deutsch-jüdische Geschichte. Mit Übersetzungen aus dem Jiddischen von Lilian Harlander und Lara Theobalt*, ed. Bernhard Purin, and Ayleen Winkler (Berlin/Leipzig, 2021), 60–67, especially 60.

50 Mordechai Wolf Bernstein, *Dos iz geven nusekh ashkenaz* (Buenos Aires, 1960, Yiddish), 12 and 343; Bernstein, *Nisht derbrente shaytn*, see note 48, 13.

51 Bernstein, *Dos iz geven nusekh ashkenaz*, see note 50, 344; in English: "Do not let us waste the heritage of Ashkenaz."

storing objects in museums. This might be explained by the "transformation," as Bernstein calls it, that museum objects undergo, from objects of utility to objects of representation.[52]

For example, the Torah crown from Laupheim does not actually function as a Torah crown in the current exhibition "In the Labyrinth of the Times" in the Jewish Museum Munich, but as representative for Bernstein's work in Germany, the Jewish community of Laupheim and, due to its fire damage, for the November pogroms. This transformation from an object of utility to an object of representation might contradict the JCR's aspiration for continuity of Jewish culture through the objects. Instead of being used in its original context, the Torah crown represents all that is lost. However, the JCR did place objects in museums outside of Germany, so the transformation of the object's function apparently was no general problem. If this transformation of function was relevant for Bernstein, his approach would have deviated in this aspect from the JCR's. Also, Bernstein did create a *musée imaginaire* by writing his books on German Jewish communities. He explicitly says in one of his forewords that the objects and places he describes were supposed to retell the beginnings of Ashkenaz, and hence function as objects of representation.[53] Therefore, it seems highly unlikely that he would have regarded musealization in general – in the sense of using objects as representatives – as a discontinuation of Jewish culture and thus negative. Moreover, in some instances, he even suggests that certain objects actually belong in a museum, such as when he talks about *mizrahim*, which he considers to have a highly artistic quality.[54]

Upon a closer look, it transpires that the negatively evaluated cases of pre-war collections are connected to instances of persecution and destruction other than that under National Socialism. In category A3, two Hebrew manuscripts had been reused as book covers,[55] and in a museum in Baden-Württemberg, Bernstein found wooden figurines from the fourteenth century covered with a layer of remains of Hebrew manuscripts.[56] The one negative evaluation in category C, museums in other countries, concerns a pair of shoes which had been produced by using destroyed Torah scrolls.[57] In these cases, the form of appropriation appears to be the central issue.

Thus, while the two aspects of the JCR's attitude toward restitution considered in this chapter – location outside of Germany and continuity – seem unlikely to be

---

52 Karl-Heinz Kohl, *Die Macht der Dinge. Geschichte und Theorie sakraler Objekte* (München, 2003), 122 and 257; Susanne Claussen, *Anschauungssache Religion. Zur musealen Repräsentation religiöser Artefakte* (Bielefeld, 2009), 46.

53 Bernstein, *Dos iz geven nusekh ashkenaz*, see note 50, 9.

54 Bernstein, "'Zwei Misrachim' im Fürstlichen Museum Amorbach," see note 27, 131.

55 Bernstein, "Verbrannte Tora-Rollen und geschändete Pergamentblätter," see note 49, 61 and 62.

56 Bernstein, "Die 'Gottesmutter' im Schnaittacher Tora-Schrein," see note 17, 282.

57 Bernstein, "Verbrannte Tora-Rollen und geschändete Pergamentblätter," see note 49, 60.

decisive in Bernstein's evaluation of the musealization of Jewish cultural objects, the form of appropriation might be the determining factor. When stemming from a persecution context – be that of the Shoah or another case of persecution – the placement of objects in museums – regardless of their location – might have been considered as continuing the rupture caused by the persecution. This is indicated in the text about Laupheim, where Bernstein appeals for salvation of the museum objects. In contrast, the restitution, as indicated in the text about Gunzenhausen, is perceived as returning the objects to their rightful place – which one might call salvation. Since continuity apparently is not a decisive factor for this notion, it might be a general sense of justice: returning what has not been rightfully appropriated. As Bernstein writes about the restitution by the JCR: "Un dos eigentlekh is take mayn skhar far yenem koshmar-shpatsir, wos ikh bin gegangen tsvishn di dosike udim mutsalim me'esh."[58]

A final assessment of Bernstein's view on the musealization of Jewish cultural objects, however, would require more extensive research of all the articles in his books as well as his other writings. Since such a study would be of larger scope, another or an additional method might be considered for the purpose, such as employing a historical discourse analysis.

58 Bernstein, *Nisht derbrente shaytn*, see note 48, 11 in English: And this is actually my true reward for that nightmarish walk I took among the logs rescued from the fire.

Lea Weik

"In the religious field great strides have been made" – Jewish Relief Organizations and the Supply of Religious Objects to Jewish Communities in the British Zone (1945–1950)

After the liberation by Allied troops in 1945, there were about 80,000 to 90,000 surviving Jews on German territory. The majority of them were so-called Displaced Persons (DPs) from Eastern Europe, who were housed in various DP camps.[1] In addition, it is estimated that about 28,000 German Jews had survived in interconfessional marriages, in hiding or in camps.[2] For the most part, they returned to their homes and families, if possible, or sought shelter elsewhere. In the British zone, which included the present-day German states of Schleswig-Holstein, Hamburg, Lower Saxony and North Rhine-Westphalia, the majority of Jewish DPs were housed in the Bergen-Belsen camp. The situation of the survivors in the completely overcrowded former concentration camp was catastrophic and in the first weeks after the liberation thousands died of hunger, debilitation and disease.

For all these people, the first priority was to continue to survive, i.e. to secure food, clothing and housing. However, it soon became clear that many also felt a need for religious practice. This chapter attempts to reconstruct how Jewish survivors in the British zone were enabled to practice their religion and the ways in which they obtained the religious accessories or ceremonial objects necessary for worship. The focus will be on the role of Jewish aid organizations in acquiring such objects and establishing a religious infrastructure. Essential sources are the files of the Henriques Collection in the Wiener Library London.

Shortly after the end of the war, various Jewish aid organizations became active in Germany. In the British zone, these were primarily the British Jewish Committee for Relief Abroad (JCRA) respectively its operative arm, the Jewish Relief Unit (JRU), and the American Jewish Joint Distribution Committee (JOINT).[3] Both organizations began their work in June and July 1945, and were required by the British military government to work exclusively for the DPs in the camps. The JOINT directed its

1 Hagit Lavsky, *New Beginnings. Holocaust Survivors in Bergen-Belsen and the British Zone in Germany, 1945–1950* (Detroit, 2002), 27 on.

2 Lavsky, *New Beginnings*, see note 1, 29.

3 In addition the Chief Rabbi's Religious Emergency Council (CRREC), the Organization through Training (ORT), the Hebrew Sheltering and Immigrant Aid Society (HIAS), the Jewish Agency for Palestine, the Jewish Brigade and the Bricha were active in the British Zone.

https://doi.org/10.1515/9783110750812-009

work in the British zone from Belsen until the end of 1949. The headquarters of the JRU was initially located in Celle and thus in the immediate vicinity of Bergen-Belsen.[4] In the second half of 1945, however, it was moved to Eilshausen in Westphalia, since the United Nations Relief and Rehabilitation Association (UNRRA) had its headquarters there.[5] The Germany Division of the JRU was headed by Rose Henriques and Leonard Cohen. From the end of 1945 they were subordinate to the Director of Germany, Henry S. Lunzer.[6]

Initially, the most important task of the Jewish relief organizations, besides providing food, clothing and housing, was to help the survivors trace relatives. However, the possibility of being able to practice their religion freely again also became a high priority for many Jews. On issues of religious rehabilitation and care for the surviving Jews, the JCRA worked closely with the Chief Rabbi's Religious Emergency Council (CRREC), also based in London. The CRREC had sent four rabbis to the British zone in June, even before the first JCRA relief workers arrived in Germany, and from the beginning was concerned to provide the survivors with religious supplies such as kippot, prayer shawls, phylacteries and prayer books. This organizationally and logistically complex undertaking was prepared even before the end of the war and demanded great commitment from those involved. In a letter dated December 7, 1944, the Secretary General of the CRREC, Henry Pels, addressed Leonard Cohen of the JCRA with the following lines:

> [W]ith regard to the item of 1.000 pairs of phylacteries which was agreed upon by your Finance Committee, I would like to mention that after consideration we find that it is not possible to distribute these Tefillin to the Jewish populations on the continent without proper bags. We've therefore tried to get some blackout material, which is available free of coupons for us and found a person who is prepared to make these 1.000 bags for us.[7]

In his reply, Cohen was convinced of the need to have bags made for the phylacteries, but since the sum of £50 seemed too high, he had the bags made free of charge by his relative, Rita Cohen, who also worked for the JCRA.[8] This episode not only demonstrates the scarcity of money in the Jewish relief organizations and the great personal commitment of their employees, but also shows the important role that was given to religious requisites. For the tefillin that were sent out would of course have fulfilled their function even without the corresponding bags. However, being able to hand them out to the survivors as a set in a bag can be understood on the one hand as a revaluation of the tefillin and on the other hand it also expresses respect for the survivors, because after years

4 Donate Stratmann, "'In the field' – Die Arbeit der internationalen jüdischen Hilfsorganisationen in der britischen Besatzungszone Deutschlands (1945–1951)," in *Deutschland - trotz alledem? Jüdische Sozialarbeit nach 1945*, ed. Helga Krohn, and Gudrun Maierhof (Frankfurt am Main, 2006), 65.
5 Stratmann, "'In the field,'" see note 4, 72.
6 Stratmann, "'In the field,'" see note 4, 73.
7 Wiener Library London, Henriques Collection, HA14-2 (Post-war religious Reconstruction), fol. 81.
8 Wiener Library London, Henriques Collection, see note 7, fol. 88.

of persecution in which they had been denied their humanity by the National Socialists, they were now once again seen as individuals and respected as believers. Thus, the relief workers also made sure, as far as possible, to listen to the concerns and needs of the survivors in personal one-on-one conversations, and relief goods were also individually packaged and handed over to the respective recipient. That this approach was intentional becomes clear from a report by Rose Henriques from September 1945, in which she writes: "This is a deliberate policy destined to re-awaken individualism in each of the DP's, and helping them to forget the 'mass existence' which has been their unfortunate lot lately."[9] That relief workers were concerned about the mental state of survivors is also clear from a letter from Rabbi Solomon Schoenfeld to Leonard Cohen from January 1945, in which he writes: "Our people on the continent seem to go in for talesim, and although they are not, from the point of view of our religious law, as important as tefillin and other requisites, they seem to possess a strong psychological appeal, which is, after all, also one of our main considerations."[10]

Supplying the survivors with religious accessories was a challenge for the aid organizations not only in view of the large quantities required, but also because procuring the ritual items was not easy in itself. After all, the manufacture of tefillin and mesusot is subject to strict religious specifications – the leather and parchment used must be kosher and can only be inscribed by a trained sofer. The high demand for these products led to an enormous increase in prices within a short period of time and the relief organizations, financed purely by donations, looked for possible alternatives to ordering them in Palestine. In a document dated September 13, 1945, Leonard Cohen wrote with regard to the mesusot needed, that "[p]archement can be obtained in London at various artists sundrymen shops. I shall enquire whilst I am in Germany whether it may be used and whether there are people amongst the DPs who could write them."[11] Indications as to whether this plan was pursued or even implemented could not be found. However, Judith Baumel points out, that employees of the JOINT in the US zone faced the same problems and therefore arranged that tefillin were produced in the DP camps Weilheim and Plattling from mid-1947.[12]

Another way for the CRREC to obtain religious supplies was through collections of such items in British Jewish communities. For example, the North London Relief Co-ordination Committee, in cooperation with CRREC, organized a relief drive in September 1946 in which prayer books were collected as well as

9 Wiener Library London, Henriques Collection, HA6A-4/1 (Further report on the work at Celle), fol 55a.

10 Wiener Library London, Henriques Collection, HA14-3 (Post-War Religious Reconstruction 1945 Jan.–June), fol. 13.

11 Wiener Library London, Henriques Collection, HA14-3 (Post-War Religious Reconstruction 1945 July–December), fol. 195.

12 Judith Tydor Baumel, "The Politics of Spiritual Rehabilitation in the DP Camps," *Simon Wiesenthal Center Annual* 6 (1989): n.p.

religious requisites.[13] Details of the success of such collections are not available, but in a letter to Rose Henriques in September 1947, her colleague E.G. Lowenthal complained about the books provided:

> I sometimes feel that people are clearing out their lofts where they apparently find the oldest stuff for transmission on to the Jews in Germany, instead of letting us have books not only in good condition but up to the date literature suitable for Jews in towns over here. What I mean is this: We obtain [...] old Hebrew-English prayer books, partly in a rotten state, which for the majority of people, are unsuitable [...].[14]

The books collected in London received a stamp before being sent to Germany, which identified them as a gift from the JCRA or the CRREC and thus makes them identifiable to this day. For example, it was possible to locate several prayer books in the Gelsenkirchen Jewish Community that bear a stamp of the CRREC (Fig. 1).

Identifying other objects from these donations today is much more difficult or impossible. Although dedication sheets were often placed in the parcels, the objects themselves were usually not marked.

These examples give a rough idea of how enormous the survivors' need for religious objects was and the difficulties relief organizations faced. The difficult situation was aggravated by the fact that from the beginning the British military government had only allowed the Jewish relief organizations to take care of the Jewish DPs in the camps but not of the, mostly German Jews, who lived outside the camps.[15] The justification for this directive was the British decision not to recognize Jews as a separate victim group. In the DP camps, too, all survivors had been grouped according to their respective countries of origin and, unlike in the US zone, no separate camp was set up for Jewish survivors. Although this practice was changed soon after massive protests by the Central Committee of Liberated Jews, for German Jews outside the camps the regulation still meant that they were treated equally to non-Jewish Germans and received only the subsistence level of food rations.

From the beginning, however, both JOINT and JRU circumvent the prohibition to operate outside the DP camps, arguing that they also had to take care of those DPs who had settled outside the camps.[16] In this way, JRU staff soon extended their work to the newly founded Jewish communities in the British zone, which numbered 37 by the end of 1947.[17] As the emigration of the vast majority of Jewish DPs proceeded, JRU and CRREC focused more and more on supporting the communities.

---

13 Wiener Library London, Henriques Collection, HA2-6/5 (Correspondence, 1946. JCRA Organisation: Supplies), fol. 75/R.

14 Wiener Library London, Henriques Collection, HA16-1/13 (Collections in the UK, Jewish libraries and books,1946–1947), fol. 5/B.

15 Stratmann, "'In the field,'" see note 4, 72.

16 Lavsky, *New Beginnings*, see note 1, 53.

17 Wiener Library London, Henriques Collection, HA22-1/2 (Mrs Henriques Confidential, 1946–1949. Miscellaneous: Journals, Photographs, etc.).

Fig. 1: Stamp of the Chief Rabbi's Religious Emergency Council London (CRREC) in a Prayer book for the Jewish High holidays found in the Jewish Community of Gelsenkirchen (Photograph: Lea Weik, Braunschweigisches Landesmuseum, 2021).

Rose Henriques (1889–1972), who had come to Celle with the second group of relief workers immediately after the liberation, headed the German department of JRU and was especially committed to the Jewish survivors. Since she and her work for the JRU are almost unknown today, her role will be examined in more detail below. In the East End of her hometown London Henriques, together with her husband Basil, ran the Bernhard Baron Settlement for Jewish people of all ages. The couple offered various services for children, young people and their parents, as well as support for the elderly. Medical assistance and free legal counseling for low-income people were also provided. In the settlement's own synagogue, religious classes took place as well as activities for adults. Her social commitment played an essential role in Rose Henriques' life and so it was probably a logical conclusion for her to become actively involved in the JCRA from 1943 onwards.

Shortly after her arrival in Germany, Henriques expressed her concern for Jewish survivors outside the DP camps:

> The German Jews need the support of the authorities as do the DPs; and those of them who struggle to re-establish their congregations and re-dedicate their synagogues should have the advice of persons versed both in German law and German congregational history, so that when the British Authorities are approached, they receive properly prepared and technically correct information for their consideration.[18]

From the beginning, Henriques regularly visited the newly emerging communities and met with their representatives to get a picture of their situation and needs. Her numerous reports from the first five years after the war provide a profound insight into the situation of the communities and at the same time are a powerful testimony to Henriques' tireless commitment to the concerns of the survivors. Her regular visits in the field meant that she was able to evaluate the situation of the Jewish communities comparatively realistically:

> [...] and although we have to face the fact that, to all intents and poses, the history of the Jews in Germany rests in the past rather than in the future. One cannot, in common humanity, say to these brave, struggling middle-aged and elderly men and women – "You are only there to die off: it's waste of time for you to try to live a full life again" – which, in effect, is what we should be doing if we withdraw, or even lessen our moral and practical support. Both by the leaders of the Central Jewish Committee and by their own Gemeinde representatives are they constantly being urged in forceful language – "Get out of Germany whilst there is still time. German Jewish life must not be re-established in Germany." The majority cannot emigrate, it is cruel to seek to cast a still deeper gloom over their last few years and to minimise their brave efforts.[19]

With this view, Henriques, consciously or unconsciously, opposed the World Jewish Congress' call to Jews, shared by much of the world Jewish community, to "never again settle on blood-soaked German soil."[20]

In the following two years, until the final withdrawal of the JRU from Germany, Henriques and her colleagues did their utmost to strengthen and support the communities: "Wherever there is a German Jewish Community in the British Zone, be it ever so small, the JRU workers make periodical visits and attend to the queries put to them by the committees and representatives of communal affairs."[21]

The establishment of a religious infrastructure in the communities included not only the supply of individual believers with religious accessories, but also the establishment of synagogues and prayer halls and to equip them with ceremonial objects.[22] Almost all synagogues and community centers were destroyed. Ceremonial objects had also often been destroyed or looted during the November pogroms and were

---

18 Wiener Library London, Henriques Collection, HA6A-4/1 (Mrs Henriques reports 1945. Jews in Germany), fol. 38. (HA6A-4/1/38).

19 Wiener Library London, Henriques Collection, HA6A-4/4 (Mrs. Henriques reports 1948), fol. 20/a.

20 Michael Brenner, *Nach dem Holocaust. Juden in Deutschland 1945–1950* (München, 1995), 99.

21 Wiener Library London, Henriques Collection, HA6A-4/4 (Mrs. Henriques reports 1948), fol. 8.

22 A main aim was also to send out rabbis and offer the possibility of celebrating the Jewish holidays appropriately as well as offering circumcisions, bar mitzvahs and weddings according to tradition.

considered lost at the end of the war. Some of these objects had been incorporated into the collections of German museums and archives and had survived the war there. In the British zone, such cases are documented from Hamburg and Lübeck, among others.[23] In Hamburg, survivors had come together immediately after the end of the war to found a new congregation. They used the small house synagogue in the former Oppenheimer Stift in Kielortallee as a prayer room, which had been misused and damaged during the war, but which could be reconstructed as a provisional building within a short time.[24] Shortly before the planned grand opening of the synagogue, the congregation turned to the Hamburg Senator for Culture on August 21, 1945, with the request that for the upcoming High Holidays "some cultic equipment such as Torah crown, shields, pointers, etc., which at the time had been taken into custody by Dr. Spierling [sic!][25] director of the Altona Museum and subsequently housed in the bunker Heiligengeistfeld, could be obtained, even if only on loan, subject to clarification of the legal situation."[26] On August 31, G.F. Wilimot of the Monuments, Fine Arts & Archives Branch approved this loan, but stipulated that the objects would remain property of the Altona Museum "pending a decision by a higher authority."[27] That the transfer of the objects actually took place becomes clear from a "List of the ceremonial objects from the possession of the former Jewish Religious Association e.V. Hamburg, which were given on loan for use by the Altona Museum to the Jewish Religious Commission Hamburg Rothenbaumchaussee 38 on September 5, 1945," which was signed by the Jewish Religious Commission on September 18.[28] This inventory includes a total of 84 ceremonial objects. Where these museum objects originally came from has not yet been conclusively clarified. As Karin Walter points out in her article on the Jewish cult-room in the Altona Museum, some objects might have been part of the synagogue silver confiscated by the German Reich in 1939.[29] In Hamburg, an exemption was granted for all objects made of silver, gold or platinum confiscated by Reich decree in February 1939. In contrast to the usual practice, such objects were not melted down or given to public purchasing agencies, but cultural institutions such as museums, were enabled to secure objects of "scientific value that

23 The Monuments, Fine Arts & Archives Branch also discovered Torah scrolls and clothing in the Suermondt Museum Aachen and approximately 1,000 volumes of Hebraica in the Hanover Municipal Library.

24 Heinz Goldstein, "Harry Goldsteins Bericht über den Wiederbeginn jüdischen Lebens in Hamburg 1945–1948 aufgezeichnet von seinem Sohn Heinz Goldstein," in *„Schließlich ist es meine Heimat ..." Harry Goldstein und die Jüdische Gemeinde in Hamburg in persönlichen Dokumenten und Fotos*, ed. Uwe Lohalm (Hamburg, 2002), 19.

25 This refers to Hubert Stierling (1882–1950), who was director of the Altona Museum from 1932 to 1949.

26 Staatsarchiv Hamburg, 522–2_1237 (Kultus 1945–51), fol. unnumbered; translated by LW.

27 Staatsarchiv Hamburg, 522–2_1237 (Kultus 1945–51), fol. unnumbered; translated by LW.

28 Staatsarchiv Hamburg, 522–2_1237 (Kultus 1945–51), fol. unnumbered; translated by LW.

29 Karin Walter, "Der jüdische Kultraum im Altonaer Museum (1914–1933). Eine Spurensuche," in *Schatten. Jüdische Kultur in Altona und Hamburg*, ed. Gerhard Kaufmann (Hamburg, 1998), 25.

should be preserved".[30] Director Stierling of the Altona Museum had ordered some Judaica objects for his institution from the responsible administration for art and cultural affairs in April 1940 and also received them. Although it is not yet reconstructed exactly how many objects Stierling had received from the confiscated silver at that time, it was in any case considerably less than the 84 objects that the Hamburg Jewish Community received from him in 1945.[31]

The fact that the objects were initially given to the community only on loan had two reasons: on the one hand, questions of restitution had not yet been regulated by law at that early point in time.[32] On the other hand, no one could know then how long the Jewish communities would exist at all for many thought of them rather as "Liquidationsgemeinden" than as "Aufbaugemeinden." With this large number of properties, the Jewish Community of Hamburg was a rare exception so soon after the end of the war. Most other congregations lacked the ritual objects necessary for worship.

As it became more and more apparent that Jews settled in numerous places and would not leave Germany, Rose Henriques saw the need to provide the congregations with ceremonial objects for worship in synagogues and prayer halls. But this was no easy task, especially since the vast majority of the Judaica objects discovered after the end of the war were located in the US zone.[33] At the end of March 1949, she wrote to the editor of the *Jewish Chronicle* in London:

> I am most anxious that before we finish our work in Germany, we shall know that every Gemeinde however small and however primitive their premises for Divine worship may be, they will all have the minimum of Religious Requisites at their disposal. There is, as you probably know, a large store of these in the US Zone, and that is why our JRU workers are making special note of the needs of the small groups of German/Jewish residents.[34]

The "large store" to which Henriques refers, is the Offenbach Archival Depot (OAD), which served as a collecting point for looted books and Jewish ceremonial objects since March 1946 (Fig. 2–4). In the little more than three years of its existence, more than 3.5 million books and manuscripts as well as several thousand Torah scrolls and other ritual objects passed through the sorting and distribution procedure of

30 Quoted in Walter, "Der jüdische Kultraum im Altonaer Museum (1914–1933)," see note 29, 25; translated by LW.

31 According to Karin Walter, Stierling had ordered fifteen Judaica objects, although it is not clear whether he received them. The museum received nineteen objects. Whether these came into the museum instead of the ordered fifteen objects or in addition to them remains unclear. See Walter, "Der jüdische Kultraum im Altonaer Museum (1914–1933)," see note 29, 25.

32 In the British zone, the Military Government Act No. 59 on the "Restitution of Identifiable Property" to Victims of National Socialist Suppression did not come into effect until May 1949.

33 The vast majority of Judaica looted by the National Socialists and hidden during the war were located in tunnels, bunkers, castles or chateaus in the area that became part of the US zone after the war ended.

34 Wiener Library London, Henriques Collection, HA7/4-16 (Hannover 1 Reports 1947–49), fol. 59/A.

the depot. The primary goal was, of course, to return the objects to their former owners or their rightful heirs, but this was only achieved in very few cases. The majority of the Jewish ceremonial objects and books stored in the OAD were categorized as "heirless cultural Jewish property." In order to prevent cultural property from falling into the hands of the German state, various international Jewish organizations in the United States founded the Jewish Restitution Successor Organization (JRSO).[35] From June 1948, it acted as a trust organization for heirless Jewish assets and subsequently endeavored to ensure their restitution.[36] In February 1949, the Jewish Cultural Reconstruction (JCR) was finally authorized as a sub-organization of the JRSO to search for heirless Jewish cultural assets and to forward them to Jewish institutions, primarily in Israel and the USA.

Fig. 2: Books and other archival material as they arrived at the Offenbach Archival Depot, 1946 (Yad Vashem Photo Archive, ID 73_2_18).

35 The JRSO consisted of the following organizations: Agudas Israel World Organization, American Jewish Committee, American Jewish Joint Distribution Committee, Anglo-Jewish Association, Arbeitsgemeinschaft der Süddeutschen Landesverbände Jüdischer Gemeinden, Board of Deputies of British Jews, The Central British Fund for Jewish Relief and Rehabilitation, Conseil Représentatif des Juifs de France, The Council of Jews from Germany, The Jewish Agency for Israel, Jewish Cultural Reconstruction Corporation and World Jewish Congress.

36 Ayaka Takei, "The 'Gemeinde-Problem' The Jewish Restitution Successor Organization and the Postwar Jewish Communities in Germany 1947–1954," *Holocaust and Genocide Studies* 16.2 (2002): 271.

Fig. 3: Offenbach depot, display of confiscated silver Torah crowns, Torah pointers and other ritual objects looted from European synagogues, ca. 1945–1947 (United States Holocaust Memorial Museum, courtesy of S. J. Pomrenze, Photograph Number: 48726).

Between July 1949 and January 1952, the JCR distributed a total of 1,024 Torah scrolls and 7,867 ceremonial objects to museums and synagogues worldwide.[37] Israel and the US each received about forty percent of the objects, and the remaining twenty percent went to other Western countries, primarily France and Great Britain. Only 89 ceremonial objects were distributed to synagogues in Germany, because the representatives of the JCR were quite reluctant to give them to Jewish communities in Germany. They were of the opinion that the history of Judaism in Europe, and in particular the continued presence of Jews in Germany, had been terminated by the Shoah. In addition, the JCR feared that the newly established communities, out of financial necessity, might sell the heirless property given to them or that the property might be lost forever if the communities were dissolved.[38] Rose Henriques apparently did not share this view to the same extent. Even after her return to London she continued to advocate that the communities in the British Zone were provided with ceremonial objects.

37 Georg Heuberger, "Zur Rolle der Jewish Cultural Reconstruction nach 1945," in *Was übrig blieb. Das Museum Jüdischer Altertümer in Frankfurt 1922–1938*, ed. Felicitas Heimann-Jelinek (Frankfurt am Main, 1988), 101a.

38 Takei, "The 'Gemeinde-Problem,'" see note 36, 276.

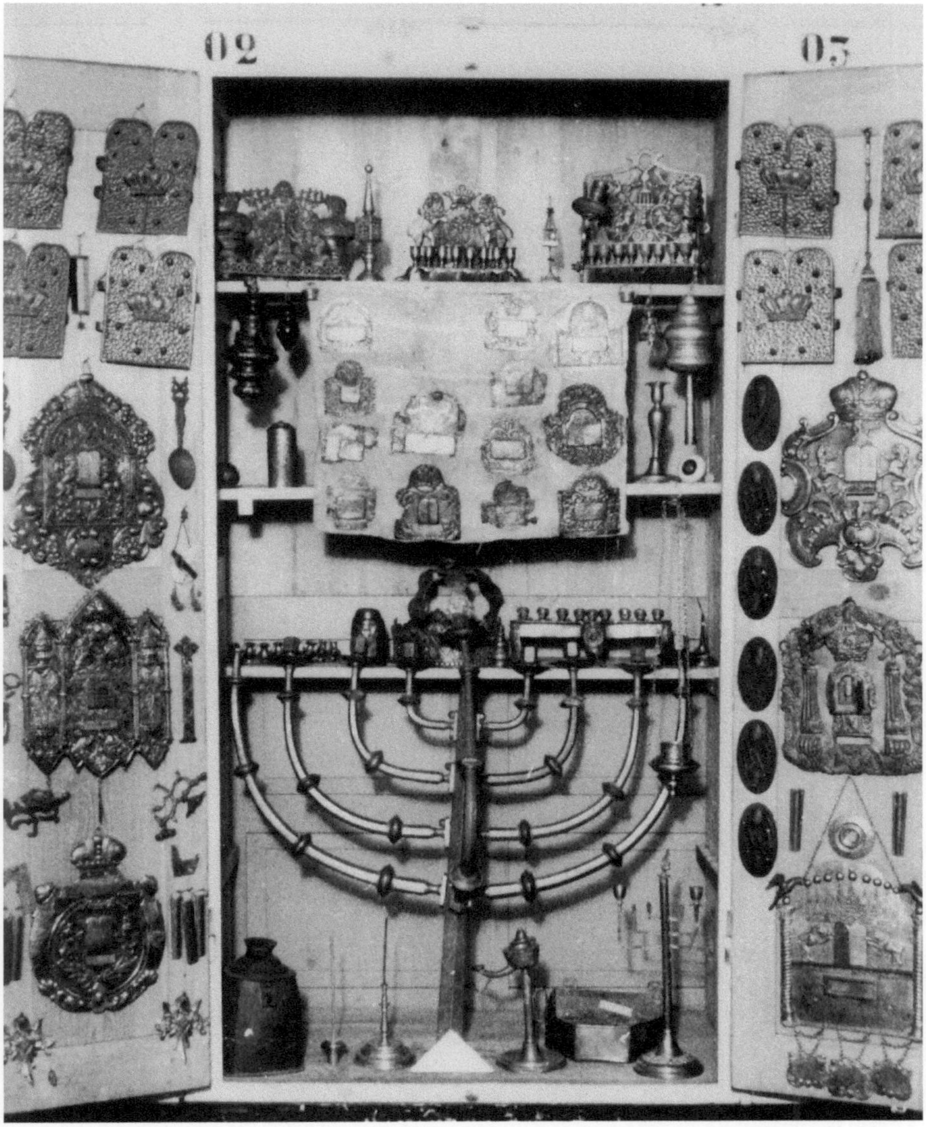

Fig. 4: Offenbach depot, display of silver Hanukkah menorahs, Torah breast plates and other ritual objects confiscated by the Nazis (United States Holocaust Memorial Museum, courtesy of S. J. Pomrenze, Photograph Number: 48734).

In March 1950, after nearly five years, the JCRA ended its work in Germany and withdrew its Relief Units. Henriques, believing this withdrawal to be premature, sent a circular from London to the Jewish communities in the British zone in May 1950. It stated:

> During my recent visit to Germany, I was informed by several of the communities that their Synagogues or Betstuben had insufficient silver ornaments and covers for the scrolls and the reading desks. In order to try and obtain these from accumulated stores in Germany for the use of German Jewish places of worship I should require a complete list of what is still necessary to complete the essential equipment of Synagogues and Betstuben.[39]

Probably to avoid raising expectations too high, Henriques added: "You will realise, I feel sure, that this is in no way a firm promise to produce the articles required [...]."[40] Nevertheless, the response was great and within the next few weeks Henriques received feedback from nineteen communities, in which they announced their needs.[41] Based on these responses, an extensive list was compiled that summarized the communities' total needs to nearly 180 ceremonial objects.[42] At the end of November 1950, Henriques then sent the list to the head of the JCR, Salo Baron, in New York, with the request to send ceremonial objects from the Offenbach Archival Depot to the communities:

> [F]rom my own frequent visits to Germany ever since 1945 to this date, I have become convinced that the most urgent desire of the few thousand remaining German Jews is to set up whatever "Betstube" or little Synagogue now taking the place of the former edifices with as perfect an outfit as possible. Their craving for spiritual rehabilitation and their earnest efforts to achieve this are most moving an awe-inspiring to the beholder and should receive every help and encouragement it is possible for their co-religionists outside Germany to offer them.[43]

Despite the above-mentioned skepticism of the JCR towards the establishment of Jewish communities in Germany, and although the OAD had already been dissolved by that time, Henriques received the hoped-for commitment as early as December 11. In a short letter, Hannah Arendt, then executive director of the JCR, confirmed to her: "we have instructed Dr. Lowenthal to let you have the ceremonial objects which you need for the communities in the British zone and your request will be filled as far as possible."[44]

---

39 Wiener Library London, Henriques Collection, HA18-3/15 (Religious Requisites Purchases, 1947–52), fol. 3.

40 Wiener Library London, Henriques Collection, HA18-3/15, fol. 3.

41 Only the Jewish communities in Bielefeld, Braunschweig, Koblenz, Lippstadt/Soest wrote that they did not need any supplies. Wiener Library London, Henriques Collection, HA6E-6 (Requisitions, 1950), fols. 1–22.

42 The Wiener Library London, Henriques Collection, HA18-3/14 (Religious Requisites Loot, 1946–1951), fols. 16–18.

43 Wiener Library London, Henriques Collection, see note 42, fol. 23a.

44 Wiener Library London, Henriques Collection, see note 42, fol. 25.

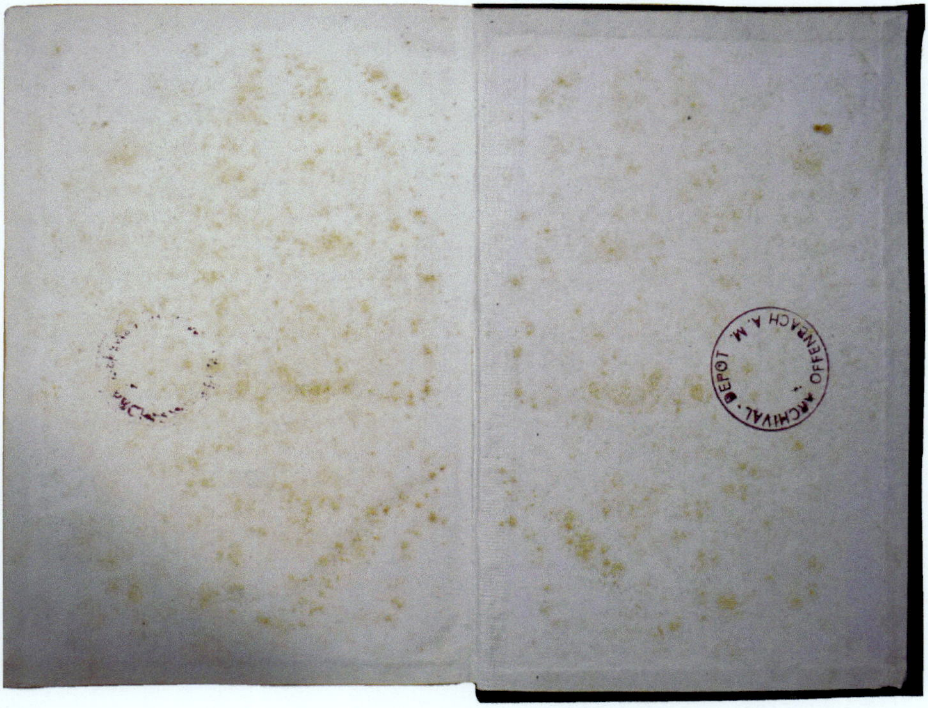

Fig. 5: Stamp of the Offenbach Archival Depot in a prayer book for the Jewish high holidays found in the Jewish Community of Gelsenkirchen (Photograph: Lea Weik, Braunschweigisches Landesmuseum, 2021).

Whether and to what extent the objects promised by the JCRA actually went to the communities remains unclear in the end. At the beginning of September 1951, nine months after receiving Arendt's confirmation, Henriques addressed the following inquiry to Norbert Wollheim, chairman of the Association of Jewish Communities in Northwest Germany since 1946: "I should be very much obliged, if you would let me know as soon as ever possible, whether the Communities have yet received the ceremonial objects from the American sources."[45] Unfortunately no response from Wollheim could be found in the files of the Henriques Collection.[46]

As in the above-mentioned case of objects sent from the CRREC, the objects sent from the OAD prayer books are the most likely to be identifiable today. Thus at least two prayer books can still be found in the holdings of the Gelsenkirchen Jewish community that bear a stamp of the OAD (Fig. 5).

---

45 Wiener Library London, Henriques Collection, see note 42, fol. 33.

46 It is also possible that the request no longer reached Wollheim, as he emigrated to the USA with his family in September 1951.

In the course of the withdrawal of the JRU from the British zone and the closure of the Bergen-Belsen DP camp in July 1950, the Jewish communities entered a new phase. Although they continued to receive support from Jewish aid organizations in the years that followed, they were more or less on their own. At the same time, the founding of the *Zentralrat der Juden* in Deutschland in July 1950 marked a clear signal, both internally and externally, to build a longer-term infrastructure. The foundation for this had been laid by the numerous employees of the various Jewish aid organizations, one of whom was Rose Henriques, who, shortly before her departure from Germany, drew the following conclusion:

> In the religious field great strides have been made. Every Gemeinde has some sort of a place of worship, ranging from a tiny room in an old age home, which has also to be used as a quiet room by the residents; through all degrees of "Betstube", which are usually rooms in a communal building, which have been redecorated and furnished with makeshift equipment. Then the standard rises, to a few newly built synagogues which will remain as permanent synagogues, sufficient for the decimated population.[47]

47 Wiener Library London, Henriques Collection, HA7/4-16 (Mrs. Henriques reports, 1950), fols. 5/b–6/a.

Sarah König

Between Rite and Musealization. Judaica in the Jewish Communities of Southern Germany after the Shoah, Using the Example of Augsburg and the Person of Julius Spokojny

The final victory of the Allied armies over the National Socialists and the German *Wehrmacht* in the spring of 1945 was not only greeted with joy in large parts of the Jewish world public, it also revealed the indescribable extent of the extermination and led to bewilderment among those affected and among observers. The triumph at the end of the reign of terror was accompanied by a sense of powerlessness and disorientation among those persecuted, which was to shape the identity of Jewish life in Germany for some time after 1945. The same applies to the need for self-assertion resulting from the circumstances. Nevertheless, it was precisely this phase, in the immediate aftermath of ostracism, persecution and murder, that formed the foundation for the rebuilding of a Jewish community in Germany.

Against this background, the following chapter deals with the question of the ritual objects looted and destroyed during the National Socialist era and their significance for the newly constituted communities. This will be demonstrated by the example of Augsburg, which is special in that it has combined a museum and synagogue in one building since 1985. The central figure of this very unusual constellation is the Polish-born Julius Spokojny, who first came to Augsburg as a DP in the 1950s. He relatively quickly acquired a leading role in the congregation, which had already been re-established in 1946, and he was finally elected to the board of directors in the 1960s. In this position he contributed significantly to the reconstruction of the synagogue, which had been damaged in 1938, and, in 1985, with the inauguration of the large synagogue, he founded the first Jewish Museum to be newly opened in the FRG.

In addressing the question of the non-Jewish museology of Jewishness in museums, Jens Hoppe has for the first time dealt in detail with a research desideratum that has long eked out a shadowy existence.[1] One question that has preoccupied "Jewish" museology since its early days was whether Judaica should be exhibited in decidedly and exclusively Jewish museums, or should be quasi-integrated in separate departments in already existing museums of cultural history. Interestingly, according

1 Jens Hoppe, *Jewish History and Culture in Museums. Zur nichtjüdischen Museologie des Jüdischen in Deutschland* (Münster, 2002).

https://doi.org/10.1515/9783110750812-010

to Hoppe, this was a discussion conducted exclusively in Jewish circles. This discussion very clearly reflects the fundamental question of the role of Judaism in German society and the inner-Jewish development of the time. The two poles oscillated between, on the one hand, the view that the Jewish past was an inherent part of the German past and that the Jews saw themselves as Germans and, on the other hand, a desire to increasingly include their own, Jewish aspects in the considerations.

After 1945, the question of how to exhibit Jewish culture in museums arose again. This time, however, against the background of the Shoah. Apart from the question of whether and in what framework to exhibit and to what extent the Shoah should be presented or dealt with, a new question was that of the target audience. Whereas before 1933 the respective discussions had calculated with Jewish visitors, the exhibition organizers had to adjust to a primarily non-Jewish audience.

Augsburg takes on a special role in these considerations. Not only is it the first Jewish Museum to be newly opened in the Federal Republic of Germany, it also has its very own history of relations with the local community. Both institutions are located under the same roof. In order to better understand the origins and genesis of the museum, however, a brief historical outline of the community after 1945 will first provide information about the importance of ritual objects in the community and how the later musealization is to be classified.

Returnees and survivors of the camps – both Displaced Persons from all over Europe and Jews originating from Germany – formed new Jewish communities from 1945 onwards, whereby the prospect of a permanent stay "in the land of the perpetrators" seemed unlikely for the vast majority of those involved.[2] They regarded themselves as a "liquidation community," and emigration was at the forefront of the efforts of those survivors in particular who had been deported to the camps by the Germans from all over Europe.

The heterogeneity of the Jewish communities, the various religious orientations and the different perspectives of their members gave rise to a large number of provisional synagogues, prayer halls, religious schools and other institutions of religious and cultural Jewish practice. They were set up in camps, partly in barracks, in assigned houses or also in synagogues that had not been completely destroyed in 1938; partly historical ritual objects were reused, partly new facilities were created; Torah scrolls and prayer books were procured from various sources.

Jewish relief organizations played an important role in this context, especially in Palestine and the USA. One of these organizations was the United Nations Relief

2 On this see generally Michael Brenner, *Nach dem Holocaust. Juden in Deutschland 1945–1950 (Beck'sche Reihe 1139)* (München, 1995); and Michael Brenner, and Norbert Frei, "Second Part: 1950–1967. Consolidation," in *Geschichte der Juden in Deutschland von 1945 bis zur Gegenwart*, ed. Michael Brenner (München, 2012). Angelika Königseder, and Juliane Wetzel, *Lebensmut im Wartesaal. Die jüdischen DPs (displaced persons) im Nachkriegsdeutschland* (Fischer Die Zeit des Nationalsozialismus 16835) (Frankfurt am Main, 2004).

Fig. 1: Chuppa, made by the A.J.D.C. – Joint, Eretz Israel, before May 1948 (Jewish Museum Augsburg Swabia).

and Rehabilitation Administration (UNRRA), which was founded in 1943, and in the immediate post-war period was not only responsible for providing the DPs with the necessities of life, but also saw itself as responsible for the repatriation of the DPs. The work of the American Joint Distribution Committee, or JOINT, should also be mentioned here, as well as that of Vaad Hatzala, which operated from Palestine. The latter was originally founded with the aim of getting rabbis as well as yeshiva students out of war-torn Europe during World War II. After the end of the war, the organization played a crucial role in the spiritual rehabilitation of the survivors and, like the JOINT, provided the communities with ritual objects, among other things. Thus, a chuppah made by the JOINT in Erez Yisrael can still be found in the collection of the Jewish Museum Augsburg (Fig. 1). Other hastily procured objects are unfortunately no longer preserved today, or were later replaced by more suitable and valuable ritual objects in the communities.

In order to be able to maintain the numerically small congregations despite all their cultural and religious diversity, the idea of the "unified congregation" took on a new form, although it remains to be asked to what extent the desired unification originated in the congregations themselves or was politically desired from outside. Differences existed between the members not only in linguistic terms, but also in their expectations of congregational life and worship. In worship, liturgy and music, and the synagogue rooms, compromises therefore had to be found between the religious and cultural traditions, from Orthodoxy with its different manifestations in Eastern and Central Europe, which shaped most of the DPs, to the Reform movement, which had defined the Liberal community in Augsburg until its dissolution by the National Socialists.

In Augsburg, for example, initial attempts in 1945 and 1946 to found a joint congregation of surviving Jews from Augsburg and DPs stranded in the city failed. As a result, two congregations developed which existed in parallel and used the community rooms in Halderstraße. Thus, the board of the congregation coming from Augsburg wrote to the former Rabbi Jacob:

> On the whole we get along well with [the foreign co-religionists], although we have two congregations here in Augsburg [:] 1., the Israelitische Kultusgmeinde as the legal successor recognized by the government 2. Juedische Gemeinde consisting of different nations. It has become apparent that although we are of one faith, we have different interests and views.[3]

The early 1950s were marked by the clash of German Jews with those DPs who had decided to stay in Augsburg. The leaders of the Jewish community feared for their standing in the Jewish community, but above all in their own community. Granting the "foreign co-religionists" the demanded active and passive right to vote was rejected with repeated reference to the community's statutes.

Nevertheless, there were repeated attempts to bring both parties to the table. After the earliest of these attempts in the 1940s had repeatedly failed and two communities had established themselves in parallel, the desire for a connection on the part of non-German Jews with their German co-religionists seemed to grow. The decisive framework conditions in this respect were formed by overriding socio-cultural and political processes in Germany as well as in the entire (Jewish) world. The Jews living in or immigrating to Germany developed an increasingly strong self-confidence both externally and within the Jewish communities in the Federal Republic. The Central Council of Jews in Germany, founded in 1950, gave these new developments and above all this new self-image and self-awareness a face and a voice.

In the early 1950s, Jews living in Augsburg who were not originally from German (Reich) territory also began to identify more strongly with their new homeland. Whereas until then the intention at the end of the war had been primarily to emigrate, more and more decided consciously to stay in Germany. However, this intention to stay was bound to certain conditions and caused problems as well as opportunities both in everyday and religious life. In order to be able to build up a lasting existence, many were dependent on (start-up) help. However, the primary goal of the "foreign co-religionists" was to become full members of the Jewish Community (IKG, Israelitische Kultusgemeinde). It was only with the emigration of most

3 Gernot Römer, ed. *To my congregation in the Dispersion. Rundbriefe des Augsburger Rabbiners Ernst Jacob 1941–1949* (Augsburg, 2007), 134.

Fig. 2: Senator Julius Spokojny with the new Sefer Torah at the dedication of the small Augsburg Synagogue in 1963 (Jewish Museum Augsburg Swabia).

of the DPs after the founding of the state of Israel in 1948 and easier entry conditions to the USA that the Jewish community consisting of the DPs finally disbanded and the members still remaining in Augsburg for various reasons were finally integrated into the Jewish community and recognized as full members. In June 1963, Spokojny took over the chairmanship of the IKG, which he held with a short interruption until 1996.[4]

Julius Spokojny (Fig. 2) was probably the most prominent figure on the path of rapprochement between German and non-German Augsburg Jews. In order to better understand his person and role in the IKG and in relation to his ambitions for the museum, his curriculum vitae will be briefly discussed below.[5] Spokojny was born on September 23, 1923 in Miechów near Krakow in Poland. At the age of sixteen he was deported to a labor camp, and on April 11, 1945, he was liberated in Buchenwald.[6] He volunteered for

4 Andrea Sinn,/et al., *Zukunft im Land der Täter? Jüdische Gegenwart zwischen "Wiedergutmachung und "Wirtschaftswunder" 1950–1969* (Augsburg, 2013), 17.

5 See Archive of the Jewish Museum Augsburg Swabia, personal file Julius Spokojny.

6 Julius Spokojny, "Der Wiederaufbau der jüdischen Gemeinde in Augsburg-Schwaben," in *Geschichte und Kultur der Juden in Schwaben II. Neuere Forschungen und Zeitzeugenberichte (Irseer Schriften)* (Stuttgart, 2000), 413–421, here 413.

the Red Cross and finally arrived at the DP camp in Landsberg am Lech in 1946. "Once there, it was already clear to me that we, the young people, would have to become active, take our fate into our own hands, in order to be quickly reintegrated into a free world and a normal life."[7] Spokojny also became involved in youth work in Landsberg, devoting himself to the "beautiful and meaningful task of re-education, providing orientation and a vision of a better world [...]." With his wife and first son, born in the camp in 1950, Spokojny moved to Augsburg after the dissolution of the Landsberg am Lech camp. At the annual Irsee conference of the district of Swabia on the history and culture of the Jews in Swabia, Spokojny spoke on the reconstruction of the community.[8]

> We were faced with a huge mountain of tasks. It was not only a question of reorganization, but above all of many everyday things. [...] You can imagine that first the need had to be alleviated, economic and social need of the people. But of course we also wanted to have a religious and cultural life again. [...] The Holocaust had torn families apart, one was suddenly all alone, one was lonely. The congregation was not only an aid organization. It was a place of encounter. [...] There one experienced help and comfort, there one made plans for the future together [...] The clearest sign of new hope, new beginnings were the marriages [...] Children were born as a physical expression of new courage to live and faith in the future. With their steadily increasing number, the question of a parish kindergarten was raised. [...] Then we thought of establishing a religious school. Our children should grow up in the faith of their fathers, be educated according to our tradition.[9]

One of his most urgent and important concerns was "reconciliation between Jews and Christians."[10] He became a founding member of the Society for Christian-Jewish Cooperation in Augsburg and subsequently established a close friendship with Archbishop Stimpfle of Augsburg. In the first years after its founding, the Society was to fulfill political tasks in particular, to restore the confidence of the world public in the young Federal Republic and to help reestablish diplomatic relations. Today, the Society "works for understanding between Christians and Jews, the fight against anti-Semitism and right-wing radicalism, and for peaceful coexistence between peoples and religions [...]."[11]

Already in the 1950s, shortly after his arrival in Augsburg, Spokojny had the memories and desire to rebuild the large synagogue and make it usable for worship. His efforts were rewarded on September 1, 1985, when the synagogue was rededicated in a festive atmosphere. However, the renovation and restoration of the temple hall was not enough. The peaceful coexistence of the denominations in the city, which

7 Spokojny, "Der Wiederaufbau der jüdischen Gemeinde in Augsburg-Schwaben," see note 6, 414.
8 Spokojny, "Der Wiederaufbau der jüdischen Gemeinde in Augsburg-Schwaben," see note 6, 414.
9 Spokojny, "Der Wiederaufbau der jüdischen Gemeinde in Augsburg-Schwaben," see note 6, 414 on.
10 Spokojny, "Der Wiederaufbau der jüdischen Gemeinde in Augsburg-Schwaben," see note 6, 416.
11 https://augsburg-schwaben.deutscher-koordinierungsrat.de/gcjz-augsburg-ziele. Accessed February 12, 2019.

Fig. 3: Augsburg, the interior of the Augsburg Great Synagogue, inaugurated in 1917 and restored in 1985 (Jewish Museum Augsburg Swabia).

was a lifelong concern of his, he also thought further at the same time and attached importance to the fact that especially the youth should come to the synagogue and get to know Judaism. To this end, the Jewish Cultural Museum was opened at the same time as the synagogue was rededicated. The synagogue became the main exhibit of the new museum, which "may interest the youth of all peoples in open-minded understanding of the culture and religion of the Jews."[12]

His services to Jewish life in Augsburg are certainly exceptional and call for in-depth treatment. However, the factors and components underlying his biography can also serve as an example for an entire generation of young Jews who, originally from Eastern Europe, found a new, permanent home in Germany after 1945. The religiousness, but also the cultural imprint and not least the energy that the young DPs put into building their future, contributed essentially to the fact that Jewish life was able to establish itself in the young Federal Republic. The fact that this new beginning was not easy can be seen particularly clearly in Spokojny's biography. The not only anti-Semitic, but also racist reservations against the Jews coming from Eastern Europe were not only met with from the German majority society, but sometimes also from the resident German-Jewish community. But it was not only cultural and social integration that presented difficulties. In economic aspects and monetary matters, too, the Eastern European Jews in particular did not have it easy. The concept of "reparations" increasingly became the central buzzword of the post-war period.

Spokojny was also aware that the number of congregation members would initially hardly reach that of the pre-war congregation and therefore saw in the founding of the museum an opportunity to make the building accessible not only to the congregation but also to the non-Jewish urban population. In the preface to its opening, Spokojny says the following:

> So now that [...] we can no longer fill the synagogue, this magnificent building is still to be used for services on holidays, but otherwise we have placed it as the main exhibit in a museum which is to bring the culture of the Jewish religion closer to our fellow men. The museum and synagogue are open to the entire population of Germany and abroad, and we especially hope that the youth of all nations will take an interest in the culture and religion of the Jews with an open mind.[13]

The focus Spokojny placed on teaching the religious aspects of Judaism is evident in the first permanent exhibition.

---

12 See foreword by Julius Spokojny in: *Stiftung Jüdisches Kulturmuseum Augsburg-Schwaben, 10 Jahre Wiedererrichtung der Synagoge Ausgburg. 10 Jahre Gründung des Jüdischen Kulturmuseums Augsburg-Schwaben* (Augsburg, 2001), 5.

13 Jüdisches Kulturmuseum Augsburg Schwaben, *Zeugnisse jüdischer Geschichte und Kultur* (Augsburg, 1985).

Figs. 4–5: Augsburg, view of the first permanent exhibition of the Jewish Culture Museum in 1985 (Jewish Museum Augsburg Swabia).

But what kind of objects were they and where did the exhibits on display come from? The municipality and the museum were in principle supposed to be separate institutions. However, in the person of Spokojny, there was a practically inevitable overlap. This is the reason why the museum's collection still contains objects that previously belonged to the municipality or were on permanent loan to the museum. Spokojny himself also built up a private collection over time, which he then gave to the museum on permanent loan.

Another exciting core collection of the museum consists of around twenty Torah shields (*tas*) from former Jewish rural communities of Bavarian Swabia.

Since the community in Augsburg was the only Jewish community in the immediate post-war period, it was also the point of contact for the return of Jewish objects region.

In addition, there is a collection that came to the museum under completely different circumstances. Spokojny wanted to fill his museum as quickly as possible and, therefore, in addition to the acquired ritual objects from former rural communities, he also exhibited objects that were purchased specifically for the purpose of the exhibition. These included objects from the art workshop of Shuki Freiman in Israel.

Fig. 6: Object from the Spokojny Private Collection. Hanukkah candlestick in bench form with shamash and small jug with turned handle for oil, late nineteenth century (Jewish Museum Augsburg Schwaben).

Fig. 7: Object from the Spokojny Private Collection. Pair of rimonim from the Binswangen synagogue, Augsburg 1823 (Jewish Museum Augsburg Swabia).

Fig. 8: Torah shield (tass) from the Ichenhausen Synagogue; Augsburg 1765–1767 (Jewish Museum Augsburg Swabia).

The objects, which combine traditional form with modern design, now form a core part of the collection. Numerous permanent loans also came from the Bavarian National Museum in Munich, which had already displayed a small collection of Judaica from 1881.

The founding of the museum in Augsburg was a welcome occasion for the Free State to once again permanently exhibit Jewish ceremonial objects from Bavarian collections.

The aforementioned practice of making Judaica especially for museum purposes has existed since the founding of the first Jewish museums or collections. It is therefore interesting to distinguish first of all which objects were in active ritual use at a given time and were subsequently museumized, and which objects were made purely for museum purposes. A concrete example of the former is a *parochet* that has been in the museum's collection since the 1990s.

The lower part reads: "In cherished Memory of David and Sophie Weber." Further research finally made it possible to retell the story of the *parochet*. David and Sophie Weber lived in Augsburg until their emigration in 1939. Their children had the Torah curtain made after their deaths and gave it to the congregation in Rhodesia, where the family lived after their emigration. There, according to the family, it was in active use until the synagogue closed. In 1997, the son of the family decided to bring the *parochet* to his parents' former hometown and gave it to the museum on permanent loan.

Fig. 9: Purim scroll with pull-out scroll Book of Esther from the workshop of Yehoshua Freiman, Israel ca. 1980 (Jewish Museum Augsburg Swabia).

Fig. 10: Wedding ring, on permanent loan from the Bavarian National Museum, sixteenth century (Jewish Museum Augsburg Swabia).

Fig. 11: Torah curtain donated "In Cherished Memory of David and Sophie Weber," South Africa ca. 1960 (Jewish Museum Augsburg Swabia).

The museology of the "Jewish," especially in connection with Jewish museums in post-war Germany, often also had a compensatory function for museum makers and audiences. Religious traditions and objects that had a very clear ritual meaning in the pre-war period often stood in the post-war period only as a proxy for this ritual use and the people who had given them meaning through their actions. It is precisely these religious traditions that Spokojny wanted to represent in his museum. Accordingly, the first permanent exhibition was not intended to explicitly represent the life and customs of the Augsburg and Bavarian-Swabian Jews, but rather to present the beauty and diversity of religious customs. More important to the museum's founder than the documentation of the exhibition and the historical contextualization of the exhibits was thus rather the presentation of Judaism as a time-honored and creditable religion that deserved the same respect as Christianity.

This recourse to traditional values is also very often found outside the museum context. Particularly with the influx of Jews from the former Soviet Union from the 1990s onwards, these values and traditions advanced to become a central theme, often illustrating the search for or finding of one's own new identity while taking the historical context into account. The effects of these developments can be traced to the present day. Having themselves become a "tradition," the forms established in the post-war period have experienced and continue to experience a renewed change since the influx of Jewish immigrants from the states of the former Soviet Union after 1990, which is also expressed in a diversification of the religious practices of today's communities.

Part 3: **Liturgy and Music**

Samuel Weigel

Introduction to Part 3: Community, Religious Practice and Synagogue Music in Post-War Germany

Regarding Jewish religious communities, religious practice, community and the music of the synagogue are closely interwoven. For example, in synagogue services, prayers, psalms, *piyyutim* and the reading of the Torah are recited in song. Also, some congregations involve musical instruments, depending on their interpretation of the *halacha*. Usually, the *hazzan*[1] represents the link between the liturgical practice, God, and the community, who, as the prayer leader, has the necessary musical knowledge to lead the service. Likewise, many Jewish communities have their repertoire of melodies and specific ways of reciting prayers, for example certain improvisational and ornamental frameworks (*nusachot*). Thus, the affiliation of a congregation to particular religious streams of Judaism is also reflected in synagogue music.

This introduction will provide an overview of the transformations of music, religious practice, and community in Jewish congregations of post-war Germany and highlight overarching public, internal Jewish and academic discourses, such as practices of remembrance and questions of cultural heritage: Issues that will also be explored in the following contributions from a variety of perspectives. While parts one and two of this edited volume look at the tangible manifestations of Jewish religious practice, primarily through architecture and a wide variety of objects, these cannot be seen in isolation from cultural contexts and associated practices. Therefore, this chapter is devoted to the intangible dimension of Jewish life and related Jewish practices.

Transformations of music and ritual in Germany after the Shoah

Shortly after 1945 and mainly in larger German cities, surviving Jews came together for praying, often in improvised prayer rooms, with changing cantors and rabbis. Over the decades, synagogues were renovated, or newly built and community structures consolidated: Cities, such as Frankfurt am Main developed into centers of Jewish life in Germany. Despite this new beginning, the history of Jewish communities in Germany since 1945 has been marked by various disruptions, which had a decisive

1 In Liberal contexts also referred as cantor.

https://doi.org/10.1515/9783110750812-011

influence on the composition of the communities, the rite, and denominational affiliations. In particular, several periods will be emphasized here: The immediate post-war period, the following time of consolidation, the collapse of the former USSR and the associated effects on the communities in reunified Germany.

Due to the aftermath of the Shoah and the emigration of Jewish survivors, West Ashkenazic traditions had all but disappeared from Germany, both the German Reform Judaism and the German Orthodox Judaism.[2] The post-war communities were made up mainly of Displaced Persons and survivors of the Shoah from Poland and other areas of Eastern Europe[3] who re-established the *minhag polin*,[4] especially in southern Germany.[5] With the increasing consolidation of Jewish life in Germany after the Shoah communities in larger cities were re-established as *Einheitsgemeinden nach orthodoxem Ritus* (unified communities). The *Einheitsgemeinden* held their service according to the Orthodox rite, so that Jews of all religious streams, Orthodox members in particular could attend.[6] The larger communities nowadays offer their members several prayer rooms and synagogues of various denominational affiliations. For example, the Frankfurt community maintains an Egalitarian *minyan* in addition to the Orthodox main synagogue.[7]

Besides the changing community structures, the zoning after the war also influenced further transformations regarding the communities' composition and institutionalization. In the immediate post-war period and due to newly occurring pogroms in Eastern Europe many Jews from primarily Poland and Hungary came to the US zone, favored by comparatively Liberal immigration and emigration policies. Thus,

2 Jascha Nemtsov, "Synagogenmusik im heutigen Deutschland: Alte Vorbilder, neu Tendenzen, internationaler Vergleich," in *Der eine Gott und die Vielfalt der Klänge: Sakrale Musik der drei Monotheistischen Religionen*, ed. Michael Gassmann (Stuttgart, 2013), 33–55, especially 41–43.

3 Atina Grossman, and Tamar Lewinsky, "Erster Teil: 1945–1949: Zwischenstation," in *Geschichte der Juden in Deutschland von 1945 bis zur Gegenwart*, ed. Michael Brenner (München, 2012), 67–152, especially 67.

4 Also known as Polish tradition and one of the two directions of Ashkenazic Judaism. The other *minhag* is called *minhag ashkenaz* and is related to areas of Western Europe, especially Germany.

5 Michael Brenner, and Norbert Frei, "Zweiter Teil: 1950–1967: Konsolidierung," in *Geschichte der Juden in Deutschland von 1945 bis zur Gegenwart*, ed. Michael Brenner (München, 2012), 152–287, especially 164.

6 Nemtsov, "Synagogenmusik im heutigen Deutschland," see note 2, 43–44.

7 As was found in the aforementioned associated research project, "Objects and spaces reflecting religious practice: traditions and transformations in Jewish communities in Germany after the Shoa" and within the sub-project "Music, Tradition," the researchers of the European Centre for Jewish Music (EZJM) conducted several interviews with *hazzanim* and rabbis from Berlin, Stuttgart, Frankfurt am Main, Niddatal and Cologne. Part of the results can be found in this volume's essay "Jewish Musical Heritage in Post-War Germany: Negotiating Jewish Self-Understanding through Synagogue Chant," by Sarah M. Ross. Another part will also be included in the cultural heritage platform Soundscape Synagogue. See Europäisches Zentrum für Jüdische Musik, Soundscape Synagoge, https://www.soundscape-synagoge.de/. Accessed September 20, 2021.

survivors and adherents of the pre-war German traditions mainly remained[8] in the minority in the communities of the American zone, while the majority of members cultivated the Polish tradition.[9] In northern Germany, predominantly in the British zone, the situation was entirely different. Here, Jews from Eastern European areas were mainly outnumbered.[10] The communities in the French zone were in close contact with communities in France and Switzerland. In the case of the community of Saarbrücken, many members who had previously fled to France were able to return and, with the assistance of a surviving rabbi, were able to continue the local pre-war tradition.[11]

In general, the various local traditions of the pre-war period and their liturgical music had largely disappeared from Germany after the Shoah. In consequence, synagogue music in the post-war *Einheitsgemeinden* depended strongly on the personal backgrounds of single *hazzanim*, rabbis, or community members, who led the services.[12] In some cases, there were efforts to recreate the melodies of the pre-war congregation; in others, a new local tradition was established, as I will elaborate on later. In addition to the overall transformations in local traditions, Jascha Nemtsov observes a general shift in most German communities from an Ashkenazic to a Sephardic pronunciation of prayers.[13]

From the 1960s onwards, interest in Judaism in the Federal Republic of Germany (FRG) moved more and more into the foreground, especially in a historical examination of the Shoah.[14] However, waves of anti-Semitic incidents increased in the following years.[15] Until the 1990s, the communities that had solidified after the war also had to contend with declining membership and an aging population.[16] Furthermore, the dichotomy between staying and leaving was still present in internal Jewish discourse, as expressed in the metaphor of the packed suitcases (*gepackte Koffer*) that had become popular.[17]

In the German Democratic Republic (GDR), on the other hand, only a small number of Jewish communities existed after the division of the state. The increasing state repression and dwindling membership from the 1950s onwards intensified this

8 By the terms pre-war rite/tradition, I refer to the liturgical practice of the two major streams of Judaism represented in Germany before the Shoah: the Western Ashkenazi Orthodox and the Liberal Reform tradition.

9 Brenner, and Frei, "Zweiter Teil: 1950–1967," see note 5, 164.

10 Grossman, and Lewinsky, "Erster Teil: 1945–1949," see note 3, 126–128.

11 Grossman, and Lewinsky, "Erster Teil: 1945–1949," see note 3, 174–175.

12 Nemtsov, "Synagogenmusik im heutigen Deutschland," see note 2, 50.

13 Nemtsov, "Synagogenmusik im heutigen Deutschland," see note 2, 49.

14 Brenner, and Frei, "Zweiter Teil: 1950–1967," see note 5, 264.

15 Brenner, and Frei, "Zweiter Teil: 1950–1967," see note 5, 274 on.

16 Karen Körber, "Zäsur, Wandel oder Neubeginn? Russischsprachige Juden in Deutschland zwischen Recht, Repräsentation und Realität," in *Russisch-jüdische Gegenwart in Deutschland*, ed. Karen Körber (Göttingen, 2015), 13–36, especially 29.

17 Körber, "Zäsur, Wandel oder Neubeginn?," see note 16, 13.

effect. In part, this led to fundamental difficulties in holding services, with the result that the number of members required for a minyan was temporarily lowered.[18] Additionally, support was sought from cantors from the FRG, such as Estrongo Nachama.[19] As a consequence of a general shortage of cantors, the office of chief cantor of the Jewish communities in the GDR was created in the 1960s and was held by Werner Sander. Due to the circumstances and decreasing possibilities of holding services religious practice in the communities also receded into the background. Partly, the *hazzanim* held the services according to Orthodox rite. In several cases also an organ or harmonium was added, referring to the Liberal tradition.[20] In particular, the German-Jewish Reform tradition experienced high popularity in concert form through the *Leipziger Synagogalchor* led by Werner Sander – especially among non-Jewish audiences.[21]

The fall of the Berlin Wall and the subsequent collapse of the Soviet Union led to a massive increase in the number of members in Germany's Jewish communities. Against the background of the so-called *Kontingentflüchtlingsgesetz* (Law on measures for refugees admitted in the context of humanitarian aid operations[22]), Jews from Eastern Europe were able to emigrate to the FRG. However, the overall process bore several conflicts: On the one hand, stereotypes of the refugees were established in public discourse; on the other hand, their integration also led to tensions in the communities.

In the Soviet Union, living Judaism in a *halachic* sense was made difficult in many ways. For example, in the context of issuing identity cards in the Soviet Union, being Jewish was considered by the authorities to be a purely ethnic-national construct. Resulting from this, many Jews from the affected parts of Eastern Europe brought a secular understanding of Judaism to Germany. Thus, in the 1990s, there was a clash between two different understandings of Jewishness, which continue to cause conflict in German communities today: On the one hand, post-war German Jews with a religious understanding of Judaism and, on the other, Soviet Jews who had had little contact with religious practice.[23]

---

18 Melanie Eulitz, "Die jüdisch-Liberale Bewegung in Deutschland nach 1990," in *Russisch-jüdische Gegenwart in Deutschland*, ed. Karen Körber (Göttingen, 2015), 37–59, especially 42.

19 Esther Slevogt, *Die Synagoge Pestalozzistrasse: 'Deinem Hause gebühret Heiligkeit, Ewiger, für alle Zeiten,'* Jüdische Miniaturen 127 (Berlin, 2012), 105–106.

20 Eulitz, "Die jüdisch-Liberale Bewegung in Deutschland nach 1990," see note 18, 42–43.

21 Tina Frühauf, *Werner Sander: 'Den Frieden endgültig zu festigen': Ein großer Vertreter der jüdischen Musik in der DDR,* Jüdische Miniaturen 213 (Berlin, 2017), 76–77.

22 Bundesgesetzblatt, "Gesetz über Maßnahmen für im Rahmen humanitärer Hilfsaktionen aufgenommene Flüchtlinge vom 22. Juli 1980," *Bundesgesetzblatt* 1.41 (1980): 1057–1058, http://www.bgbl.de/xaver/bgbl/start.xav?startbk=Bundesanzeiger_BGBl&jumpTo=bgbl180s1057.pdf. Accessed September 20, 2021.

23 Yfaat Weiss, and Lena Gorelik, "Die russisch-jüdische Zuwanderung," in *Geschichte der Juden in Deutschland von 1945 bis zur Gegenwart*, ed. Michael Brenner (München, 2012), 295–375, especially 386–388.

As a result of the 1990s, the German congregations had to meet the demands of their new members. Consequently, social support services were created, but the language barriers between members, in particular, posed a problem.[24] In addition, the increase in membership had another significant effect, from which Liberal Judaism in Germany notably benefited. The rising membership numbers enabled congregants interested in Liberal Judaism to seperate themselves from the *Einheitsgemeinden*. Consequently, many new Jewish congregations were founded, especially in the 1990s, which maintain a Liberal rite.[25] Despite the increase in membership in the 1990s, many communities struggle nowadays with declining numbers due to progressive aging.[26]

Especially in the first decades after the end of the war, many Jewish communities had no permanent cantors. For a long time, training centers did not exist in Germany, so the congregations depended on support from abroad.[27] The cantors of the post-war period oscillated between emigration countries and Germany and were regularly engaged for the High Holidays. However, a specific cantorate, as Tina Frühauf notes in her monograph *Transcending Dystopia: Music, Mobility and the Jewish Community in Germany, 1945–1989*, did not emerge in post-war Germany. As she sums up, the cantors' influence on the communities is of high importance. Thus, along with the cantors, musical repertoire, aesthetics, and liturgical practice moved from congregation to congregation, which also played an essential role in consolidating a denominational identity.[28]

In the course of the research related to this volume, two poles have emerged that are of particular relevance for the orientation of religious practice in post-war Germany up to the present day: The recommencement and the revitalization of pre-war traditions. Two Jewish communities researched as part of the project, in which context his publication was published, show how different the engagement with the pre-war tradition can be.

In keeping with the spirit of revitalization, the Pestalozzistrasse Synagogue of Berlin‘s Jewish Community offers its members services in the German-Jewish Reform tradition. Thus, the repertoire consists almost entirely of liturgical compositions by Louis Lewandowski, which is recited with the support of a mixed synagogue choir and organ accompaniment. This form of service not only refers to the Liberal practice of pre-war services there but it also references another local historical legacy: Louis Lewandowski, one of the most influential composers of the German-Jewish Reform

---

24 Körber, "Zäsur, Wandel oder Neubeginn?," see note 16, 29.

25 Eulitz, "Die jüdisch-Liberale Bewegung in Deutschland nach 1990," see note 20, 51.

26 Karen Körber, "Einleitung," in Karen Körber, ed., *Russisch-jüdische Gegenwart in Deutschland* (Göttingen, 2015), 7–12, especially 8.

27 Tina Frühauf, *Transcending Dystopia: Music, Mobility, and the Jewish Community in Germany, 1945–1989* (New York, 2021), 146–147.

28 Frühauf, *Transcending Dystopia*, see note 27, 154.

tradition. The Frankfurt am Main community in the Westend Synagogue shows a different perspective: One that involves a break with the pre-war tradition, entirely in the sense of a new beginning. After the war, the synagogue services in the Westend were adapted to suit the Polish majority, meaning a break with the German-Jewish Reform tradition from the pre-war period. The current cantor of the congregation continues the tradition established after the war but also implements melodies from the North American Modern Orthodox tradition to meet the changing needs of the congregation members.[29]

Interviews with cantors from other Jewish congregations have shown the different ways of dealing with the past. These depend on a wide variety of factors, such as overarching socio-political developments and interests, demographic and structural changes within the community, and the personal interests of the cantors, rabbis, or the community council.

Intangible dimensions of Jewish life after the Shoah in Germany

Within academic contexts, the immaterial dimensions of Jewish life after the Shoah are researched and discussed in different ways. While the other two parts of this volume focus on the history and material heritage of German Jews after the Shoah, this part also refers to two overarching discourses regarding Jewish cultural practices in Germany. One of the two discourses I will shortly elaborate on is the *Erinnerungskultur* (remembrance culture) regarding the Shoah and post-war Judaism in Germany. Additionally, this introduction will look at the connected concept of (Jewish) cultural heritage, which also plays a significant role in identity formation and representation of Jewish life in Germany.

The term *Erinnerungskultur* has various meanings[30] and is used by the Aleida Assmann to refer to practices of remembrance that are characterized by a "Pluralisierung und Intensivierung der Zugänge zur Vergangenheit"[31] (pluralization and intensification of access to the past). These can have an identity-forming effect and fulfill ethical functions, such as coping with (state) violent crimes.[32] With the historical examination of the Shoah, specific remembrance practices have emerged in Germany and Europe, which are supported and mobilized primarily by memorial sites and events, Jewish museums, and political discourses. Regarding the atrocities of the

29 Personal interview with I.A. in Berlin, June 2021; with Y.R. in Frankfurt am Main, June 2021.

30 Aleida Assmann, *Das neue Unbehagen an der Erinnerungskultur: Eine Intervention*, 3rd edition (München, 2020 [2013]), 30.

31 Assmann, *Das neue Unbehagen an der Erinnerungskultur*, see note 30, 32.

32 Assmann, *Das neue Unbehagen an der Erinnerungskultur*, see note 30, 32.

Shoah, that way of remembering Judaism in Germany before 1945 represents an important step in historical examination and the prevention of antisemitism. Yet, in academic discourse, some positions see problems in representing the Jewish present in the German memorial landscape. At the center of these criticisms is the observation that Jewish life in Germany is predominantly researched and represented by non-Jewish actors, as Ruth Ellen Gruber and Y. Michal Bodemann are stating.[33] Following this critique, the absence of Jewish actors involved in public acts of remembrance leads to a portrayal of Jewish culture fed by the museum and the creation of an imagined or "virtual" Judaism,[34] as Gruber depicts it. Furthermore, as Bodemann describes concerning the Shoah, the *Erinnerungskultur* also serves political functions, such as a guarantor of democracy in the FDR[35] or in constructing a specific image of Judaism in Germany, an image with which the majority of the German public can identify but disregards Judaism's present heterogeneity.[36] Based on the memorial site at Flossenbürg, Timo Saalmann's contribution in this volume looks at recent changes in the practice of remembrance that involve Jewish survivors to a greater extent.

The term cultural heritage is often used in political discourses in the context of safeguarding the tangible dimension of heritage, particularly monuments and artifacts.[37] For a few decades, UNESCO[38] and several cultural heritage initiatives have emphasized safeguarding intangible cultural heritage. However, in the context of Jewish cultural heritage in Germany, there is also a tendency to refer mainly to tangible manifestations, while the engagement with intangible Jewish heritage through cultural heritage initiatives is mostly neglected.[39] Sarah M. Ross, against the background of various definitions of Jewish cultural heritage, distinguishes primarily between two

---

33 Ruth Ellen Gruber, *Virtually Jewish: Reinventing Jewish Culture in Europe* (Berkeley/Los Angeles/London, 2002), 10–11.

34 Gruber, *Virtually Jewish*, see note 33, 21.

35 Y. Michal Bodemann, "The State in the Construction of Ethnicity and Ideological Labor: The Case of German Jewry," *Critical Sociology* 17.3 (1990): 35–46, especially 41.

36 Y. Michal Bodemann, "Reconstructions of History: From Jewish Memory to Nationalized Commemoration of Kristallnacht in Germany," in *Jews, Germans, Memory. Reconstructions of Jewish Life in Germany*, ed. Y. Michal Bodemann (Ann Arbor, 1996), 179–226, especially 209.

37 Janet Blake, "UNESCO's 2003 Convention on Intangible Cultural Heritage: The implications of community involvement in 'safeguarding'," in *Intangible Heritage: Key Issues in Cultural Heritage*, ed. Laura Jane Smith, and Natsuko Akagawa (Oxford and New York, 2009), 45–73, especially 46.

38 UNESCO, *Basic Text of the 2003 Convention for the Safeguarding of the Intangible Cultural Heritage 2020 Edition* (Paris, 2020), 5, https://ich.unesco.org/doc/src/2003_Convention_Basic_Texts-_2020_version-EN.pdf. Accessed September 20, 2021.

39 Regina Randhofer, "Wiedergeburt, nicht Erbe. Überlegungen zum jüdischen Kulturerbe am Beispiel der Lieder der Sefarden," in *Jüdisches Kulturerbe MUSIK – Divergenzen und Zeitlichkeit: Überlegungen zu einer kulturellen Nachhaltigkeit aus Sicht der Jüdischen Musikstudien*, ed. Sarah M. Ross (Berlin/Bern/Brussels/New York/Oxford/Warsaw/Vienna, 2021), 73–87, especially 75–76.

terms: *Jüdisches Kulturerbe* (Jewish cultural heritage)[40] and Jewish heritage. *Jüdisches Kulturerbe* describes the past-oriented practice of researching and presenting Judaism, which non-Jewish actors in Germany primarily cultivate. In contrast, the term Jewish heritage, especially in English-speaking parts of the world, refers to the totality of expressions of Jewish life, including aspects such as ritual or music.[41] In this sense, she argues for a concept of cultural heritage and cultural sustainability that focuses more on the future and considers the processes of transmitting and preserving Jewish life in the present.[42]

Thus, the individual contributions of this part of the publication tangent in different ways to the discourses mentioned above on remembrance culture and cultural heritage. The spectrum ranges from changes in remembrance practice at a memorial site (Saalman) to the continuation of the cultural heritage of the German-Jewish Reform tradition using the example of synagogue organs (Frühauf) to identity-finding processes in Jewish communities, especially concerning cultural heritage and local *nusachot* (Ross).

The contributions

The following contributions are devoted to transformations in liturgical(-musical) practice from different perspectives. From the history of synagogue organs in post-war Germany, these range thematically through changes in ritual and linked identity-finding processes to the significance of the Kaddish recitation in a memorial site.

Especially in the German-Jewish Reform tradition, the Shoah caused a massive rupture. In her contribution "A Relic of the Past? The Organ and the Jewish Communities in Post-War Germany," **Tina Frühauf** precisely investigates this rupture in the history of Jewish communities in Germany by examining the changing role of synagogue organs. Within the framework of her research, she refers specifically to the history of the organ in Frankfurt's Westend Synagogue and looks at other communities based on interviews, archival material, and various iconographic representations. Furthermore, she shows what role organs played in the service as a vehicle for acculturation efforts, from pre-war Germany until the late 1990s. Finally, she notes that due to various factors, including changes in ritual, they now only lead to a shadowy existence in Jewish communities – both in the FRG and the GDR. Thus, starting from the tangible

40 Sarah M. Ross, "'Jüdisches Kulturerbe' vis-á-vis 'Jewish heritage:' Einleitende Überlegungen zur Idee einer kulturellen Nachhaltigkeit in den jüdischen Musikstudien," in *Jüdisches Kulturerbe MUSIK – Divergenzen und Zeitlichkeit: Überlegungen zu einer kulturellen Nachhaltigkeit aus Sicht der Jüdischen Musikstudien*, ed. Sarah M. Ross (Berlin/Bern/Brussels/New York/Oxford/Warsaw/Vienna, 2021), 1–39, especially 22.

41 Ross, 'Jüdisches Kulturerbe' vis-á-vis 'Jewish heritage,' see note 40, 22.

42 Ross, 'Jüdisches Kulturerbe' vis-á-vis 'Jewish heritage,' see note 40, 35–36.

representatives of the German-Jewish Reform tradition, Frühauf's contribution provides an insight into the transformations of the music of the synagogue from 1945 to 1989 in divided post-war Germany.

The following two essays also deal with Jewish cultural heritage and remembrance culture, albeit from different perspectives. First, **Sarah M. Ross'** article "Jewish Musical Heritage in Post-War Germany: Negotiating Jewish Self-Understanding through Synagogue Chant" sheds light on the complex negotiation processes of belonging within Jewish communities and how these are reflected at the level of liturgy and synagogue music. Her research bridges the gap between liturgical-musical practice and the broader discourses around Jewish intangible cultural heritage in Germany, which influence the search for Jewish identities in complex ways.

Timo Saalmann devotes his essay "Kaddish in Flossenbürg. On the Genesis of the Memorials to Jewish Victims of the Concentration Camp" to how the memorial site of the former concentration camp Flossenbürg in Bavaria deals with remembering the victims of the Shoah. Starting with the construction of the Jewish Memorial Stones in 1949/50 and 1985, he looks at the history of the Flossenbürg Memorial and its relationship to linked cultures of remembrance. Then, beginning with a restructuring of the memorial in 1995, Saalmann describes certain transformations in remembering the past: away from a Christian-influenced culture of remembrance that commemorates nationally defined groups of victims, towards that of a prayer and memorial site for former Jewish prisoners from Flossenbürg. In this respect, Saalmann emphasizes the changing role of the Kaddish prayer in commemorative events at Flossenbürg.

Tina Frühauf

A Relic of the Past? The Organ and the Jewish Communities in Post-War Germany

With the pogroms of November 1938, the vast majority of the 200 organs and harmoniums that had become an integral part of synagogue architecture, and of musical and liturgical practice in Central Europe were destroyed. Some had been "sold" to churches; smaller instruments, such as harmoniums, were buried for safekeeping in the soil of graveyards, only to be unearthed after liberation in May 1945. With these junctures, the use of the organ in synagogue services during the post-war era was largely sealed. Embraced as instrument and object by few communities and often in idiosyncratic ways, the organ now had a comparatively minor presence in worship. Only a few congregations in occupied, East and West Germany, used organs or harmoniums, driven by the wish to continue pre-war practices or due to unique happenstance.

Being a nearly immovable artifact and a constituent of Jewish culture in later modernity, in the post-war era the organ came to embody the near absence of Liberal Judaism on German soil. Indeed, the organ quarrels that had stirred up Jewish communities in the nineteenth and early twentieth centuries in a fundamental conflict about acculturation versus Jewish autonomy no longer had relevance for the post-war communities, many of which followed the *minhag Polin*. As one of the least fixed elements of Jewish musical practice, the organ still left its mark in the post-war Germanys and in different ways: absence, silent presence, and adapted or modified presence. This essay discusses this three-fold representation of the organ, focusing on the period between 1945 and 1989 and drawing on representative case studies that rely on the interpretation of archival documents and other sources, interviews, and iconographic analysis.

In July 1945, two months after the official surrender of the German armed forces on May 7, and the end of the Holocaust, some two hundred people gathered for a memorial service in the British sector of Berlin in the cleared ruins of the Pestalozzistraße Synagogue. It was one of the few synagogues that had outlived the November pogroms of 1938 and the bomb raids of World War II. In a letter, the Jewish Lithuanian-born GI Kieve Skidell described this service to his wife, saying it was "impressive in the extreme," "everyone wept" and "one of the men switched back on the Eternal Light." The ceremony was a conscious reassertion of German-Jewish identity: It began with the *Sheheḥiyanu*, a blessing that has been recited by Jews for nearly 2,000 years to celebrate special occasions and to give thanks for unusual experiences. According to Skidell, there was either an organ or harmonium accompaniment throughout the service, and the musical repertoire with compositions by Louis Lewandowski and Georg Friedrich Händel, leaning on Liberal customs, showed an "unmistakable attempt to return

https://doi.org/10.1515/9783110750812-012

to the olden days." This is doubly remarkable as before 1945 the Pestalozzistraße Synagogue, then following conservative customs, had not installed an organ.[1]

During the war years, preacher Martin Riesenburger together with assistants had saved a great number of *Kultus* items in Berlin, among them two valuable organ-harmoniums, hiding them at the Weißensee cemetery. Although the Nazis damaged 4,000 graves and destroyed the mourning hall, the cemetery provided a safe space for Jews to hide. The buried objects miraculously survived and after the war they were immediately retrieved, transported via horse carriage to Rykestraße Synagogue in the Prenzlauerberg neighborhood, and from there, redistributed. A similar story about buried objects and the role organ-harmoniums played therein could be told for Munich and perhaps similar is true for other communities even if not documented. As such these episodes are a testimony of the planned survival of a practice that had lasted just a mere one hundred years – that of the organ and organ music in the synagogue. In the post-war era, this practice, however, would experience transformation. This essay explores this transformation, not so much as a process than as a product. It focuses on the period between 1945 and 1989, when Germany was first occupied and then divided along East–West lines. It does so by drawing on representative case studies, the Westend Synagogue in Frankfurt am Main being at the forefront.

After the Second Rabbinical Conference of 1845, the Great Synagogue installed three sizable organs in succession beginning in 1859; Philantropin and the Westend Synagogue followed suit. Nothing remained of them after the war. The Westend Synagogue at Freiherr-vom-Stein-Straße was the only synagogue that survived Kristallnacht and the bombings of World War II, but its sizable three-manual Walcker organ did not. Facilitating provisional repairs of the space, the military government insured the synagogue's reinstatement in time for the High Holidays of 1945. And indeed, the day before Rosh Hashanah, Westend Synagogue was re-inaugurated during a festive service. The service made the front-page of the *Frankfurter Rundschau*, which highlighted the importance of this moving hour. There was a sense of hope in the statement that "the space as yet was without the organ, the old seating."[2] The article specifically referred to the absence of the emblem of Reform and alluded to the possibility of its reinstatement in the future. A leaflet about the synagogue notes that nothing had remained of the original instrument and that the first services after the war were "still without organ."[3] It thus suggests the loss of pre-war musical practices, while anticipating their revitalization.

---

1 See Tina Frühauf, *The Organ and Its Music in German-Jewish Culture* (New York, 2012). The fact that Skidell mentions an organ reveals his lack of detailed knowledge of keyboard instruments; either a transportable harmonium or an organ-harmonium (a reed organ of large capacity and power) was used during the service.

2 rk, "Wiederweihe des ersten jüdischen Gotteshauses in Frankfurt a. M.," *Frankfurter Rundschau* (September 12, 1945).

3 See Zentralarchiv zur Erforschung der Geschichte der Juden in Deutschland, Heidelberg, B. 1/13 (Frankfurt), (Westend Synagoge: Einweihung), 05.03 Synagoge 140 (K).

Five years later, on September 6, 1950, Frankfurt publicly celebrated the reinauguration of the Westend Synagogue after its complete renovation. It was an important affair for post-war West Germany, attended by about one thousand people, among them prominent American officers and German politicians.[4] The musical program, reminiscent of Liberal pre-war services with choir and organ, was certainly in accord with the political message the reconstruction of the space to its original specifications had wanted to convey. At the time, the Westend Synagogue was the largest and most prominent Jewish sanctuary in West Germany and home to the second largest community (after Munich). It remained the only synagogue fully reconstructed in the course of *Wiedergutmachung*. The Hessian government had not only sponsored the renovation, it also financed the new organ, which E.F. Walcker & Cie., Ludwigsburg, built as its opus 2967. With three manuals and 36 stops, it was only slightly smaller than the Walcker instrument built for the synagogue in 1910 and destroyed during Kristallnacht, but did not seek to replicate the disposition of the previous instrument.

The installation of the organ was deemed important enough to be mentioned in the mainstream press. The *Frankfurter Presse* opened its coverage of the ceremony with the line: "To the celebratory sounds of the organ, on Wednesday, twelve years after its destruction through the National Socialists, the newly erected Frankfurt Westend Synagogue was inaugurated."[5] During the ceremony, however, the organ never performed a solo part as it had done when Siegfried Würzburger (1877–1942) served as organist during pre-war times.[6] For the inauguration, an organist visiting from France merely accompanied the choral works of Louis Lewandowski and Samuel Naumbourg sung by the Oratorio de Paris as well as the closing "Hatikvah," all under the baton of Max Moses Neumann (1894–1960).[7]

Following the Westend Synagogue and supported by government funds, many Jewish communities were able to renovate or build new synagogues beginning in the 1950s, a development that peaked around 1960. Indeed, in West Germany, the consecration of new synagogues became a fundamental endeavor. The organ, however, once a

---

4 The inauguration festivities received worldwide attention; see, for example, "News from Germany," *AJR Information* 5.10 (1950): 7. For a detailed report, see "Einweihung der Westend-Synagoge in Frankfurt a.M.," *Allgemeine Wochenzeitung der Juden in Deutschland* 5.23 (September 15, 1950): 5.

5 "Unter feierlichen Orgelklängen wurde am Mittwoch, zwölf Jahre nach ihrer Zerstörung durch die Nationalsozialisten, die neuerbaute Frankfurter Westend-Synagoge eingeweiht," *Frankfurter Presse* (September 7, 1950).

6 For the program, see Zentralarchiv zur Erforschung der Geschichte der Juden in Deutschland, Heidelberg, B. 1/13, Serie A (Frankfurt) (Vorbeter), A.140.

7 The programs variously misidentified the ensemble as synagogue choir of the Consistoire de Paris and Paris synagogue choir; see "Frankfurt Synagogue Dedicated," *Information Bulletin: Monthly Magazine of the Office of US High Commissioner for Germany* (November 1950), n.p. As with the choir, divergent names circulated for the organist, perhaps due to last minute changes. Instead of Henriette Roger, organist at the Grand Synagogue Rue de la Victoire, Maria-Louise Girod of the Radio National Paris may have performed on the occasion.

visual and aural symbol of Reform and acculturation could rarely be found in the new sacred spaces and was even removed from existing ones. Westend Synagogue in Frankfurt was one of the few to have an instrument (it also had a harmonium).[8] But the instrument was only built due to government efforts, not because the community pressed for it. From the outset, it was rarely heard, as the main sanctuary of the synagogue was only used on the High Holidays.[9] Though initially there must have been expectations that the organ would be played during services, as the Walcker firm received a contract to maintain the instrument in the years 1951 and 1952.[10] By 1954, the organ was only sporadically used, attesting to the congregation's shift toward Orthodoxy.[11] Not only was it not heard, but it had no visible presence. Unlike its pre-war predecessor, whose façade had been placed above the ark, the new organ at Westend was in the rear of the synagogue and barely noticeable (Fig. 1). In this way it became a physical symbol: its relative silence and lesser visibility made it a monument rather than an instrument. As a museum piece it memorialized nineteenth-century native Jewry.

Fig. 1: Frankfurt am Main, western view of the Westend Synagogue, with Walcker organ opus 2967 in the back (Photograph: Dontworry, 2010, Wikipedia, CC BY-SA 3.0).

8 For the harmonium's use, see "Chanukka-Feier im Altersheim," *Allgemeine Wochenzeitung der Juden in Deutschland* 5.36 December 15, 1950 11.

9 From 1959 on, the main sanctuary was used also on the Sabbath. Eastern European Jews held their own services in the Trausaal; see Helga Krohn, *Es war richtig, wieder anzufangen: Juden in Frankfurt am Main seit 1945* (Frankfurt am Main, 2011), 114.

10 See Zentralarchiv zur Erforschung der Geschichte der Juden in Deutschland, Heidelberg, B. 1/13 (Frankfurt) (Westend Synagoge: Einweihung), 05.03 Synagoge 140 (K).

11 See Zentralarchiv zur Erforschung der Geschichte der Juden in Deutschland, Heidelberg, B. 1/13, Serie A (Frankfurt), A.804, (Korrespondenz Max Meyer mit Kantoren [Anstellung]), 14. The organ's use is last documented on Hanukkah 1961, during a service on December 7, with Frankfurt's cantor Avigdor Zuker, Aladar Fuchs, and organist Herbert Manfred Hoffmann, see *Allgemeine Wochenzeitung der Juden in Deutschland* 16.36 (December 1, 1961): 9. For a program, see *Allgemeine Wochenzeitung der Juden in Deutschland* 16.39 (December 22, 1961): 11.

Salomon Korn (*1943), a descendent of Displaced Persons who became an architect and served the Jewish community in Frankfurt as chairman, had his own thoughts on the silent organ. He confirmed that congregants saw it as a non-Jewish instrument tied to Christianity, thereby ignoring its over 100-year long presence in synagogues.[12] According to Korn, during the quarrels surrounding the "positive definition and demarcation of Judaism" between Liberal Jews and those tightly adhering to Jewish law, the *halacha*, the organ had become a symbol that ignited the underlying issue of identity – as if the continuity of native Jews hinged on organ pipes.[13] But ultimately its presence or absence had neither contributed to the dissolution nor revitalization of Judaism. The organ had merely accompanied Jewish life. For Korn it had become a relic of the past, whose "sphinx-like deafening silence" is testimony to what it once was, stood for, and still represents.

The organ quarrels that had stirred up Jewish communities in the nineteenth and early twentieth centuries in a fundamental conflict about acculturation versus Jewish autonomy no longer had relevance for the post-war communities, many of which followed the *minhag Polin* practiced by the majority of its membership. Naturally, there were exceptions, such as in Düsseldorf, which planned to install an organ. For the inauguration of the new synagogue on September 7, 1958, the community used a cost-efficient harmonium which, played by Hertha Berthold-Plaat, "contributed to the festive ambiance."[14] After the inauguration, a briefing took place on October 23, 1958. Point 6 of the agenda, "Miscellaneous," reads that the instrument was up for discussion, though no further details are recorded.[15] One and a half years later, in February 1960, Julius Dreifuß, at the time president of the Landesverband der Jüdischen Gemeinden von North Rhine-Westphalia, privately wrote to the board, arguing against instrumental accompaniment. He stemmed from a Liberal family and did not argue on halachic grounds (although they indirectly played a role). Rather, he shared his fear that the Eastern European Jews who quite regularly attended services would stay away or even break with the community if an organ would play an integral part in worship.[16] Although nothing further is reported, it seems that the instrument was removed sometime after the commemoration of the November pogroms that year out of respect for the Orthodox minority. While the community continued with the repertoire conceived by Louis Lewandowski for

---

12 See Salomon Korn, "Die schweigende Orgel in der Westendsynagoge," *Frankfurter Jüdische Nachrichten* 59 (September 1983): 3–4.

13 Korn, "Die schweigende Orgel in der Westendsynagoge," see note 12, 4.

14 See "Triumph des Geistes über den Ungeist," *Allgemeine Wochenzeitung der Juden in Deutschland* 13.24 (September 12, 1958): 6.

15 See Zentralarchiv zur Erforschung der Geschichte der Juden in Deutschland, Heidelberg, B. 1/5 (Düsseldorf), (3.3 Kultus, Kultur, Gedenken: Kantor Grabowski, Gottesdienst), 213 (K).

16 See Donate Strathmann, *Auswandern oder Hierbleiben? Jüdisches Leben in Düsseldorf und Nordrhein 1945–1960* (Essen, 2003), 171.

Liberal services, it did so without instrumental accompaniment to ensure unity of its diverse congregants.

Already in the early twentieth century, Düsseldorf, unlike many other communities, had admitted and to some extent integrated Eastern European Jewish immigrants.[17] Liberal Jews had constituted the majority, while the Orthodox (both natives and from abroad) celebrated separately without choir and organ in line with their customs.[18] The small size of the community after 1945 (by July 1960 it counted just over 900 registered members)[19] did not allow for separate services, and the harmonium had to vanish for the sake of an integrative post-war community – a true *Einheitsgemeinde* as it were. After all, it was possible for Liberal Jews to do without organ than for Orthodox Jews to accept its use during Sabbath and holidays.

Another unique case with regard to the organ (and otherwise) was the Jewish community of Saarbrücken. Its musical practices were in line with its distinctive path, which mirrored the political situation of the Saarland in the post-war period. Initially under French occupation and administration, the Saar region did not immediately become one of the federal states. France even considered establishing an independent Saarland. Between 1947 and 1956 the region was known as the Saar Protectorate and only joined West Germany in January 1957. The Jewish community thus reconstituted itself in a city that belonged to a quasi-autonomous state after the French military relinquished control. Fifty-one remigrants, for the most part, congregated on June 2, 1946, to establish the so-called Synagogengemeinde Saar, an undertaking that was officially sealed on August 1, 1946, by the chief administrator of the Saar region, Hans Neureuter.[20] After using provisional prayer rooms, foundations for a new synagogue were being laid at Beethovenplatz in 1948 and with good foresight, for by the end of the year membership had risen to four hundred, mostly remigrants and a few Displaced Persons. By the end of that year, Walter Kasel assumed the position of cantor and teacher of the growing community.

With a cantor and plans for a new synagogue in place, the community hired Edmond Alexandre Roethinger to build an organ. The choice of this Strasbourg-based firm was historical given that it had already built a 23-stop instrument for the synagogue of Metz in 1895, and in 1925 an instrument with 62 stops for the Synagogue de la Paix in Strasbourg. As the community board and council supported a

17 See Strathmann, *Auswandern oder Hierbleiben?*, see note 16, 30.

18 See Strathmann, *Auswandern oder Hierbleiben?*, see note 16, 31.

19 For detailed statistics on Düsseldorf's community, see Strathmann, *Auswandern oder Hierbleiben?*, see note 16, 36.

20 See Anne Gemeinhardt, "Der Saarländische Sonderweg: Die Synagogengemeinde Saar 1947–1955," *Münchner Beiträge zur jüdischen Geschichte und Kultur* 4.1 (2010): 26–41. On music in the Jewish community of Saarbrücken before 1933, see Ricarda Wackers, "Verstummte Lieder: Musik in der jüdischen Gemeinde vor dem Holocaust," in *Musik in Saarbrücken: Nachklänge einer wechselvollen Geschichte*, ed. Nike Keisinger and Ricarda Wackers (Saarbrücken, 2000), 127–146.

Fig. 2: Saarbrücken, synagogue interior with view on the Roethinger organ (Photograph: Ulrich Knufinke, Bet Tfila – Research Unit Braunschweig, 2007).

synagogue architecture that followed Liberal aesthetics (with the bimah in the front), the new organ was visibly placed with façade pipes left and right of the ark (Fig. 2); the pre-war harmonium remained in the choir loft.[21] The instrument was small with 19 stops on two manuals. It was built in the Alsatian style, following French tonal design, but with fewer reeds. It employed an electric cone valve chest and a number of aids to provide flexibility in registration, such as manual and pedal couplers, two free combinations, fixed combinations labeled Plein Jeu, Reed Voices, Mixtures, a general crescendo pedal, and swell shutter pedal for expression – a vast improvement over the pre-war harmonium owned by the community. No quarrels regarding the instrument's installation are known.[22]

The organ was first heard during the consecration ceremony of the new synagogue on January 14, 1951. Organist Joachim Krause, in addition to playing solo pieces, accompanied the visiting chief cantor Joseph Borin (1893–1970) of Strasbourg's Synagogue de la Paix, La Chorale "Le Chant Sacré," its resident all-male choir under Robert Kahn, and local mezzosoprano Felicie Ermann.[23] Although the Synagogengemeinde

21 See Wackers, "Verstummte Lieder," see note 20, 140.

22 Marcel Wainstock, e-mail message to the author, August 19, 2014.

23 See "Neues Symbol der alten Liebe: Saarbrücken hat ein neues Gotteshaus," *Allgemeine Wochenzeitung der Juden in Deutschland* 5.41 (January 1, 1951): 5; on the one-year anniversary

Saar was not the first community in West Germany to install an organ, it was the first and initially the only one to use it on a regular basis. As with most communities in the FRG, from the outset the Synagogengemeinde Saar understood itself as *Einheitsgemeinde*, a configuration specifically found in Germany where, driven by laws issued in 1813 and 1847, a locality's various religious denominations would incorporate under one umbrella community. This model continued after 1945; however, in contrast to pre-war times, the post-war *Einheitsgemeinden* did not always have to unite different strands of Judaism. Instead, they largely modeled themselves on Eastern European customs and generally identified as Orthodox having congregants from across the spectrum. However, this was not the case with the Synagogengemeinde Saar, which embraced selected Liberal customs without overtly defining itself as Liberal. In this vein, the organ accompanied all parts of the service sung by both cantor and congregation, on Sabbath and holidays. Later, however, one native Jew in particular together with several Eastern European Jews opposed use of the organ, forcing the community to seek a compromise. Pursuing an idiosyncratic route, the community continued to offer services with organ accompaniment, except on Yom Kippur, when the instrument remained silent (with the exception of accompanying the *Kol nidrei*), all in an attempt to find common ground with those who followed a stricter observance of Jewish law.

The use of the organ in Saarbrücken's synagogue reflects the community's flexibility, which perhaps was reinforced by its political and geographic setting; it did not quite belong to what Rabbi Schlomo Rülf himself called the "actual Germany."[24] A community predominantly of remigrants, rather than former Displaced Persons or migrants from the East, it sought a flexible middle ground in-between Liberal orientation and conservative observance. This is also evident in the repertoire used during service, with compositions by Lewandowski and Sulzer representing Liberal and conservative customs. Performances of prayer songs by Naumbourg attest to the cultural proximity to France. Each cantor, however, also introduced new melodies. Benyamin Z. Barslai (1923–2003), who served as cantor and teacher from 1965 to 1969, brought with him an Eastern European melody for *Unetaneh toḳef* and *Hayom te'amzenu* on Yom Kippur, and his successor Chaim Lipschitz (1923–2003) introduced tunes he had learned in Israel.[25]

---

celebration, see *Allgemeine Wochenzeitung der Juden in Deutschland* 6.41 (January 18, 1952): 11. Until 1935, the Saarbrücken community had a Jewish organist and choir director, who played a central role in developing the synagogue's musical program; see Wackers, "Verstummte Lieder," see note 20, 141. Joachim Krause was not Jewish. In order to offer festive music in the pre-war fashion, the community invited Borin and La Chorale "Le Chant Sacré" to sing on special occasions; see Schlomo Rülf, *Ströme im dürren Land: Erinnerungen* (Stuttgart, 1964), 245.

24 "Lange hatte ich gezögert, ins eigentliche Deutschland zu fahren," Rülf, *Ströme im dürren Land*, see note 23, 259.

25 Marcel Wainstock, e-mail message to the author, August 19, 2014.

The community's dealings with the organ would remain largely unchanged until 1988. A pivotal point arrived with the hiring of Ariel Rothschild, who succeeded Lipschitz in 1987. Born into an Orthodox family from Alsace (though his father was born in Frankfurt am Main), he initially embodied Saarbrücken's middle ground. When his father died in 1988, he asked to serve without organ accompaniment for the duration of the year-long mourning period. The community complied. Shortly thereafter Rothschild left. In their search for a successor, the board members agreed to not hire a Liberal cantor. But no other cantor could be found who was willing to serve with accompaniment. Worship continued without organ music, but the instrument was serviced and occasionally used during synagogue concerts and Kristallnacht commemorations.[26]

Aside from Frankfurt am Main and Saarbrücken, only a few other communities in West Germany acquired an organ or a harmonium, each under unique circumstances. The building of the synagogue in Unna-Massen was originally a Protestant church and equipped with a small five-stop one-manual instrument. When in 1960 the space was remodeled and consecrated to become home to the Jewish congregation, the organ remained.[27] But whether it was actually used is unknown. (Similar spatial conversions in Hanover, Bielefeld, and Speyer at the beginning of the new millennium led to synagogues being equipped with organs). "Organ" music is documented in the synagogue of Minden on the occasion of the Kristallnacht commemoration in November 1958 (the instrument was a harmonium).[28] When the Jewish youth of Westphalia visited the new synagogue in the spring of 1959, Händel's "Largo" served as a prelude and "Tochter Zion" as postlude.[29] The communities of Bonn and Trier, too, occasionally used a harmonium for recitals or weddings.[30] Sporadic documentation might attest to the fact that harmoniums were used infrequently, often only during the inauguration of rebuilt synagogues, perhaps as a

---

26 During the 1990s, some members expressed the wish to have organ accompaniment and the community reverted to its previous compromise to use it with exceptions, but in reverse. It has only been used once a year, on Hanukkah, to accompany the *Maoz tsur*.

27 See Achim Seip, "Die Orgel in der Synagoge – Fast vergessen und wiederentdeckt," in *Jüdische Vielfalt zwischen Ruhr und Weser: Erträge der dritten Biennale Musik & Kultur der Synagoge 2012/2013*, ed. Manfred Keller, Jens Murken, and Diethard Aschoff (Berlin, 2014), 274.

28 See "'Wir dürfen niemals vergessen!': Gedenkfeiern zum 20. Jahrestag der Synagogen-Zerstörung," *Allgemeine Wochenzeitung der Juden in Deutschland* 13.34 (November 21, 1958): 5.

29 See *Allgemeine Wochenzeitung der Juden in Deutschland* 13.5 (May 1, 1959): 11.

30 In Bonn, a recital with Manfred Moshe Korn and pianist Heinz Geese is documented on November 28, 1959, with a broad variety of Jewish song repertoire and a prelude played on the harmonium; see *Allgemeine Wochenzeitung der Juden in Deutschland* 14.37 (December 11, 1959): 11. The wedding in Trier on May 16, 1965, featured local cantor Eugène Fettmann (1917–1983), who came from Luxembourg, and an unnamed organist on the harmonium; see *Allgemeine Wochenzeitung der Juden in Deutschland* 20.10 (June 4, 1965): 11.

reminder of the organ's pre-war existence.[31] Indeed, the harmonium, as a smaller and moveable instrument, served as a proxy for the organ, which would have to be permanently installed. In this way the harmonium was a compromise, though most communities tacitly agreed on leading services without instrumental music, avoiding a second *Orgelstreit*.

To be sure, reasons for not including instrumental accompaniment or gradually abandoning the organ varied. The majority of the congregations gathered in newly constructed synagogues, not in existing structures with an integrated organ. Even if the communities had wanted to preserve the pre-war establishment of the *Orgelsynagoge*, the high expense of an instrument was an impediment to acquiring one and maintaining it, especially in the wake of the desolate economic situation in the years after 1945. Additionally, there were logistical issues (the difficulty of finding a qualified organist) and demographic changes (the large number of Displaced Persons and new immigrants who were mostly rooted in the Eastern Ashkenazic rite without organ accompaniment).[32] Although many congregants were not strictly observant and did not regularly attend Sabbath services, the *Einheitsgemeinde* changed from the predominant pre-war Liberal constituent with organ music, mixed choir, and German-language sermon, to a community without organ. Prayer and song in Hebrew were generally preferred and sections for women and men became the norm.[33] With the exception of the Pestalozzistraße Synagogue in West Berlin, which after the war resumed the legacy of the New Synagogue at Oranienburger Straße with its core musical program established by Lewandowski, the congregations of West Germany largely turned away from pre-war customs. Liberal services, which in 1968 took place at Frankfurt's Baumweg and the Grand Hotel, were temporary. Shlomo Lewin from Erlangen visited to sing prayer melodies by Lewandowski, though initially without

---

31 Another example of the one-time use of the organ at a synagogue's inauguration is Cologne, where Hans Knäbel played a prelude on Psalm 30 and a festive fantasy; he might also have accompanied the children's choir, which sung under Manfred Moshe Korn (see Wilhelm Unger, *Zur Weihe der wiederhergestellten Synagoge Roonstrasse und des jüdischen Kulturzentrums in Köln 20. September 1959* [17. Elul 5719] [Cologne, 1959]). When the Jewish community in Essen inaugurated its new synagogue on October 21, 1959, a harmonium is documented as well, but it is unclear if it continued to be used; see Hermann Lewy, "Ein glücklicher Tag: Neues Gotteshaus geweiht," *Allgemeine Wochenzeitung der Juden in Deutschland* 14.31 (October 30, 1959): 5. The same is true for Stuttgart ("Neue Stuttgarter Synagoge eingeweiht," *Allgemeine Wochenzeitung der Juden in Deutschland* 7.7 [May 23, 1952]: 4); Mülheim (*Allgemeine Wochenzeitung der Juden in Deutschland* 15.5 [April 19, 1960]: 5); and Worms (see E.G. Lowenthal, "Tat der Gesinning – Tag der Besinnlichkeit," *Allgemeine Wochenzeitung der Juden in Deutschland* 16.37 [December 8, 1961]: 5).

32 In Munich, for example, DPs constituted eighty percent of the Jewish population by 1959; see Anthony D. Kauders, *Democratization and the Jews: Munich, 1945–1965* (Lincoln, 2004), 42.

33 See Michael Brenner, *After the Holocaust: Rebuilding Jewish Lives in Postwar Germany* (Princeton, 1997), 71 and 147.

organ accompaniment.[34] When the third Liberal service was held in 1970, it counted 63 congregants. By 1973 services were held with organ accompaniment, but without a mixed choir.[35] Services after 1974 are not documented.

By 1982 at least one reader of the *Allgemeine jüdische Wochenzeitung* bemoaned the absence of Liberal worship, responding to Nathan Peter Levinson's report on the musical customs in Leipzig's synagogue ("professional synagogue choir," singing "traditional melodies by Lewandowski and Sulzer," and "accompanied on the harmonium") with the rhetorical question: "Why is the tradition of Liberal German Jewry otherwise [i.e. outside of West Berlin] not being preserved?"[36] Due to the increasing presence of the Eastern European cohort and Orthodox customs gaining a stronghold, prayer services changed indefinitely.

In East Germany the situation looked similar, though for different reasons. For one, the size of the Jewish community was miniscule from the outset, with only eight Jewish communities, in Chemnitz, Dresden, Erfurt, Halle, Leipzig, Magdeburg, and Schwerin, counting altogether approximately 3,000 members if including East Berlin (the number would steadily decline). While many of the congregations preserved pre-war customs, they did so without the organ, due to limited funds. An exception was the above-mentioned Israelitische Religionsgemeinde zu Leipzig, which in 1950 hired Werner Sander (1902–1972), formerly from Breslau. In 1951, he informed the board of a unique opportunity to purchase a used two-manual instrument for 8,000 marks built by the Hörügel firm.[37] He made a strong case for buying the instrument, arguing that only first-rate *Friedensmaterial* (literally "peace material," as opposed to materials used in warfare) had been used; such an instrument would replace the Wilhelm Sauer organ destroyed in 1938; it would elevate services and synagogue concerts. Musically, Sander tried to continue the Leipzig tradition on all possible counts. Two months later, in November 1951, the community had located a keyboard instrument for use during service, though quality concerns prevented its purchase.[38] Another exception was the synagogue of Erfurt, which by 1953

34 See "Liberaler Gottesdienst in Frankfurt," *Allgemeine unabhängige jüdische Wochenzeitung* 23.10 (June 7, 1968): 11; see also announcements in *Allgemeine unabhängige jüdische Wochenzeitung* 24.22 (August 29, 1969): 9; *Allgemeine unabhängige jüdische Wochenzeitung* 25.7 (February 13, 1970): 9; and *Allgemeine unabhängige jüdische Wochenzeitung* 25.13 (March 27, 1970): 11.

35 See *Allgemeine jüdische Wochenzeitung* 25.43 (October 26, 1973): 9.

36 Klaus Herrmann, "Ein Besuch in Leipzig," *Allgemeine jüdische Wochenzeitung* 37.13 (March 26, 1982): 6. For Nathan Peter Levinson's report on the use of the organ in Leipzig's synagogue, see "Besuch in der Messestadt Leipzig," *Allgemeine jüdische Wochenzeitung* 37.1–2 (January 1 and 8, 1982): 7.

37 See Archiv der Israelitischen Religionsgemeinde zu Leipzig 458, "Aktennotiz" (September 24, 1951).

38 See Zentralarchiv zur Erforschung der Geschichte der Juden in Deutschland, Heidelberg, B.1/38 (Jüdische Landesgemeinde Thüringen) (Werner Sander to Günter Singer, November 5, 1951), no. 332.

owned a harmonium, frequently played by a Mr. Alsdorf and later by Walter Köhler (Fig. 3).[39] These developments, however, were short-lived. While synagogue music with organ continued its slow recovery under Werner Sander in Leipzig and Günter Singer in Erfurt, Jewish life in the newly founded Republic took an unforeseen turn that would largely bring its course to a halt – the purges between November 1952 and March 1953, which severely decimated the Jewish communities.

Still, a few months later, on August 30, 1953, Riesenburger rededicated Rykestraße Synagogue in time for the High Holidays. It would remain the sole functioning synagogue in GDR's capital until the late 1980s – an emblem as it were. The reinauguration, however, did not happen without hindrance. The previous day, arson in the sanctuary made the news:

> What a curious smell, so we thought ... incense? No, the Jewish rite does not use it. But there, out of the cracks from the closed reed organ billowed smoke, clouding toward us. In horror, the community secretary opened the lid of the instrument: underneath it gave off clouds of smoke.[40]

That of all places the reed organ was a site of arson, provides grounds for questions. If fascists wanted to burn down the synagogue, why start underneath the lid of an instrument? And why would the *Berliner Zeitung* share the news so soon after the purges? Community members against the organ had no reason. At the time, the instrument was not used on the Sabbath. The fire was discovered early enough to prevent major damage. The building and its visitors were unharmed. The condition of the instrument remains unknown.

A decade later this event was history. The magistrate of Berlin had contributed 24,000 East marks (the average monthly income at the time was 450 marks) to build a new organ for Rykestraße Synagogue. It was inaugurated during a synagogue concert on March 11, 1962, by Martin Riesenburger himself, who was a gifted keyboardist.[41] Built by the Sauer firm, the instrument was small, with only one keyboard, but sufficient for accompanying concerts and wedding ceremonies, and religious services (it is still extant, but rarely used). In his inaugural speech, Riesenburger expressed hope that the organ's "sounds will rise to the honor of God as a

39 See the announcement of his passing in *Nachrichtenblatt der Jüdischen Gemeinde von Groß-Berlin und des Verbandes der Jüdischen Gemeinden in der Deutschen Demokratischen Republik* (March 1967): 10.

40 "Was ist das für ein merkwürdiger Geruch, dachten wir ... Weihrauch? Nein, der jüdische Ritus verwendet ihn nicht. Doch da, aus den Ritzen des geschlossenen Hamoniums quoll Rauch, wölkte uns entgegen. Entsetzt riß der Sekretär der Gemeinde den Deckel des Instrumens hoch: darunter qualmte es." M.J., "Brandstiftung in der Synagoge," *Berliner Zeitung* (August 29, 1953).

41 See "Präludium für Stefan," *Berliner Zeitung* (May 22, 1964). Riesenburger played the instrument for Stefan Jerzy Zweig (*1941) when he visited the synagogue. A Buchenwald survivor, he is the subject of the GDR bestseller *Nackt unter Wölfen* (1958) and moved to East Berlin in February 1964 to study cinematography.

Fig. 3: Erfurt, harmonium situated on the gallery behind the Torah ark (Photograph: Katrin Keßler, Bet Tfila – Research Unit Braunschweig, 2019).

herald of peaceful times."[42] As such, the concert was nostalgically embraced as a reminder of "the old days" and a "great, moving music event."[43] It brought back two elements Liberal Jews cherished in- and outside worship: a mixed choir, which was brought in from Budapest, and an organ. The inauguration of the new organ took place just six months after Pestalozzistraße had bought an electronic organ.

In spite of these exceptions, the fate of the organ in synagogues on German soil was nonetheless sealed. This transformation had originated with the pogroms of November 1938, when the vast majority of the two hundred organs that had become an integral part of synagogue architecture and musical and liturgical practices in Central Europe were destroyed. Around the same time, some Jewish communities "sold" (that is gave away far below their value and for various reasons) their instruments to churches, such as in Augsburg, Dortmund, and Munich.[44] Following these junctures and in light of the post-war communities' economics and demographics,

42 See G.S., "Künder friedvoller Zeiten," *Neue Zeit* (March 15, 1962).

43 See G.B. "Das war ein Konzert," *Nachrichtenblatt der Jüdischen Gemeinde von Groß-Berlin und des Verbandes der Jüdischen Gemeinden in der Deutschen Demokratischen Republik* (April 1962): 11.

44 On the impossibility to reclaim ownership of an organ solder under value, see the Augsburg organ affair, Tina Frühauf, *Transcending Dystopia: Music, Mobility, and the German-Jewish Community, 1945–1989* (New York, 2021), 47–48; on the case of Munich, see 40.

the reintroduction of the organ into synagogue service in the post-war era became a non-subject. Embraced or merely accepted as instrument and object by few communities and often in idiosyncratic ways, even as a museum piece (Fig. 4), the organ had hardly any presence in the synagogues of post-war Germany at large. As one of the least fixed elements of Jewish musical practice, it left a threefold mark of a different kind, signifying absence, (silent) presence, and adapted or modified presence. As an almost immovable artifact and integral constituent of Western Jewish culture in later modernity, after 1945 it ultimately came to symbolize the absence of Liberal Judaism on German soil.

Fig. 4: Augsburg, today a section of the Augsburg Synagogue at Halderstraße hosts a museum, where the prewar harmonium is exhibited, attesting to keyboard instruments having become museum pieces (Photograph: Pryor Dodge. Private collection of the author. Printed with permission).

Sarah M. Ross

Jewish Musical Heritage in Post-War Germany: Negotiating Jewish Self-Understanding through Synagogue Chant

In 1972, German-Jewish sociologist Alphons Silbermann (1909–2000) stated that in recent years (meaning between 1945 and the 1960s), there had been few sociological studies on Jews and Judaism in German-speaking countries. According to Silbermann, scholars chose instead to work on descriptive historical works based on diverse (archive) materials on single issues, mostly subjects concerning World War II and the Holocaust.[1] In light of the recent historical circumstances at that time, the lack of sociological – of empirical and ethnographic – studies on Jews and Jewish life in Germany was not surprising. Four decades later, however, Silbermann‘s observation is still true, despite the fact that Jewish communities in Germany have grown again, due to the immigration of Jews from the former Soviet Union between 1990 and 2005. There is a particular lack of scholarship involving ethnomusicological studies on Jewish communities in Germany today. Ethnographic fieldwork in disciplines such as Sociology, Ethnology, Cultural Anthropology and also Ethnomusicology require face-to-face encounters involving researchers and research partners in the here and now. The face-to-face interaction required for effective fieldwork poses a dilemma for many (non-Jewish) researchers in Germany owing to fears of contact and misunderstanding, little knowledge about Judaism as lived and living religion and culture, Jewishness as an ethnic identity and – most importantly – societal, social, political, and academic structures that contribute to the lack of research on Jewish contemporary issues.[2] As anthropologist Dani Kranz points out, it is relevant "[if] they [the anthropologists] are Jews or non-Jews [...], in particular in a charged context as in post-Shoah Germany, and in regard to the issues, and questions they raise."[3] Against this backdrop, it is relevant that the data on synagogue chant (*nusach*) in German Jewish communities today, in this chapter, is based on talking with Jewish community members and cantors in Germany, and not about them. This approach is

---

1 Alphons Silbermann, "Soziologie des Judentums," *Kölner Zeitschrift für Soziologie* 24 (1972): 417–419; 417.

2 Dani Kranz, and Sarah M. Ross, "Tektonische Verschiebungen in der Judaistik und Jüdische Studien nach 1990 durch die Integration der Jüdische Theologie und eine jüdische Selbstermächtigung in Deutschland," in *Die Shoah in Bildung und Erziehung heute – Weitergaben und Wirkungen in Gegenwartsverhältnissen*, ed. Marina Chernivsky, and Friederike Lorenz (forthcoming).

3 Dani Kranz, "Intersecting Allopolitics, or the Quest for Jewish Anthropology in Germany," *Modern Jewish Studies* (forthcoming).

https://doi.org/10.1515/9783110750812-013

therefore participant-centered. Quoted statements of my interview partners are anonymized at the request of my research partners.

The respective data was mainly collected through music-oriented ethnographic fieldwork in Jewish communities in Mannheim and Frankfurt am Main within the context of a larger, interdisciplinary research initiative on traditions and transformations of Judaism and Jewish practices in Germany after the Shoah.[4] In addition, qualitative interviews with cantors of other synagogue communities in Germany, such as in Berlin and Stuttgart, were conducted and their musical practices have been recorded. The data collection was primarily guided by the questions of how Jewish self-understanding in post-war Germany is expressed in Jewish liturgical music today, and thus, how the latter is interrelated with diverging ideas about Jewish cultural heritage in Germany.

"German-Jewish" cultural heritage

In the immediate aftermath of the Shoah, Jewish cultural heritage in Germany became 'contested heritage.'[5] The restituted remains of German-Jewish heritage, such as library collections, ritual and art objects as well as other 'ownerless' Jewish assets,[6] were transformed by international Jewish organizations[7] into a collective property belonging to Jewish people globally; they were distributed to Jewish communities abroad. This endeavor was spearheaded by the idea that future Jewish life in Germany was impossible. As such, German-Jewish heritage became, in the words of Dan Diner, "a holy sign of Jewish collective affiliation after the catastrophe."[8] This act of collecting led to disagreements between international Jewry and representatives of the reestablished Jewish communities in Germany.[9] One could say that the Jews residing in Germany felt as if they faced a double expropriation. In the decades following the Shoah, Jewish communities in Germany had to deal not only with social, cultural and economic hardship, but with the consequences of the *cherem*,[10] the ban imposed by the international

4 The project was entitled "Objects and spaces reflecting religious practice: traditions and transformations in Jewish communities in Germany after the Shoa," and funded from September 2018 until August 2021 by the German Ministry of Education and Science.

5 See Elisabeth Gallas, et al., ed. *Contested Heritage. Jewish Cultural Property after 1945* (Berlin, 2020), 10–12.

6 An exemption are the few rare library collections and ritual objects located, for example, in the former British zone. These cultural assets stayed in Germany.

7 Like Jewish Cultural Reconstruction Inc. (1945–1952).

8 Dan Diner, "Im Zeichen des Banns," in *Geschichte der Juden in Deutschland von 1945 bis zur Gegenwart*, ed. Michael Brenner (München, 2012), 15–66; 29.

9 Diner, "Im Zeichen des Banns," see note 8, 26–31.

10 Diner, "Im Zeichen des Banns," see note 8, 20. See also Anthony Kauders, *Unmögliche Heimat. Eine deutsch-jüdische Geschichte der Bundesrepublik* (München, 2007).

Jewish collective on those Jews who decided to stay in the country. The latter group quite often developed a distorted self-understanding as "absent attendees."[11]

Small Jewish communities were re-established shortly after World War II, a 'Jewish void' was left that had to be filled with new cultural-political significance. Throughout the second half of the twentieth century, this vacuum was to be filled with a new concept of 'Jewish cultural heritage.' This heritage was intended to serve the idea of a 'New Germany' as well as of a 'New Europe,' and it did not necessarily include Jews as agents. Since the late 1960s, German – not Jewish – society has been increasingly involved in the discovery and preservation of 'Jewish cultural heritage,' not only with the intention of distancing itself from its history, from the former Nazi dictatorship, but also to lay the foundation for the revival of Jewish life. The problematic aspects of the 'Jewish revival' in Germany have been discussed in detail elsewhere.[12] It was, however, precisely in this context that a new German concept of Jewish cultural heritage took shape. 'Jewish heritage' in this sense no longer referred to the totality of all forms of expressions of Jewish life, of being Jewish and doing Jewish things; rather, the German term for Jewish cultural heritage, *Jüdisches Kulturerbe*, became a symbolic construction of Jews and Judaism reconfigured as a political tool for fighting anti-Semitism, promoting cultural diversity and Christian/German-Jewish dialogue, and for preserving fundamental new European values such as democracy and tolerance.[13] Moreover, Jewish cultural heritage sites have since been exploited as items of general public interest, and thus, became an important economic resource for Jewish heritage tourism in Europe. The German idea of *Jüdisches Kulturerbe* thus refers primarily to a specific modus operandi adopted by experts in the fields of monument preservation, tourism, museums and politics etc. These experts limit their definition of 'doing heritage'[14] almost exclusively to tangible forms of Jewish cultural heritage of the past, ascribing contemporary and political values and meanings to it, and selectively reintroducing it as a resource for (non-Jewish) society, global heritage markets as well as the academic community.[15] The 'objects' of interest included under the umbrella of the German

---

11 Diner, "Im Zeichen des Banns," see note 8, 44 on.

12 See for example the book by Ruth Ellen Gruber, *Virtually Jewish – Reinventing Jewish Culture in Europe* (Berkeley/Los Angeles/London, 2002); see also Miranda Crowdus, and Sarah M. Ross, "Applied Ethnomusicology and Jewish Music Studies: Negotiating 'Third Mission' Requests in Germany Today," in *Diggin' up Music: Musikethnologie als Baustelle*, ed. Michael Fuhr, Kerstin Klenke, and Julio Mendivil (Hildesheim, 2021), 120–144; 109.

13 For a more detailed discussion on this topic, see Sarah M. Ross, "'Jüdisches Kulturerbe' vis-à-vis 'Jewish Heritage': Einleitende Überlegungen zur Idee einer kulturellen Nachhaltigkeit in den Jüdischen Musikstudien," in *Jüdisches Kulturerbe MUSIK – Divergenzen und Zeitlichkeit. Überlegungen zu einer kulturellen Nachhaltigkeit aus Sicht der Jüdischen Musikstudien*, ed. Sarah M. Ross (Bern, 2021), 19–39; 20, 22–23.

14 See Keith Emerick, *Conserving and Managing Ancient Monuments. Heritage, Democracy, and Inclusion* (Woodbridge, 2014), 5.

15 Laurajane Smith, *Uses of Heritage* (London/New York, 2006), 44.

term *Jüdisches Kulturerbe* are abandoned and converted synagogues, municipal buildings of former Jewish communities, as well as ritual objects from the time before the Shoah etc. Intangible forms of Jewish heritage, such as music, ritual and knowledge, are mostly excluded from this discourse. Even within academic scholarship, new and relevant discourses in Critical Heritage Studies such as the integrative turn that understands tangible and intangible values of cultural property as interrelated, are hardly applied to studies on *Jüdisches Kulturerbe.*[16] In Critical Heritage Studies, there is no common concept of 'Jewish cultural heritage' (only an 'authorized heritage discourse'),[17] and as such as there is – owing to the historical situation in Germany and Europe since 1945 – not only one heir and stakeholder of Jewish heritage, but many different ones. These stakeholders include the Jewish communities themselves – on a national and international level – as well as the non-Jewish societies and their scholars, (Jewish) museums, non-academic history societies, monument conservationists and other actors in the field of heritage management, and last but not least, those involved in the German culture of Holocaust commemoration.

The constructed German product *Jüdisches Kulturerbe* is thus, for the most part, disconnected from actual Jewish life. In order to understand, how Jewishness is lived and negotiated in Germany today, it is, however, necessary to take a closer look at intangible, lived forms of Jewish heritage, such as Jewish liturgical music. Intangible cultural heritage refers to cultural expressions that are directly supported by human knowledge and skills. It is a cultural phenomenon of the present that is passed down from generation to generation, usually by oral transmission, and is constantly recreated and changed in the process.[18] A sustainable heritage process requires a sufficiently large group of stakeholders who are willing and able to accept and negotiate the heritage and pass it on to future generations – also in a modified form. Furthermore, this process requires a growing Jewish cultural and religious community that ensures the persistence of intangible Jewish heritage: thus, it is directly dependent on a stable Jewish self-understanding.[19] The latter is, however, one of the most contested and unstable aspects of contemporary Jewish life in Germany.

---

16 Fiorella Dallari, "The Heritage from Cultural Turn to Inclusive Turn. The Cultural and Sacred Landscape of the UNESCO List: A Sustainable Track to overcome the Dichotomy between Tangible and Intangible Heritage," *Proceedings of TCL 2016 Conference* (2016): 129–141; 129, 131.

17 Smith, *Uses of Heritage*, see note 15, 11.

18 UNESCO, "What is Intangible Cultural Heritage?" https://ich.unesco.org/en/what-is-intangible-heritage-00003. Accessed October 13, 2021.

19 See Huib Schippers, "Sound Futures: Exploring the Ecology of Music Sustainability," in *Sustainable Futures for Music Cultures. An Ecological Perspective*, ed. Huib Schippers, and Catherine Grant (New York, 2016), 1–17; 3, 12–13.

Being Jewish in Germany

Being Jewish and expressing one's individual Jewishness in Germany in the twenty-first century is still fraught with challenges. The "Biller-Czollek debate" is the most current example for an interpretation *ex cathedra* of how Jewish one has to be in order to be counted as a legitimate Jew in Germany, and most importantly, in order to carry the "moral message" of Jews in the country.[20] Essayist and lyricist Max Czollek (born in East Berlin in 1987) is one of the most popular publicists in Germany today. Some would say that he gained his popularity because of his "brilliant analyses of the Jewish condition in Germany" that were "reviewed far beyond the German-speaking world, even in the *New York Times*."[21] Others argue that his bold Jewish identity marketing made him famous: "[T]here is hardly a tweet, hardly a text, in which the publicist, [...] does not mention his alleged Jewishness."[22] In a column in the weekly magazine *Die Zeit*,[23] Jewish writer and columnist Maxim Biller spoke out on what many suspected but only few knew for sure: according to the *halacha* (Jewish law) of many denominations of contemporary Judaism, Czollek is not Jewish as he has only one Jewish grandfather. So what? As sociologist Y. Michal Bodemann states in his response to the debate, outside Germany, in any other country that is home to a Jewish diaspora, a public debate of this kind would be inconceivable, because Germany is the only country in the Western hemisphere where Judaism holds such a politically charged position.[24] Particularly in Germany, but also in other countries such as Poland, Jews are required to conduct "ideological labor" as Bodemann calls it elsewhere. By this, he refers to Jews in (West) Germany as an ethnic group that performs a specific ideological function within larger society, namely the reclamation of Jewish identity and culture in post-Shoah Germany:[25] Already "in 1949, US High Commissioner John McCloy addressed the reestablished Jewish communities in

20 For the debate, see Jacques Schuster, "Von der deutschen Sehnsucht, Jude zu sein," *Die Welt* (September 6, 2021), https://www.welt.de/kultur/article233489632/Falsche-Identitaeten-Von-der-deutschen-Sehnsucht-Jude-zu-sein.html#Comments. Accessed August 7, 2021. With regard to the dimensions of the dynamic interplay between being and doing Jewish in Germany, and individually lived out ideas about being Jewish outside of a formal Jewish community, see Dani Kranz, "Shades of Jewishness. The Creation and Maintenance of a Liberal Jewish Community in Post-Shoah Germany," PhD dissertation, University of St. Andrews, 2009.

21 Y. Michal Bodemann, "Die Causa Max Czollek: Wer ist hier eigentlich Jude? Und wer nicht?," *Berliner Zeitung Online* (September 2, 2021), https://www.berliner-zeitung.de/wochenende/die-causa-max-czollek-wer-ist-hier-eigentlich-jude-und-wer-nicht-li.179949?pid=true. Accessed October 13, 2021.

22 Schuster, "Von der deutschen Sehnsucht, Jude zu sein," see note 20.

23 Maxime Biller, "Der linke Intellektuelle Max Czollek und seine komplizierte Biografie," *Die Zeit* 33 (August 11, 2021).

24 Bodemann, "Die Causa Max Czollek: Wer ist hier eigentlich Jude? Und wer nicht?," see note 21.

25 Y. Michal Bodemann, "The State in the Construction of Ethnicity and Ideological Labor: The Case of German Jewry," *Critical Sociology* 17.3 (1990): 35–46.

Germany. He stressed that Germany's relation to the Jews would be a 'real touchstone' of the new democracy."[26]

Thus, for critics such as Biller, the problem is that Czollek does not fit with the local interpretation of the *halacha*. The problem is that Czollek – who was socialized in a Jewish environment and thus feels close to Judaism – legitimizes his public activities by means of his affiliation with the Jewish community that upholds the *halacha* as the decisive boundary of a Jewish status, even though he is obviously not *halachically* Jewish. The problem is that there is more value attached to the performance of Jewishness in Germany than to being and doing Jewish, that one Jew denies the other the speaker position, and that "this debate is also fed by non-Jewish Germans, who obviously feel qualified to interpret the genealogies of Jews."[27] To put it differently: Actual lived traditional *halachic* observance is widely understood as the epitome of "doing Jewish" – orthopraxis – in contrast with prevalent (often non-Jewish) definitions of "legit" Jewishness. This debate gives the impression that Biller and others are using *halachic* stipulations as an excuse for discrediting the currency that Czollek gains through his affiliation with Judaism. For what purpose exactly is unclear: Perhaps to bolster their own currency as Jews, for the sake of policing legit Jewish identity, or to bring people forward who perform Jewish identity to boost their careers. Notwithstanding, the question of who is a Jew, or what is Jewish heritage, is of central importance in Germany. It is subject to a constant competition of self-attribution and attribution by others, as is the case in the broad field of Jewish musical heritage discussed in the following.

This debate, which expresses to some degree also Jewish "in-group" biases, is not new. Again, it was Alphons Silbermann who already addressed in his article "Zur Sozial-Kulturellen Situation der Jüdischen Gemeinden in Deutschland," published in 1960, that those Jews who survived the Holocaust in Germany or re-settled in Germany for different reasons were confronted by Jews from abroad with a range of antipathies. Overall, the Jews from abroad expressed a complete lack of understanding of the motivations of those who chose to re-settle in Europe, as they doubted that Jewish life could exist in Germany again.[28] The Jewish communities that have been reestablished shortly after the Shoah, consisted of a very diverse group of people. These groups ranged from native German Jews of a formerly assimilated, educated middle class to

26 Marion Kaplan, "Antisemitism in Postwar Germany," *New German Critique* 58 (Winter 1993): 97–108; 104.

27 Bodemann, "Die Causa Max Czollek: Wer ist hier eigentlich Jude? Und wer nicht?," see note 21.

28 In his day, Silbermann recognized quite concretely different resentments: Among others, a resentment against Germany and his Nazi-past in general, as well as a resentment against the Jews living in this country (while living in mental identification and social interaction with the major non-Jewish German society): See Alphons Silbermann, "Zur Sozial-Kulturellen Situation der Jüdischen Gemeinden in Deutschland: Bemerkungen zu Fragen der geistigen Wiedergutmachung," *Kölner Zeitschrift für Soziologie* 12 (1960): 204–223; 206 and 209.

Yiddish speaking Jews originating from rural parts of Eastern Europe. Silbermann continues and states that those who stayed in or (re-)migrated to Germany "as they are," could no longer refer to a long-established 'Jewish habitus,' such as English, American or Swiss Jews still do today. They must, for lack of a 'traditional habitus,' bear the brand of resentment of apostasy, when the doors of Israel had been opened in 1948. Thus, the culturally diverse group of Jews remaining in Germany presents "an accumulation of people of the same faith, randomly, aimlessly and in a state of bewilderment, thrown together from diverse individual groups."[29] According to Silbermann, the fate and future of those Jews who remained in Germany can be considered as unessential by the wider Jewish community itself: Meaning that any kind of investment in the well-being and future of their communities is understood as a wasted effort. Alternatively, it can be recognized that this community that was thrown together by destiny will dissolve its own inner conflicts and, most importantly, will overcome its cultural differences despite the diverse resentments and prejudices coming from outside. Otherwise, "in a not too far future, this community will find itself at best in the state of a permanent vegetation."[30] Looking on Jewish (communal) life in Germany today, in 2021, it is as if Silbermann is speaking to us at this very moment, as if he had just made his observations. His realization that negotiating cultural and religious practices and identities – Jewish heritages respectively – is the key to a sustainable Jewish community in Germany holds to date.[31]

Synagogue chant as intangible cultural heritage

Worldwide, Jewish communities are held together – ideally – by their shared socio-cultural heritage such as language, customs or liturgical practice and its music.[32] Today, Jewish congregations in Germany are still a conglomeration of community members and leaders drawn from a wide variety of cultural backgrounds: Rabbis and cantors come from Israel, the UK, the USA, Switzerland or France, and the board is composed of members of the "old community," that is, of members with differing cultural backgrounds born and raised in Germany after 1945, while the majority of the

29 Silbermann, "Zur Sozial-Kulturellen Situation der Jüdischen Gemeinden in Deutschland," see note 28, 208.

30 Silbermann, "Zur Sozial-Kulturellen Situation der Jüdischen Gemeinden in Deutschland," see note 28, 218.

31 Silbermann, "Zur Sozial-Kulturellen Situation der Jüdischen Gemeinden in Deutschland," see note 28, 210–215.

32 Here, we are basically talking about the basic definition of ethnicity: see Fredrik Barth, "Introduction" and "Pathan Identity and Its Maintenance," in *Ethnic Groups and Boundaries: The Social Organisation of Culture Difference*, ed. Fredrik Barth (Bergen, 1969), 9–38.

community itself consists largely of immigrants from the former Soviet Union arriving after 1989. The central question here is how group cohesion can come about under these conditions? The most obvious answer to this question is that the common bond of Judaism should hold a community together. In German Jewish synagogue communities today, this unifying bond, this stereotypical "after all, we are all Jews" as Silbermann calls it,[33] does not consist of a common social and cultural heritage, milieu, environment and upbringing, etc. This bond is to large extent made up of a "mythologizing falsification of history."[34] The latter suggests – among others – an internal and constant cultural and religious dynamic within Jewries that follows the laws of a centuries-old tradition.

The most prominent example for how the cultural dynamics of Jewish musical heritage are often coated with political interests that are informed by mythologizing notions of Jewish history is the contemporary performance practices of nineteenth-century Reform synagogue music. More precisely, this discourse is embedded in the performance practice of the synagogue compositions of Louis Lewandowski (1821–1894) or Salomon Sulzer (1804–1890), which are characterized by a combination of mixed choir, cantorial solo and the use of the organ. The contemporary idealization of nineteenth-century German Reform Judaism today, and thus the cultural promotion of its synagogue music inside and outside Jewish communities, is to a large extent driven by the German state despite the fact that the majority of Jews in Germany neither understand themselves as 'German Jews' nor do they align with Reform synagogues and the Liberal rite. The few that identify as 'native German Jews' have their "strongholds" in Orthodox-oriented Jewish communities, such as in Mannheim and Frankfurt am Main, or are not affiliated with any community at all.[35] According to historian and political scientist Julius Schoeps, "[the] German government is fond of the Reformers, because according to them, these are people one can talk to. The behavior of Orthodox rabbis serving in the state is perceived by the German public as problematic, because it contradicts the expectation that Jews behave as an integral part of Germany's Liberal society."[36]

33 Silbermann, "Zur Sozial-Kulturellen Situation der Jüdischen Gemeinden in Deutschland," see note 28, 210.

34 Silbermann, "Zur Sozial-Kulturellen Situation der Jüdischen Gemeinden in Deutschland," see note 28, 210–211.

35 Hannah Tzuberi, "Jewish Studies in Berlin: Two Different Schools and Their Missing Jews," *Mandolinaforpresident* (11 May, 2016): 1–7; 3, https://mandolinaforpresident.wordpress.com/2016/05/11/jewish-st. Accessed July 1, 2020.

36 Schoeps, quoted in Tzuberi, "Jewish Studies in Berlin," see note 35, 4.

Outside Jewish communities

This fondness for German Reform Judaism and its music is reflected in the way non-Jewish German society understands and uses Jewish intangible cultural heritage. Outside Jewish congregations, the preference for German Reform music can be explained by a widely held perception that *Jüdisches Kulturerbe* in Germany is 'something from the past,' and thus something fixed and unchanging, as well as by its aesthetic proximity to Christian church music and the art music of Romanticism. Thus, it is no coincidence, that this type of 'Jewish music' was just added to the German UNESCO Register of Good Safeguarding Practices.[37] The entry in the UNESCO register was initiated, in 2019, by the Leipzig Synagogue Choir, which is a semi-professional concert choir with predominantly non-Jewish members and choir directors. It was the choir's belief that this music should be preserved "as it once existed" and as it is practiced today. The choir itself is not an integral part of a Jewish community and therefore does not share any original Jewish choir traditions. The choir's claim evidences the lopsided structure of German/Jewish relations, with Jews and manifestations of "legitimate" Jewish identity being constructed by non-Jewish Germans. In fact, the musical activities of the Leipzig choir can be interpreted as Holocaust commemoration. Rather than reflecting the musical practices of a living Jewish community, the choir's activities allow people to come to terms with the past, and bring non-Jews closer to Judaism. Since its foundation in 1962, the choir has been committed to the 'preservation' of European synagogue choral music, more precisely to the music of nineteenth-century Reform movement, such as the music of Louis Lewandowski. Accordingly, the common understanding of musical heritage as a dynamic and living tradition that is transmitted – *l'dor va'dor* ('from generation to generation') – by its own rules,[38] is obviously not relevant here.

Thus, the listing of Reform synagogue music in UNESCO's Register of Good Safeguarding Practices demonstrates a rather un-reflected and romanticized understanding of Jewish heritage, of cultural continuity and discontinuity respectively. The argument used in this context is that the Shoah, the great break in the history and culture of European Jewry, led not only to the decline of Reform synagogue choral music in Germany but also to the destruction of the corresponding musical literature, which is why this music is hardly "performed" in synagogue services today. Another problem aligned with the decision to include this music in the register is the ignorance of the original and primary function of this music as ritual music of Jewish worship. Furthermore, the UNESCO application and decision for registration not only clearly comes from an outsider's perspective of Jewish liturgical music, it also ignores

37 See www.unesco.de/kultur-und-natur/immaterielles-kulturerbe/immaterielles-kulturerbe-deutschland/synagogale-chormusik. Accessed October 9, 2021.

38 Huib Schippers, and Catherine Grant, ed. *Sustainable Futures for Music Cultures. An Ecological Perspective* (New York, 2016).

the fact that the synagogue music of Reform Judaism experienced many ruptures and turning points both before and after World War II.[39]

In contrast with the above-mentioned argument of "discontinuity" due to the Shoah, one could say that a certain continuity lies precisely in the continuation and further development of this music in Jewish communities in the United States, the United Kingdom, Israel and elsewhere. Here, cultural continuity emerges from the integration of the music into a living Judaism and its liturgical practice. The assumption that the performance of Jewish music of the past in musealized, mythologized and unchanging forms can be considered as successfully sustaining culture (as part of UNESCO'S mandate) is therefore an erroneous one. In addition, the ruptures and turning points in the history of the music of Reform Judaism were not only externally determined, but were as much a result of inner-Jewish debates and religious and cultural transformations. Thus, the choice not to resume the rite of Reform Judaism in the re-established Jewish communities in Germany right after 1945 was based on cultural and theological decisions, since a significant part of the post-war communities defined themselves as traditional or Orthodox.[40]

A counterexample to the efforts of the Leipzig choir and UNESCO to safeguard Reform Jewish synagogue music is the Pestalozzistrasse Synagogue in Berlin. The synagogue was inaugurated in 1912 as a place of worship for Orthodox Jews. At that time, the melodies of Louis Lewandowski were known as "Gemeindemelodien" (community melodies), and were widely used in Jewish communities throughout Germany, even beyond the realm of Reform services. In the early period of Pestalozzistrasse, when the community still identified itself as Orthodox, Lewandowski's liturgical melodies were thus sung by male choir only, and without the use of the organ. It was not until the 1930s that arrangements for mixed choir, cantor and organ entered the liturgy at Pestalozzistrasse: back than introduced by musicologist and choirmaster Arno Nadel. Despite the wide-ranging destruction of the Berlin Jewish community, after 1945, every effort was made to keep the city's tradition as one of the important centers of Ashkenazi culture alive. Thus, Sephardic cantor Estrongo Nachama, who served the community in Pestalozzistraße from 1947 until his death in 2000, familiarized himself with the German Reform tradition, in order to sustain this intangible heritage. Today, Pestalozzistraße is the only synagogue in the world whose rite still consists entirely of compositions by the important synagogue composer Lewandowski.[41] It is nowadays

39 A late draft of the application is in the possession of the author.

40 Sarah M. Ross, "Jüdisches musikalisches Kulturerbe im Kontext sozialer Zeitkonstitutionen," in *Jüdisches Kulturerbe MUSIK – Divergenzen und Zeitlichkeit. Überlegungen zu einer kulturellen Nachhaltigkeit aus Sicht der Jüdischen Musikstudien*, ed. Sarah M. Ross (Bern, 2021), 43–72; 58–62.

41 Nachama was born in Greece and raised in the Sephardic Jewish tradition. For him, preserving the Reform musical legacy of Berlin meant a considerable challenge, since he had to familiarize himself and empathize with the aesthetics of Jewish liturgical music that was a foreign sound to him. Personal interview with A.I. in Berlin, June 2021.

served by cantor and musical director Isodoro Abramowicz,[42] and is a well-known place of worship for Liberal Berlin Jews. On a regular basis, the weekly minyan consists of long-standing community members as well as of Jewish and non-Jewish visitors from all over the world, who are attracted by the performance of Lewandowski's music.[43]

In contrast to the example discussed above, in Pestalozzistrasse, it was and is the stakeholders (cantors and congregants) themselves who have taken on the musical heritage of the pre-war period, who preserve it and pass it on to future generations. Here, the music is an integral part of a living and dynamic Jewish life in Berlin, in other words of living Jewish heritage. Nevertheless, it cannot be ignored that they also benefit from the general interest of the broader (non-Jewish) public in the music of Reform Judaism and its public promotion. The opening of services to external visitors as well as the Lewandowski Festival held annually in the synagogue are examples of the extent to which the liturgical heritage of German Jews is marketed as European Jewish cultural heritage today.

Inside Jewish communities

In the communities of Mannheim and Frankfurt am Main, the tradition of Reform synagogue music was and still is a significant subject of negotiation regarding the communities' musical heritage, too. The communities of Mannheim and Frankfurt have shared similar demographic developments since 1945, which have a direct impact on the communities' synagogue rite and Jewish-liturgical music practices. Both the main synagogue in Mannheim as well as the Westend Synagogue in Frankfurt used to be known as places of German Reform Jewry, and thus for their local *minhag*. According to musicologist Philip Bohlman, the members of the Jewish community of Mannheim "had enjoyed a considerable degree of emancipation during the nineteenth century," and were thus open towards religious reforms occurring in the mid-nineteenth century: "The results of the reforms, quickly set in motion in 1854 by a new rabbi, Moses Präger (1817–1861), brought about pronounced changes in the musical activities of the

---

42 Isidoro Abramowicz was born in Buenos Aires, where his family attended a German synagogue. There, he was raised in the tradition of the Jewish Reform music of Salomon Sulzer and Louis Lewandowski. After his music studies in Buenos Aires, and later on in Germany, he took up his cantorial training at the Abraham Geiger College in Berlin. His first engagement as cantor was at the Great Synagogue of Stockholm. In 2017, he became the director of the cantorial training program at Abraham Geiger College, two years later, he was hired as the main cantor and musical director of the synagogue at Pestalozzistrasse in Berlin. Personal interview with I.A. in Berlin, June 2021.
43 Personal interview with I.A. in Berlin, June 2021.

Mannheim Jewish community,"[44] which were later on also spurred by famous reform composer Hugo Chaim Adler (1894–1955). Adler served the main synagogue in Mannheim as cantor from 1922 until his emigration to the United States in 1939. He was the primary force behind the religious musical activities generating a new, Reform-oriented Mannheimer *minhag* during a period of cultural renaissance.[45] Also the Jewish community of Frankfurt am Main used to be an important site of liturgical music: Frankfurt was known for its *hazzanut*, "which represented the archetype of the Western Ashkenazi tradition with roots in the 15th century"; it became an important center of the Reform movement in the nineteenth century and employed well-known cantors such as Fabian Ogutsch (1845–1922) or Selig Scheuermann (1873/74–1935).[46]

Between 1945 and 1989

In the post-war period, German-style Liberal Judaism neither found followers in Mannheim nor in Frankfurt. The newly-founded Jewish communities had a different membership composition, translating into a different religious character compared to the pre-Shoah communities. Between 1945 and 1952, throughout the phase of the *Sherit Hapletah* ("the remaining rest"),[47] the communities consisted of a minority of native German Jews and a majority of Eastern European survivors of the Shoah.[48] The latter had largely grown up in an Orthodox environment and wanted to hold on to this form of Judaism as a reminder of their families and the context of their lives before the destruction, even if they did not strictly observe the commandments of Orthodox Judaism beyond the confines of the synagogue.[49] The minority of the

44 Philip V. Bohlman, "The Resurgence of Jewish Musical life in an Urban German Community: Mannheim on the Eve of World War II," *Musica Judaica* 14 (1999): 107–126; 108, 121.

45 Bohlman, "The Resurgence of Jewish Musical life in an Urban German Community," see note 44, 121.

46 See Tina Frühauf, *Transcending Dystopia. Music, Mobility, and the Jewish Community in Germany, 1945–1989*, (New York, 2021), 51.

47 Bodemann, "The State in the Construction of Ethnicity and Ideological Labor," see note 25, 39–45.

48 The description 'native Germany Jews' refers to those who survived the Holocaust in the country, or returned from exile in the postwar period (mostly during the 1950s and 1960s) after a failed attempt to emigrate. The majority of Orthodox-oriented Eastern European Jews were mostly dropouts from the Displaced Persons camps located in the former American occupation zone (1945–1949). Personal interview with A.S. in Mannheim, December 2018 and June 2021; with R.A. in Mannheim, July 2019; with Y.R. in Frankfurt, November 2019 and June 2021, with F.A. in Frankfurt, November 2019; see also Jan Mühlstein, "The Return of Liberal Judaism to Germany," *European Judaism: A Journal for the New Europe* 49.1 (Spring 2016): 44–48; 44.

49 Interview with F.A. and Y.R. in Frankfurt, November 2019, with R.A. in Mannheim, July 2019; see also Frühauf, *Transcending Dystopia*, see note 46, 52.

surviving German Jews found themselves in difficult negotiation position vis-a-vis the Eastern European majority concerning issues such as resuming the German Reform tradition of synagogue music of the pre-war period or turning towards an Orthodox, Eastern European rite. At that time, Eastern European *nusach* was deemed incompatible with German Jewish practices by the native German Jews. In Frankfurt, in the late 1940s, it was almost impossible to find a cantor, who was familiar with the Liberal order of worship, the repertoire of local *hazzanut*, willing to come to Germany.[50] In order to be able to function as a Jewish community, the 'Liberal group' had to rely on amateurs and visiting cantors. Eventually, they had to hire an Eastern European cantor. In this regard, musicologist Tina Frühauf states: "The wish for continuity, in spite of the absence of suitable synagogue musicians, reflects the need to preserve and to maintain prewar expressions of identity establishing a 'normality' in the midst of chaos by holding on to what seemed familiar."[51] Even though the 'Liberal group' later adjusted to Orthodox Eastern European rite, the hope for a cantor who would reconnect the community to its musical heritage, to the former *Frankfurter Minhag*, was pronounced, as evidenced by archival material including job advertisements, applications of cantors and internal community correspondences of the 1960s as well as later evidence.[52]

Both German-Jewish sociologists, Alphons Silbermann and Harry Maor, stated in the 1960s that one could not expect a group of miscellaneous Jews to return, almost overnight, to a "newly created" Jewish religious life. They had just laid the foundation for their new institutions, in which, whatever latent Judaism still existed, should be given the chance to survive and perhaps to develop. The lack of almost any common Jewish tradition, of rabbis and cantors, of books and spiritual sources, of teachers and mentors, eventually spurred ignorance in Jewish matters. This lack of educational and sustainability-related resources caused synagogue services and their music to turn into a syncretic mix of Jewish religious elements.[53] Thus, it was not before the phase of consolidation, between 1952 and 1989,[54] that the Eastern European Orthodox rite, including the Sephardic/modern Hebrew pronunciation of the Hebrew language, prevailed. As Silbermann further explains, at that time it was not a question of taste or of desirable or undesirable Orthodoxy,

50 There have been cantors who survived the Shoah in exile, and who knew the *Frankfurt Minhag*, but did not plan to live and work there. Such as cantor Kaufmann, who later served the Jewish community in Bern, Switzerland.

51 Frühauf, *Transcending Dystopia*, see note 46, 58.

52 See archival material at the Zentralarchiv zur Erforschung der Geschichte der Juden in Deutschland, B1/13 series, A 748 and 803.

53 See Silbermann, "Zur Sozial-Kulturellen Situation der Jüdischen Gemeinden in Deutschland," see note 28, 214; Harry Maor, "Über den Wiederaufbau der Jüdischen Gemeinden in Deutschland seit 1945," PhD dissertation, University of Mainz, 1961, 11, 14.

54 Bodemann, "The State in the Construction of Ethnicity and Ideological Labor," see note 25, 39–45.

but of the adaptation of the rite and synagogue chant to social changes:[55] This adaptation did not reinforce a sense of religiosity among the community members, but led to a reinforcement of participation in synagogue services. The decision to turn away from pre-war German-Jewish tradition of synagogue music served to prevent an increasing distance from Judaism: People who needed the support of a faith seek it primarily in the social-spiritual milieu in which they live, as Silbermann concludes. By no means do they seek it in the "excesses of an inappropriate historicism; for historicism and tradition are neither the same thing nor do they have the same inner quality."[56] The latter becomes increasingly important the more we progress in time towards the present day, and take a look at how cantors serving Jewish communities in Germany today deal with the musical legacy of German Jewry in contemporary synagogue music practices.

Between 1990 and today

The years from 1989/1990 until today are called the phase of representation.[57] It is characterized by "reform efforts" and the return of Liberal Judaism to Germany, but also by a revival of *Minhag Ashkenaz*, the liturgical rite of Southwest and South Germany,[58]

---

55 In Mannheim, Italian-Israeli cantor Raffaele Polani served the congregation from 1985 to 2014. Throughout this period, the community faced some major demographic challenges, and had to deal with the lack of a common local Jewish history, a common Jewish self-understanding and of shared cultural values and musical practices. Polani contended with these challenges musically with the re-invention of the *Mannheimer Nusach*, which, in his view, is a musical tradition that emphasizes the cantor's voice and "the power of music," with less emphasis on the Hebrew liturgical text as is the case in the Orthodox rite. This change responded to the needs of the Russian-speaking Jews, the majority of whom came to Mannheim with little knowledge of Judaism and Jewish liturgy, and were not able to read and understand the Hebrew prayer texts. He thus replaced most of the Eastern European *nusach* the community used to sing between the 1950s and early 1980s, with a mixture of aesthetically pleasing synagogue songs and melodies that attracted people to come to the services and motivated them to sing along. From then on, the melodies of the Jewish Reform composer Louis Lewandowski dominated the services in Mannheim; however, these were sung without the use of choir and organ, since the congregation still considered itself Orthodox. For a more detailed discussion on the *Mannheim Nusach*, see Ross, "Jüdisches musikalisches Kulturerbe im Kontext sozialer Zeitkonstitutionen," see note 40, 54 on.

56 Silbermann, "Zur Sozial-Kulturellen Situation der Jüdischen Gemeinden in Deutschland," see note 28, 214–215.

57 Bodemann, "The State in the Construction of Ethnicity and Ideological Labor," note 25, 35–46; 45–46.

58 For a detailed discussion on *Minhag Ashkenaz* see, for example, Goeffry Goldberg, "Hazzan and Qahal: Responsive Chant in Minhag Ashkenaz," *Hebrew Union College Annual* 61 (1990): 203–217.

which is hardly practiced in synagogue services in Germany today.[59] In 1995, in some places earlier,[60] independent Liberal Jewish initiatives started in some German cities (such as Hanover, Munich, and Cologne, etc.) aiming the establishment of own egalitarian Jewish communities. They were, among others, supported by the World Union for Progressive Judaism.[61] According to Jan Mühlstein,

> [an] important contributing factor was most certainly the fall of the Iron Curtain, followed by the German reunification, which brought about significant changes in the public and personal life of Germans including its Jews. Many people were looking for a more open, egalitarian Jewish identity and community, which they were able to find in the newly founded Liberal communities.[62]

Further important factors spurring these efforts were, at least within communities located in the former American occupation zone (1945–1949), the withdrawal of the US Army, whose military rabbis used to lead non-Orthodox services that welcomed Jews from off-base,[63] but also increasing "intervention into Jewish affairs" by German politicians that were motivated by an "unattached concern for Jewish 'diversity,'" and by "their need for a particular *kind* of Jewish leadership," as Jewish Studies scholar Hannah Tzuberi states.[64]

With regard to synagogue music, and thus the promotion of the musical legacy of nineteenth-century German Reform Judaism, the founding of the Abraham Geiger College (AGC) as rabbinic seminary at the University of Potsdam,[65] which was extended by a cantorial program in 2008, plays an important role. The latter is the first cantorial school in Germany since the Shoah and aims to train male and female cantors for Jewish communities in Europe, mostly within the confines of the *Einheitsgemeinden*,

59 Particularly after the Shoah, German Jews established communities throughout the world, where they continued to practice their traditions, Minhag Ashkenaz respectively. Most of these communities were, however, not able to sustainably maintain neither their liturgical customs nor their particular German-Jewish identity. It is against this background that Machon Moreshes Ashkenaz, the Institute for German Jewish Heritage, was founded. The institute is dedicated to the research, preservation and transmission of *Minhag Ashkenaz*, its religious values, and customs, as well as the folklore of German Jewry as it once existed. For further information on the institute, see https://moreshesashkenaz.org/en/. Accessed October 11, 2021.

60 See, for example, the Liberal Jewish community of Cologne that was founded in 1982. See Kranz, Shades of *Jewishness*, see note 20.

61 In 1997, the Union of Progressive Jews in Germany was founded in Munich. At the same time, the later founder of the Abraham Geiger College in Berlin/Potsdam, Dr. Walter Homolka, was installed into the rabbinate. See Mühlstein, "The Return of Liberal Judaism to Germany," see note 48, 46.

62 Mühlstein, "The Return of Liberal Judaism to Germany," see note 48, 44–45.

63 Mühlstein, "The Return of Liberal Judaism to Germany," see note 48, 45.

64 Tzuberi, "Jewish Studies in Berlin," see note 35, 4.

65 In 2001, the Abraham-Geiger College joined the World Union for Progressive Judaism. See www.abraham-geiger-kolleg.de/personal-journey/practical-vocational-training/cantorial-track/. Accessed October 10, 2021.

which were founded in Germany after 1945.[66] The strong connection of the rabbinic seminary and cantorial school of the Abraham Geiger College to the Union of Progressive Jews in Germany resulted in increased political recognition of Liberal Judaism in Germany at the beginning of the twenty-first century. This affiliation also arguably privileges the College in relation to other (independent) Jewish organizations in terms of its "access to generous state funding available for Jewish communities" in the country.[67]

In personal interviews, several graduates of the cantorial program stated that the liturgical and thus musical training at AGC is meant to prepare the students to serve any Jewish community in Europe: that is also beyond the confines of Liberal/ Reform communities. The focus of the training is, however, on German *nusach*, on *Minhag Ashkenaz* respectively, and on the German Reform rite and musical repertoire.[68] The AGC's decision to focus on this particular tradition of synagogue music is underpinned by the wish to salvage at least some of the displaced and nearly extinguished culture and tradition of German Jewry in Germany itself. On the other hand, this decision is supported by – supposedly an un-reflected – 'liturgical acculturation' of its board members, who have been raised or trained in that tradition abroad. Yet, after graduation most cantors experience a different reality in the Jewish communities they serve, in comparison to what they were taught at school, as cantor B.M. explains:

> Most of us [cantors] are trying to re-establish that [German] musical tradition in our congregations, at least partially. [...] [Partially,] because times have changed. So first, this tradition has been forgotten. And now, when we enter a congregation, we face a tradition that's been [practiced for] 70 years or so now, where everybody who officiated here at one time after 1945 also left his mark, musically speaking. I suppose it was either [...] cantors from America or people who were trained in America or by American mentors. There you recognize a lot of melodies that don't come from Germany and don't have roots here; and that's what the community knows. That's the *minhag* by now, that's the custom, that's what people like to hear. And nobody can come into a community like an elephant in a china store. Now, as of today, it's all different. You have to do it very carefully.[69]

66 *Einheitsgemeinde* is a term for Jewish communities in German-speaking countries. The designation goes back to the German legislation of the nineteenth century, which granted Jews only one Jewish community per locality and obliged Jews to belong to it. The *Einheitsgemeinde* was retained voluntarily, which led to the formation of so-called *Austrittsgemeinden* in localities with numerically significant Jewish populations and to the strengthening of the Liberal direction under the umbrella of the local *Einheitsgemeinde*. After the end of World War II, Jewish unified congregations in Germany were rebuilt, with many breaking away from the influence of Reform Judaism and instead looking to Eastern European models. See Eva-Maria Schrage, "Die Pluralität jüdischer Gemeinden in Deutschland heute," *Jüdische Religion in Deutschland* (Wiesbaden, 2021), 45–53.

67 Mühlstein, "The Return of Liberal Judaism to Germany," see note 48, 47.

68 Personal interview with B.M., November 2018; with B.T., December 2018, with B.J., June 2021.

69 Personal interview with B.M., November 2018.

As this cantor's personal experience shows, the political ideology of the Abraham Geiger College to recreate, revive and thus safeguard the musical heritage of prewar German Jewry is guided by the same ignorance towards and misunderstanding of Jewish heritage and its transmission processes, as the heritage initiative of the Leipzig synagogue choir discussed above. Also in this context, the performance of German Jewish musical heritage carries a higher value than actually being Jewish in Germany, and how it is expressed in Jewish liturgical music. Thus, another cantorial graduate of the Abraham Geiger College reported in our personal interview:

> At the AGC one does not see and get to know 'the natural Jewish life in Germany,' because one is always surrounded by 'professional Jews' only: like the professors, the cantors (mostly from abroad) but also some politicians. It is all not authentic, rather artificial. I never understood what the real goal of the AGC is, what it is all about. There were often public services, attended by influential non-Jews from the German political scene, which were organized by several students. The AGC wanted to present the students to the public. On such an occasion, I had once, very quickly, sung a prayer in the weekday *nusach*. It was more mumbled than sung. As a result, I was strongly criticized that for what I was doing was not a spiritual experience. [One of the rabbis] jumped to my side and defended me. He said that the way I recited the prayer was as in a normal *shaharit* [morning service], as one can experience in Israel on every corner. So, against this background, experiencing and learning to understand Jewish life in Germany is very difficult for AGC students, because it is mostly about good PR, public attention and the experience, not about the reality in the communities.[70]

Regarding a sustainable transmission and maintenance of Jewish intangible heritage, of synagogue chant, it is not only relevant that the congregants have a say with regard to decisions concerning the rite and choice of *nusach*, but that they also get the chance to take agency in transmission processes of their own Jewish heritage. The biographical background of the cantorial students at AGC plays an important role. According to my interview partners,[71] a large part of the AGC cantorial students come from abroad, mostly from Eastern European countries or from Israel. Their primary educational background is grounded in musical performance, usually vocal performance. Often, having been raised in secular, non-observant Jewish homes, they choose to enroll in the cantorial program as a fallback plan, if they find that they cannot survive economically as freelance artists: "My mother had no idea about Judaism […], my family never attended synagogue services. […] First, I had to learn that I am not allowed to operate the light switch in the synagogue on Shabbat."[72] Consequently, most of the cantors trained at AGC have not been embedded in any traditional religious Jewish community, but knew their familial traditions or non-traditions as corner stones of being Jews. Yet, they lack – "unlike their

70 Personal interview with B.T., December 2018.

71 Personal interview with B.M., November 2018; with H.M., December 2018; with B.T., December 2018, with I.A., June 2021.

72 Personal interview with B.T., December 2018.

assimilated predecessors in pre-war Germany" – "memories, knowledge and experience" of traditional liturgical Jewish musical practices.[73] What Michael Friedman writes about the young rabbis trained at and graduating from the AGC is equally true with regard to the cantors:

> They are rabbis [and cantors] without a rabbinic [or cantorial] tradition, they are not the sons or grandsons of other rabbis [or cantors], they are not carriers of knowledge accumulated over hundreds of years. They are smart, but they lack the wisdom of generations and the bitter taste of destruction. They are rabbis [and cantors] without an own experience of the Holocaust.[74]

In 2021, a personal experience of the Holocaust cannot be the *sine qua non* of any discourse about Jewish musical heritage, about the perception of the same in the present and its transmission to future generations. What is relevant, however, is the degree of first-hand experience of and knowledge about this intangible heritage tied in with a strong interrelatedness of Jewish heritage and Jewish self-understanding. Without this knowledge, it would not be the stakeholders themselves (neither cantor, rabbi nor congregants) but third parties, who decide what kind of synagogue chant (of intangible Jewish heritage) meets the socio-cultural needs of a community the best. It will be Jewish officials and outsiders who decide what kind of Jewish identity will be expressed through Jewish musical heritage, which brings us back to the beginning of this article. Some graduates of the cantorial program, due to this lack of knowledge and experience, easily jump on the bandwagon of AGC's mission to return Liberal Judaism and its musical heritage to Germany. These individuals eagerly study German *nusach* and the Reform repertoire by means of printed resources and archival materials. Other foreign-born and trained cantors, who serve communities in Germany today, have a different agenda with regard to the preservation of German-Jewish musical heritage.

In another Jewish community in South Western Germany, British cantor M.H. has served the community since 2017. He was born and raised in Liverpool and Manchester, UK. His grandfather and uncle were *hazzanim* in Liverpool. As a young child, M.H. sung in the synagogue choir of the Princes Road synagogue in Liverpool, where he was introduced to the Reform repertoire of Louis Lewandowski, Salomon Sulzer, German-born synagogue composer Julius Mombach (1813–1880) and to other "classical cantorial pieces."[75] In addition to his cantorial training within the communities and the synagogue services that he regularly attended as a child and young man, M.H. entered, at the age of 16, the Tel Aviv Cantorial Institute, where he studied for six years. He came to Germany to continue his music studies at the local university of music. He had the aim of becoming the city's new cantor.[76] The history of this Jewish community is complex,

73 Tzuberi, "Jewish Studies in Berlin," see note 35, 4.

74 Friedman quoted by Tzuberi, "Jewish Studies in Berlin," see note 35, 4.

75 Personal interview with M.H., July 2021.

76 Personal interview with M.H., July 2021.

and is, until World War II, characterized by numerous discussions and negations about synagogue rite between Orthodox- and Reform-oriented Jews. In any case, the greater Jewish community in Southwest Germany was familiar with both the German Reform tradition as well as with traditional *nusach* practiced according to *Minhag Ashkenaz*. Both liturgical practices have been largely displaced with the Shoah, and replaced with post-Shoah praxes. They did survive abroad as living traditions in Liverpool and Manchester, where M.H. was raised and educated. M.H. identifies with the Germany tradition of synagogue prayer and chant due to his liturgical biography. This is different to the congregants in the community he serves today, who – for the most part – immigrated from the former Soviet Union. M.H. recognizes the difficulties most of his community members encounter on a daily basis, such as acquiring sufficient liturgical knowledge, recognizing the melodies of the different prayers and different praxes of holidays and, above all, identifying with a particular *minhag*, that is, in his mind, the German *minhag*. He describes the culture in his community as "a very non-Jewish culture," which is different to his own: "Mainly I get on with people, it is difficult. It's not easy, it's not easy because it's not my culture, you know, it is a different culture."[77]

Despite the cultural differences between cantor and congregation, and despite the fact that hardly any of the community members (cantor and rabbi included) have any German cultural background, M.H. is willing to reintroduce the German *nusach*, which he relates to as his *nusach*, and as the *nusach* belonging to Germany. He takes this approach regardless of the fact that the community had been cultivating its own – albeit, in his opinion, idiosyncratic – post-war tradition for quite some time: "I wanted to sing it [the German *nusach*], and I sang it for about six months and people, they complained about it. They said it sounded like a church."[78] According to M.H., a cantor has the responsibility to continue the tradition of his predecessors, however far back that lineage may go, even if there are tensions between preserving a specific *nusach*, a specific Jewish heritage, and the task of leading a congregation in prayer that does identify with this *nusach*. In his opinion, synagogue chant in this particular community has been greatly simplified since the 1990s, since the immigration of the Russian-speaking Jews. Much of the tradition has been lost in that time: "[M]uch of the *nusach*, the strict *nusach*, especially the German *nusach* has been lost in that time."[79] With regard to sustaining and transmitting liturgical musical heritage in Jewish communities in Germany today, the main problem is – as this example shows – that foreign acculturated and trained cantors, such as M.H., often feel obliged to come to Germany, in order to rescue, revive and transmit German Jewish intangible heritage in the name of the local stakeholders. Due to his liturgical biography, M.H. is more committed to reviving and safeguarding this tradition in his German community than to being more responsive to

77 Personal interview with M.H., July 2021.
78 Personal interview with M.H., July 2021.
79 Personal interview with M.H., July 2021.

the needs of his congregation. The question of whether the community wants to or is able to hold on to this heritage is rarely asked. The impact of the reconstruction and preservation of this Jewish musical heritage on present and future local Jewish life in Germany is so far not considered either.[80]

In the above-mentioned context of the return of Liberal Judaism to Germany, at the beginning of the twenty-first century, smaller *minyanim* were also founded, often within the structures of a *Einheitsgemeinde*. In contrast to bigger congregations, which either operate under the roof of the Central Council of Jews in Germany or the Union of Progressive Jews in Germany, these small, independent egalitarian *minyanim* went through a self-determined process of Jewish self-discovery, which enabled them to decide for themselves what heritage they wanted to affirm, accept and combine with new elements of synagogue song. Since the rededication of Westend Synagogue in Frankfurt am Main in 1950, which was initially inaugurated (in 1910) as a Reform temple, the synagogue has functioned as a mainly Orthodox institution until the *Frankfurt Model* was installed in the late 1990s/early 2000s, meaning that different streams of Judaism are united under one roof. Today, the main sanctuary of Westend Synagogue is the home of an Orthodox community that follows *Minhag Polin*, and its services are led by the American cantor Yoni Rose, who adds some "American style of *hazzanut*" to the services.[81] The *Stibl*, the *Beit Ha-Midrash*, became the synagogue of the Chassidic *minyan*, while the former weekday synagogue is now home to the egalitarian *minyan*. The egalitarian *minyan* has its predecessors in a small circle of German Jews who returned from Israel and other countries to Germany throughout the 1960s, and who started to perform Liberal services in private rooms. However, this endeavor was soon discontinued, since Liberal Judaism in Frankfurt remained limited to a small number of people and did not gain any further followers among the community members of Westend Synagogue or beyond.

After the withdrawal of the US Army in the mid-1990s, a new group of younger Jews who had regularly attended Jewish services at the US Central Chapel reestablished Jewish Liberal services in Frankfurt am Main. At first, these were held at different locations, too, until the former chairman of the Jewish community, Ignatz Bubis, invited them at the end of the 1990s to take their place in the community center, and later in the renovated weekday synagogue at Westend.[82] As "Egalitarian Minyan," this group has become an integral part of the Jewish community of Frankfurt, and is led today by Rabbi Elisa Klapheck and Cantor Daniel Kempin. Although one could say that the Liberal Jewish community in Frankfurt has returned to its roots, in terms of rite and musical *minhag* it has completely

80 Ross, "'Jüdisches Kulturerbe' vis-à-vis 'Jewish Heritage,'" see note 13, 20–21.

81 Personal interview with Y.R., November 2019.

82 Personal online group interview with D.K., J.K and L. F.-R., November 2020.

broken with the musical heritage of the prewar *Frankfurter Minhag*.[83] Both Rabbi Klapheck and Cantor Kempin were formally trained in the American Jewish Renewal Movement (ALEPH). With regard to liturgical music, the Egalitarian Minyan practices Eastern European *nusach* (as Kempin learned from the leading *hazzan* Jack Kessler of ALEPH), Western Ashkenazi *ta'amei ha-mikra* (introduced by rabbi Klapheck) alongside with American style and newly composed melodies for psalms, *zmirot* and *piyyutim*. One reason behind this discontinuity with regard to German Reform rite and music is that the members of the egalitarian *minyan* do not understand themselves as the second or third generation of Holocaust survivors, but as the first generation of German post-war Jews. According to Kempin, this self-understanding – along with many more social, cultural and political aspects of the *minyan* – has to be expressed in synagogue music.[84]

Conclusion

The examples discussed in this chapter illustrate the contemporary societal use of Jewish Heritage, of *Jüdisches Kulturerbe*, in Germany today that largely follows the idea of "past presencing"[85] that is the re-production of the past in the present. Thus, with regard to the musical tradition of nineteenth-century Reform Judaism that dominates discourses on Jewish intangible heritage within and outside Jewish communities, it becomes obvious that the main motivation behind these heritage efforts are not really a matter of continuing that specific German-Jewish musical heritage in its original context and function as ritual music. Rather, it reveals a process of "defrosting" an imagined essence of a Jewish cultural phenomenon of the past, in order to construct a virtual sense of cultural continuity for a moment, and in doing so, to serve socio-political aspirations in Germany. If the synagogue music of German-Jewish Reform Judaism (that has been widely published and distributed) had really been destroyed, as it is widely suggested and believed, it could not be reconstructed today and preserved for the future. Rather, the Leipzig Synagogue Choir and its heritage initiative, the agenda of the Abraham Geiger College cantorial program as well as the strategy of foreign cantors serving in Germany today, reveal the manifestation of a relatively new cultural phenomenon: a secular concert-life as well as a platform of Jewish professionals that elevate the liturgical music of German Reform Judaism, as well as *Minhag Ashkenaz*, as a new trade mark through

83 Participant observation of author at a Shabbat service of the egalitarian *minyan* in Frankfurt am Main in March 2019.

84 Personal online group interview with D.K., J.K and L. F.-R., November 2020.

85 Sharon Macdonald, *Sharon, Memorylands. Heritage and Identity in Europe Today* (London/New York, 2013), 12–13, 189, 214.

which people seek to increase public and political attention – hence also the desire to be supported by the UNESCO label. The decision by the German UNESCO committee to put this music on the list is perhaps a symbolic one that easily transmits the idea of successful German-Jewish cultural synthesis.

The ways in which Jews and non-Jews deal with the musical heritage of German Jewry points to ways how Jewish cultural heritage is interconnected with varying visions of the future: The AGC's and the Leipzig choir's view on their present future is full of expectations that are shaped by their idea of the future of synagogue music in Germany. This perspective on Jewish heritage inevitably obscures the view of the future present of Jewish communities in Germany: their actually occurring future reality, in which Jewish liturgical music will continue to play an essential role. As long as initiatives for the preservation of Jewish musical heritage in Germany do not take into account the difference between the conceptualizations of Jewish cultural heritage and the different forms of agency associated therewith, they will remain largely unsuccessful and backward-looking in their attempts to preserve cultural heritage in its lived sense. All along, this begs the uneasy question what living cultural heritage means in the German context. Does it need to be the pre-Shoah German Jewish *nusach*, and if so, in which form? Or can it be an Eastern European, or a Persian, or a post-Soviet *nusach*, or another variant of intangible heritages brought by post-Shoah Jewish immigrant groups to their new German home following the destruction of Jewish life in Germany?

Timo Saalmann

Kaddish in Flossenbürg. On the Genesis of the Memorials to Jewish Victims of the Concentration Camp

The memory of the Jewish victims of the Nazi concentration camp (*Konzentrationslager*, KL), which was built in 1938, is manifested in three places on the grounds of today's Flossenbürg concentration camp memorial site. The main camp and an adjoining quarry had served the extraction of the rich granite deposits in the Upper Palatinate by Deutsche Erd- und Steinwerke (DESt), one of the SS's economic enterprises. Of the approximately 100,000 registered prisoners of the Flossenbürg camp complex, with 70 subcamp locations until 1945, more than 30,000 were murdered or perished due to the harsh prison conditions.[1]

The aspect of the remembrance of Jewish victims has not yet been studied in detail for Flossenbürg. This chapter therefore aims to describe diachronically the sequence and development of the structurally manifested or memorialized forms of remembrance. The setting of two memorial stones in 1949/50 and 1985 and the construction of an architecturally designed prayer and memorial site in 1995 can thus serve as examples for the currents of remembrance culture of the respective decade in the Federal Republic of Germany. The classification of the memorial settings – the construction of the prayer and memorial site is to be understood as such here – in their contemporary historical context aims to show characteristics that on the one hand are genuine for the place of remembrance in Flossenbürg, and on the other hand fit into contexts that go beyond it. Methodologically, this approach combines an art-historical and a cultural-scientific spatial and actor-related perspective on the memorial landscape of Flossenbürg. It will become clear which community of remembrance was responsible for the monuments and how the actors and their objectives changed.

The source material is provided by the Bavarian Administration of State-Owned Palaces, Gardens and Lakes (branch office Eremitage in Bayreuth), which was responsible for the care of the so-called Valley of Death, designated as a concentration camp cemetery and memorial, since 1953. The old records are located in the archive of the Flossenbürg Memorial (AGFl) and represent the internal correspondence with the headquarters of the authority in Munich as well as the external correspondence with the State Association of Jewish Communities in Bavaria (*Landesverband der*

1 Jörg Skriebeleit, "Flossenbürg – Hauptlager," in *Flossenbürg: Das Konzentrationslager Flossenbürg und seine Außenlager*, ed. Wolfgang Benz, and Barbara Distel (München, 2007), 11–60, here 51; *Konzentrationslager Flossenbürg 1938–1945. Catalogue of the permanent exhibition*, ed. KZ-Gedenkstätte Flossenbürg (Göttingen, 2008).

https://doi.org/10.1515/9783110750812-014

Israelitischen Kultusgemeinden in Bayern), Munich, and the locally responsible offices, such as the municipality of Flossenbürg, the District Office (*Landratsamt*) of Neustadt an der Waldnaab, and the Land Construction Office of Weiden (*Landbauamt*).

The Jewish memorial stone from 1949/50

On a two-day tour in early November 1950, Philipp Auerbach visited some of the numerous concentration camp cemeteries in Bavaria with a delegation of administrative officials, functionaries of victims' associations, accompanied by changing local politicians.[2] In his function as State Commissioner for the racially, religiously and politically persecuted in Bavaria (*Staatskommissar für rassisch, religiös und politisch Verfolgte* since 1946) and as acting president of the State Compensation Office (*Landesentschädigungsamt* since November 1949), Auerbach was an exposed player in reparations policy and a high-profile figure.[3] Connected with his double function was, qua office, the task of accompanying the reverent design and care of the concentration camp cemeteries considered to be "war graves." On the second day, November 5, and Sunday after All Saints' Day, the concentration camp cemetery in Flossenbürg was officially handed over to the public.

The district administrator of Neustadt an der Waldnaab, Christian Kreuzer, had invited the public to "dedication acts" of the Christian clergy and to the "Jewish prayer for the dead."[4] Fig. 1. It was only with this act that the entire complex was completed in its first stage of development, after a memorial stone for Jewish victims had also been erected, which had been missing from the original cemetery plan.

Designed by Weiden's master builder, Josef Linhardt, the highly rectangular granite plaque with a rim and recessed mirror stands on a low pedestal and bears a six-line, engraved and red-colored Hebrew inscription:

---

2 See Bayerische Verwaltung der staatlichen Schlösser, Gärten und See, *KZ-Friedhöfe und -Gedenkstätten: „Wenn das neue Geschlecht erkennt, was das alte verschuldet…,“* ed. Constanze Werner (Regensburg, 2011).

3 Jörg Skriebeleit, *Erinnerungsort Flossenbürg: Akteure, Zäsuren, Geschichtsbilder* (Göttingen, 2009), especially 133 on; Gerhard Fürmetz, "Neue Einblicke in die Praxis der frühen Wiedergutmachung in Bayern. Die Auerbach-Korrespondenz im Bayerischen Hauptstaatsarchiv und die Akten des Strafprozesses gegen die Führung des Landesentschädigungsamtes von 1952," *Zeitenblicke* 3 (2004): 2, http://www.zeitenblicke.de/2004/2/Fuermetz. Accessed October 31, 2021.

4 AGFl, Gemeinde Flossenbürg, Az. 064 (KZ – Feiern und Veranstaltungen, 1950–1983), District Administrator Kreuzer, invitation for the festivities of the dedication of the concentration camp cemetery in Flossenbürg on Sunday, November 5, 1950.

Fig. 1: Flossenbürg, Kaddish on November 5, 1950, in front of the Jewish memorial stone. Philipp Auerbach is seen on the right with a cylinder hat (Photograph: Foto Bauer, Weiden, AGFl 2017.0297, Image 5941).

עד
הקדושים לזכרון הזאת 'המצב
על נהרגו אשר ורעב חרב חללי
ש"ימ הרשעים י"ע השם קדוש
ה"תש - ח"תרצ בשנות בפלאסענבורג
ה"תנצב

'Witness
be this stele' in memory of the holy martyrs,
'victims of sword and famine',''who were killed to sanctify the
sanctification of the (divine) name' by the wicked, their name be blotted out,
in Flossenbürg in the years 698–705.
Let their souls be bound in the bundle of life.[5]

5 AGFl, 2018.0134 (Translation to German by Nathanja Hüttenmeister and Elisabeth Singer-Brehm).

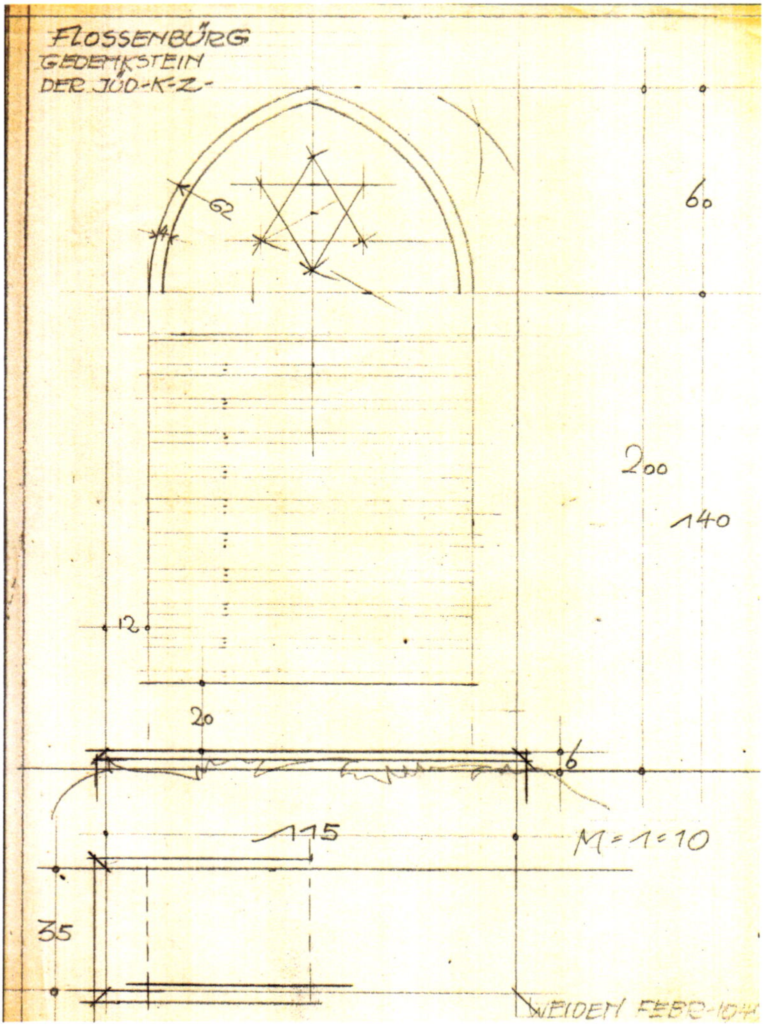

Fig. 2: Flossenbürg, design for the Jewish memorial stone by Josef Linhardt, dated February 1949 (AGFl, Josef Linhardt estate, K40.0004).

On the epitaph there is a somewhat narrower top with a pointed arch, in the lunette of which the outline of a yellow painted shield of David is carved out as a flat relief (Fig. 2).

The memorial is slightly more than two meters high and stands at the foot of the retaining wall of the actual camp area near the former camp crematorium (Fig. 3). The location is noteworthy for two reasons: It is elevated, which on the one hand

Fig. 3: Flossenbürg, Jewish memorial stone in the Valley of Death, condition March 2020 (Photograph: Timo Saalmann, Flossenbürg Concentration Camp Memorial).

makes the stone stand out from the overall landscaping concept of the Valley of Death, but on the other hand also moves it out of the longitudinal visual axis and thus makes it appear isolated.

The area adjoining the actual camp grounds, where the SS had burned the death victims and their ashes were then carelessly scattered on the embankment sloping down to the forest, became a memorial to Nazi crimes soon after the liberation by US forces on April 23, 1945. However, the need to create a memorial came less from survivors of the Flossenbürg camp complex itself than from Catholic Poles who, as former civilian forced laborers or inmates of other concentration camps, lived as Displaced Persons (DPs) in Flossenbürg, Floss, Weiden, or the surrounding area after the end of the war. The memorial committee, which had set itself the goal of making the Valley of Death worthy, mainly consisted of them.[6]

6 Skriebeleit, *Erinnerungsort Flossenbürg*, see note 3, 103–104.

Fig. 4: Flossenbürg, Valley of Death, view to the chapel above the execution site, ash pyramid, Square of Nations (Photograph: Foto Bauer, Weiden, AGFl 2017.0246, Image No. 3194).

The genesis of the Valley of Death is described in detail.[7] Josef Linhardt was responsible for the overall concept of the landscaped/cemetery-gardened Valley of Death and the "Jesus in prison" chapel (Fig. 4).

According to Jörg Skriebeleit, the site is Christian through and through. Essential for this is the eschatologically and salvation-historically charged sequence of structural relics, monuments and newly erected architectural elements. Beginning at the southeastern edge of the site, a sequence of crematorium, firing squad, the ash pyramid arranged after the liberation, the Square of Nations with cenotaphs for the victims named according to nationality, including the number of victims assumed at the time of construction, as well as the chapel "Jesus in prison," located northeast and elevated on the level of the camp site, is created roughly on a longitudinal axis. The chapel, consecrated to the Catholic Church, was built from the *spolia* of the watchtowers, some of which had been demolished. The interior design of the chapel is entirely focused on the national prisoner groups. Thus, the stained-glass windows and shields in the shape of crests again take up the naming of nationalities and numbers of victims. A wooden sculpture group on the altar depicts a martyred Jesus with attendants. The overall impression of the strongly Christian-Catholic character with a

7 See in detail Skriebeleit, *Erinnerungsort Flossenbürg*, see note 3, 116–145.

simultaneously international claim to the commemoration of the multinational prisoner society was reflected in the course of events, rituals and speeches of the inauguration ceremony on Pentecost 1947, May 25.[8]

The nationalization of the early commemoration of the majority of Flossenbürg prisoners becomes clear. Nevertheless, Jews were excluded from the main national line of remembrance, as the circumstances surrounding the installation of the first Jewish memorial stone indicate. It is symptomatic that this group of victims does not appear in the design that was planned and realized by the memorial committee or was simply omitted. Thus, Jörg Skriebeleit states about the work of the memorial committee that Jewish concentration camp survivors, unlike local and Allied decision-makers, "were apparently consciously not recruited for the committee." Although many Jewish Polish DPs were on site, on the part of the non-Jewish Polish DPs there were reservations and no sense of belonging shared with the Jewish Poles and no "willingness to cooperate with them in any way."[9] There is no evidence of any demarcation on the part of the Jewish DPs, but in fact their perspective was not taken into account. The absence of any Jewish symbolism in the new cemetery was pointed out to Auerbach by a US military rabbi in late November 1946. The social democratic second mayor of Weiden, Josef Tröger, who himself had been in KL Dachau in 1933/34 and KL Flossenbürg in 1944, and Earl F. Cruickshank (United Nations Relief and Rehabilitation Administration, UNRRA), who were members of the memorial committee, now argued that the concerns of "all" groups of victims should be taken into account, regardless of their nationality or the reasons for their imprisonment. As a result, on January 13, 1947, the monument committee approved a memorial stone for Jewish victims and decided to erect it.[10] This episode clearly shows that at least three distinct groups were represented in the memorial committee. In addition to the Polish DPs, there were also representatives of the international, de facto US dominated aid organizations or the occupation administration, as well as the group of German (political) former prisoners who came from or resided in the region.

With the memorial stone, there was then an area in the Valley of Death in which the remembrance of the Jewish victims became visible. The memorial had a special function, because now there was a place where the Kaddish could be said as a prayer for the dead. The formulaic use of the Kaddish after the Shoah as a prayer not only for deceased relatives, but for the entirety of the murdered Jews becomes recognizable here. The necessity of gathering a minyan to say the Kaddish lent special weight to the place and prayer against the background of a public culture of remembrance.[11]

---

8 Skriebeleit, *Erinnerungsort Flossenbürg*, see note 3, 135.

9 Skriebeleit, *Erinnerungsort Flossenbürg*, see note 3, 103–104.

10 Skriebeleit, *Erinnerungsort Flossenbürg*, see note 3, 103–104.

11 Andreas Lehnardt, "Kaddisch-Gebet," *WiBiLex* https://www.bibelwissenschaft.de/stichwort/22980/, paras. 3.3. Accessed October 31, 2021.

Nevertheless, Flossenbürg remained a Jewish place of remembrance only to a limited extent at the end of the 1940s, since the KL had not been a "Jewish Space" in that sense either.[12] If KL Flossenbürg is categorized and systematized, it is a main camp in the old Reich founded relatively late for the economic interests of the SS, which differed functionally from German forced ghettos or the concentration and extermination camps in occupied Poland – and thus also in memory. Jewish prisoners played a role in Flossenbürg relatively late in the war. It was not until the last year of the war that they became the largest prison group, with more than 22,000 (including female prisoners in subcamps), this after numerous transports of Jewish people from (evacuated) Eastern European ghettos and camps began arriving in August 1944, who were then used as laborers for forced labor in armaments production in the subcamps in the German Reich. The Jewish prisoners had only come to the Flossenbürg camp system as a result of forced labor in the armaments industry and its relocation back to German territory, or even after liberation as DPs, and therefore brought with them different camp experiences and needs for a commemorative culture. The routes of Jewish victims to Flossenbürg were diverse and resembled each other depending on the national or regional origin of the persecutees.[13]

The vast majority of the Jewish prisoners of the Flossenbürg main camp and its satellite camps were driven south on the so-called "evacuation" or "death marches" as the front lines approached, provided they were able to march or walk.[14] About 1,200 sick prisoners or prisoners close to death were left behind in the abandoned camp area. Unless the inmates died from the hardships of the march or were murdered by guards, they arrived emaciated at their destination. Some marching columns were left to their own devices on the way by deserting guards or had already been liberated by units of the US Army before finally reaching KL Dachau on April 29, 1945. Dachau had been the destination of the forced marches, which also seemed uncoordinated and, from today's perspective, often haphazard, due to collapsed command and command structures, partly because it was located in the center of the ever-shrinking territory controlled by German units. Some 5,500 dead from the forced marches were exhumed between 1955 and 1957 as part of the closure of various concentration camp cemeteries in Bavaria and reburied in the Flossenbürg Cemetery of Honor at what is now known as the Concentration Camp Gravesite and Memorial.

12 See, for example, Stephan Lehnstaedt, "Jewish Spaces? Defining Nazi Ghettos Then and Now," *The Polish Review* 61.4 (2016): 41–56, https://doi.org/10.5406/polishreview.61.4.0041. Accessed October 31, 2021.

13 Katarzyna Person, "Juden aus Polen im besetzten Bayern – die Erfahrung der Befreiung," in *Transporte polnischer Häftlinge in den KZ-Systemen Auschwitz, Dachau und Flossenbürg*, ed. Staatliches Museum Auschwitz-Birkenau (Oświęcim, 2020).

14 On the following, see Skriebeleit, "Flossenbürg – Hauptlager," see note 1, 51–52.

The second Jewish memorial stone from 1985

Since 1980, the Bavarian Palace Department considered erecting another Jewish memorial stone. Initially, another simple gravestone-like monument with a David shield and German inscription made of bronze was considered. Corresponding offers had been obtained from a local stonemason. In the fall, however, the Munich headquarters informed the Bayreuth branch that "an artistic design for the stone is now desired."[15] What form such a monument should take, however, remained unresolved for the time being. Drafts and executed monuments for comparable tenders were examined by the *Landbauamt*, the *Schlösserverwaltung* and the *Landesverband der Israelitischen Kultusgemeinden in Bayern*, but did not meet with approval. In the fall of 1984, Helmut Langhammer from Pressath was commissioned, a sculptor of regional renown, who had realized numerous projects for art in public spaces and whose design "seemed more contemporary and expressive than the proposals and offers received so far."[16]

An increased effort to commemorate the destruction of Jewish businesses and institutions, synagogues as well as the transfer of thousands of Jewish men to concentration camps and the murder of about 1,500 people during the November pogroms of 1938 can be seen since the fortieth anniversary of the events. Mostly based on the initiative of local actors, memorial stones or plaques have been erected at Jewish cemeteries or the former sites of destroyed synagogues since the late 1970s, bringing them back into public awareness. Frequently, prominent places were also used to commemorate the victims of Nazi persecution in a more general way.[17] It can be said with some certainty that these developments also affected the planning for Flossenbürg.

The ceremonies took place on a Sunday, May 5, 1985, relatively close to the fortieth anniversary of the end of the war or the German surrender. Yet the dedication was only one of at least four separate commemorative events organized by the Bavarian state government, the SPD, the regional council of churches of the Protestant Church in Bavaria, and precisely the regional association of Jewish religious communities in Bavaria. In the presence of local political representatives and the two Christian denominations, the sculpture was handed over to the public with speeches followed by a "Jewish prayer for the dead."[18]

15 AGFl, BSV Fl 7, Fraundorfer to the Palace and Garden Administration Hermitage, Bayreuth, September 18, 1980.

16 AGFl, BSV Fl 7, memo of Frauenhofer, September 26, 1984.

17 Christoph Daxelmüller, *Der gute Ort: Jüdische Friedhöfe in Bayern, Hefte zur Bayerischen Geschichte und Kultur 39* (Augsburg, 2009); Israel Schwierz, *Steinerne Zeugnisse jüdischen Lebens in Bayern. Eine Dokumentation* (München, 1988).

18 AGFl, BSV Fl 7, Bavarian State Chancellery (Protocol Department) to Klaß, Vice-President BSV, April 18, 1985, and letter of invitation from the BSV, April 18, 1985.

Fig. 5: Flossenbürg, memorial stone of Helmut Langhammer in the Valley of Death, condition March 2020 (Photograph: Timo Saalmann, Flossenbürg Concentration Camp Memorial).

From the running horizon of the former camp area, the cemetery and the chapel, a flight of steps leads down into the terraced Valley of Death. On a first landing of the stairs a larger plateau was built for the new memorial stone. This was aligned so that it stands in alignment with the older Jewish memorial stone in the longitudinal direction of the site. In a sense, this creates an additional longitudinal axis in the Valley of Death. The memorial stone, which is taller than a man and measures almost 2.5 meters, is made of granite typical of the site (from the Wurmstein quarry, which was also used by KL) and hewn from a single ashlar (Fig. 5).

The central design feature is a Star of David formed by two interlocking triangles with a smoothly polished surface, which is backed by an equilateral triangle in the front view, creating the association of the KL prisoners' "angle" and invoking the common iconography of memorial culture for concentration camp victims. The impression of a prisoner's angle is created by beveled triangular surfaces recessed toward the interior to the left and right of the central axis. The base plate bears in bas-relief an inscription set in capitals in the generally formulating linguistic style of the 1980s: "To the Jewish victims of National Socialist tyranny." A stylized menorah is carved on the reverse. In its outline, the memorial is reminiscent of a tree; the base is designed to be slightly wider, then the column narrows slightly and rises in clean lines before the stone transitions to more organic forms at the top and a sculptural element cantilevers out the sides and back. The roughly chipped edges and sides suggest foliage in this area.

Two leading representatives of Jewish life in Bavaria who came from Poland were instrumental in the installation of the additional memorial stone. The Munich physician Simon Snopkowski, for many years vice-president and since 1971 president of the Jewish Communities in Bavaria, who had come to the DP camp Landsberg am Lech after the liberation from KL Groß-Rosen, and Julius Spokojny, who had been imprisoned for about two weeks in KL Flossenbürg and after the liberation from the subcamp Ohrdruf of KL Buchenwald became a textile entrepreneur in Augsburg. He had been chairman of the Jewish Community of Augsburg-Swabia since 1963, a member of the Board of Directors of the Central Council of Jews in Germany since 1973, and initiated the founding of the Jewish Cultural Museum of Augsburg-Swabia, which opened in 1985. Both also belonged to the second chamber of the Free State, the Bavarian Senate (Snopkowski 1975, 1996–1999; Spokojny from 1982 until his death in 1996).[19] In the context of the culture of remembrance of the 1980s and 1990s in Bavaria, including the development of what was then called Christian-Jewish cooperation, contemporary witness work, the musealization of Jewish history and culture, and ultimately also their participation in the erection of monuments, the work of Snopkowski and Spokojny can probably not be valued highly enough. Their functions not only within their communities, but above all their activities in Jewish umbrella organizations at the state and federal level, as well as their political mandates, provided them with influence in public life. Their participation was decisive for the further genesis of the Jewish memorial sites in Flossenbürg.

The prayer and memorial site of 1995

Perhaps even more clearly than in 1985, the importance of the *Landesverband der Israelitischen Kultusgemeinden in Bayern* in shaping the culture of remembrance became apparent ten years later when a "Prayer and Memorial Site" for the Jewish Flossenbürg prisoners was opened on the grounds of the Flossenbürg concentration camp gravesite and memorial in 1995. Present and giving speeches were Hans Bradl, the District President of the Upper Palatinate, the first mayor of the municipality of Flossenbürg Johann Werner, Hugo Höllenreiner as representative of the

---

19 See the biographical sketches and testimonies in Michael Brenner, *Nach dem Holocaust: Juden in Deutschland, 1945–1950* (München, 1995), 129–132 (Spokojny), 176–178 (Snopkowski) as well as Benigna Schönhagen, *Die Augsburger Synagoge: ein Bauwerk und seine Geschichte* (Augsburg, 2010) on Spokojny.

Documentation and Cultural Center of German Sinti and Roma e. V. as well as Simon Snopkowski as President of the State Association of Jewish Communities in Bavaria and Hans Zehetmair for the State Government in his function as Deputy Minister President and State Minister for Education, Culture, Science and Art. Zehetmair's presence was due to his dual function, as his ministry had assumed responsibility for the Nazi memorials since 1991.[20]

The construction program of the small, simple building is developed together with the presidium of the regional association, Simon Snopkowski, Julius Spokojny and David Schuster (Würzburg).[21] Generationally, these men share the fate of persecution as native Polish and German Jews, respectively, who in the post-war period are professionally established and respected in their places of residence and hold

Fig. 6: Flossenbürg, view of the Jewish prayer and memorial site, 2004 (Photograph: Architect Würschinger, Weiden).

20 Unpublished sources on the construction of the prayer and memorial site is not yet accessible, so that only published sources could be evaluated.

21 Michael Trüger, *Die jüdische Gedenkstätte in Flossenbürg*, ed. Landesverband der Israelitischen Kultusgemeinden in Bayern (München, 1995).

leadership positions in their respective communities or the national association. Fifty years after the end of the war, they represented, in terms of origin and age, the two main lines of the overaged postwar German communities: Schuster, born in 1910, was the oldest of them; Snopkowski (born in 1925) and Spokojny (born in 1923) belonged to the age cohort of Eastern European Jews shaped by experience as forced laborers, who built their lives in Germany after liberation. In the mid-1990s, the growth of Jewish communities through immigration from the former Soviet republics only made itself felt.[22]

In the immediate vicinity of the "Jesus in prison" chapel, a functionalist building with cubic forms was erected, measuring just under 12 meters in length and 6.50 meters in width. It was designed by the Weiden-based architectural firm Kunnert & Würschinger, using prefabricated concrete components with whitewashed walls and a flat

Fig. 7: Flossenbürg, front view of the Jewish prayer and memorial site, 2004 (Photograph: architect Würschinger, Weiden).

22 Jutta Fleckenstein, and Piritta Kleiner, ed., *Juden 45: Von da und dort – Überlebende aus Osteuropa/Juden 90: Von ganz weit weg – Einwanderer aus der ehemaligen Sowjetunion, exhibition catalogue of the Jewish Museum Munich*, 2 vols. (Berlin, 2011/2012).

Fig. 8: Flossenbürg, Interior of the Jewish prayer and memorial site, 2004 (Photograph: Architect Würschinger, Weiden).

roof. The cubature features a metal door as openings as well as high-set, quasi skylight-giving horizontal window bands to the left and right of the vestibule. Fig. 6 and 7. Inside, the sequence of rooms begins with a covered vestibule, from which three steps lead down to the central room (Psalm 130:1), where there are columns arranged in a hexagon. The main room receives light through a tower-shaped skylight that casts the shadow of a shield of David into the room. Opposite the exit is a niche in which "Zachor" is written in Hebrew in large metal letters (Figs. 8 and 9).

The high symbolic content of the building program and the materiality in concrete and white of modernism as well as the regional granite was explained in this way: "The external bleakness of the building" stands for the "exposure of the prisoners," the "nakedness of the facade is to remind us of how the victims were deprived of their personality." Inside, "the number and quality of [...] design elements as well as the structural unity increase." The Flossenbürger granite, which was used for the floor and walls of the central room, reminds one "of the hard labor of the prisoners in the quarry."[23]

23 Trüger, *Die jüdische Gedenkstätte in Flossenbürg*, see note 21, n.p.

Fig. 9: Flossenbürg, detail (skylight) of the Jewish prayer and memorial site, 2004 (Photograph: Architect Würschinger, Weiden).

Summary

The prayer and memorial site subsequently became the location for the annual Kaddish at the commemoration ceremonies marking the anniversary of the liberation of KL Flossenbürg. Previously, the Jewish commemoration of the dead took place first at the 1949/50 memorial stone, then at the 1985 memorial. The new sculptural memorial stone was erected on the initiative of Shoah survivors and leading representatives of Jewish life, such as Simon Snopkowski, Julius Spokojny and David Schuster, who wanted to ensure a dignified remembrance of Jewish Nazi victims in Flossenbürg. This project was renewed in 1995, when the State Association of Jewish Communities in Bavaria established a "Prayer and Memorial Site" especially for Jewish Flossenbürg prisoners. The initiative of the Bavarian Jewish umbrella organization was part of the renewal of the culture of remembrance after the end of the Cold War. The previous forms of remembrance were no longer up to date by the mid-1990s, and the commemoration of one of the "forgotten camps" is beginning to realign itself with the fiftieth anniversary of the liberation. This should be understood in light of the fact that the memorial's so-called Valley of Death, which was created in the immediate post-war period, commemorates nationally defined groups of victims. At the same time, the commemoration had a distinctly Christian character, as evidenced not only by a burial ground laid out in the 1950s along with the "Jesus in the prison" chapel. Jewish victims of the Flossenbürg camp system, on the other hand, were for a long time hardly visible.

Index: Persons and Places

Persons

https://doi.org/10.1515/9783110750812-015

Places